WALLY FUNK'S
RACE for SPACE

WALLY FUNK'S RACE for SPACE

The Extraordinary Story of a Female Aviation Pioneer

SUE NELSON

CHICAGO
REVIEW
PRESS

First published in the United States of America in 2019 by
Chicago Review Press Incorporated
814 North Franklin Street
Chicago, Illinois 60610
ISBN 978-1-64160-130-6

First published in Great Britain in 2018 by
The Westbourne Press
An imprint of Saqi Books
26 Westbourne Grove
London W2 5RF UK

Printed in the United States of America
5 4 3 2 1

For Wally
and all women who aim high

Contents

Preface: Preparing for Launch ix

1. I Heard Her Through the Grapevine 1
2. Houston, We Have a Problem 43
3. Cape Canaveral 76
4. The Waiting List 107
5. An American in Paris 139
6. Spaceport America 170
7. Storage Space 201

Sources and Further Reading 237
Acknowledgments 241

Preface

Preparing for Launch

A Ford minivan rattled down a Dallas freeway at a chassis-shaking sixty miles an hour, no doubt loosening some of the aging space stickers attached to the windows. As my fingers clutched the sides of the passenger seat, I prepared to die. It occurred to me that, after the inevitable crash, at least a personalized license plate would make us easier to identify. It read "WF—A woman's place is in the cockpit."

WF stood for the driver's initials: a seventy-eight-year-old pilot called Wally Funk. Mary Wallace Funk, to be precise, but she refused to answer to Mary. Or Wallace. It didn't matter either way because it was obvious that she was better suited to flying a plane than driving a car as neither of her hands were on the steering wheel.

Her right hand groped around the back seat, searching for something. The van meandered worryingly into another lane. A piece of paper, wedged behind a visor, caught my eye. It appeared to be a medical form. The only discernible words were "Do not resuscitate." When my voice emerged it was part shout, part squeak.

"Put your hands on the wheel!"

Wally turned toward me with a mischievous smile and, all faked innocence, replied, "What? Have you never driven with your knee before?"

Meet Wally Funk. A woman born for descriptions such as force of nature, unstoppable, and, at times, woman with a death wish. Over the last few years, being in the passenger seat with Wally has aged me considerably. She's too polite to say it, but sometimes I must have driven her to distraction. Somehow we became friends.

We first met in 1997 when I was making a BBC radio documentary called *Right Stuff Wrong Sex*. The year before, I had read a couple of sentences in a US newspaper making a passing reference to the Mercury 13. At the time, like so many people today, I had never heard of them. The Mercury 13 were thirteen exceptional female pilots who, between 1960 and 1961, passed the same physical and psychological tests as the Mercury 7—America's first astronauts—as part of a privately funded program led by Dr. William Randolph "Randy" Lovelace II.

Wally Funk was one of those thirteen women with the right stuff. The funding, for reasons discussed later in the book, was cut with just a few days' notice, and none of these women ever made it to space.

As a feminist and space fan, I couldn't believe this incredible piece of hidden history had passed me by. I was determined to bring this story to a UK audience. The program's title was a direct reference to Tom Wolfe's *The Right Stuff*, a book about the selection and heroic achievements of America's first (male) astronauts. It was broadcast in the UK on BBC Radio 4 in April 1997. A shorter version later aired in the United States on National Public Radio.

The Mercury 13's efforts made it into numerous newspapers during the 1960s, but over time the knowledge of these women has ebbed and flowed. Every so often their presence, like ripples on sand, disappears from public view as if all memory of their achievements has been erased. I often give talks about women in space, and whenever I've thought, "Everyone must know about the Mercury 13 by now," a room full of people has gazed at me collectively blank. It's a stark reminder that the recognition of these trailblazing women has a long way to go.

The aim of the radio program in 1997 was to shine a renewed light on their story. I wrote a piece for the *Guardian* on the Mercury 13 and, within the following few months, *Marie Claire* and other publications followed up on the story. Years later, I met someone who had helped set up an exhibition paying tribute to the Mercury 13 at the UK's National Space Centre in Leicester. Praising the exhibition, I inquired where they'd got the idea. "I heard a program on Radio 4," she said.

Wally and I kept in contact after our interview, then lost touch, were reacquainted over the phone, and then hooked up in person almost twenty years after our first meeting. That's when she started becoming more than a work contact and became a friend. This book includes our meeting in 1997 but mainly focuses on several road trips we've made together by plane, train, and automobile in the United States and Europe in 2016 and 2017.

Most of the Mercury 13 are no longer with us, but Wally is not only alive, her energy levels are the very definition of life itself. Life doesn't just happen to Wally. She makes it happen. Her past reveals an insight into her determination, but it is also the bare bones of this particular history. Because Wally *is* living history. Defining her by the five days when she took Lovelace's tests in 1961, or even by the phrase Mercury 13, misses the extraordinary achievements she has accomplished within aviation. It also fails to recognize her lifetime's pursuit of the ultimate adventure. Wally never gave up on her dream of becoming an astronaut and remains determined to make it into space.

As you can tell, she is a formidable woman. Wally is the sort of character who could shoot, hunt, and fish from an early age.

The sort of woman more comfortable in trousers and boots than a skirt and heels. The sort of woman who can control a Ford minivan with her left knee. Wally is also the sort of woman who, if history had been kinder, might have been the first woman on the Moon. She has spent over fifty years trying to become an astronaut and get into space and is now, with the birth of commercial spaceflight, the closest she has ever been. It is a desire I can understand.

In 1974, I wrote to NASA as a British schoolgirl inquiring about how to become an astronaut. In a haze of youthful ignorance, I hadn't realized that, in order to be eligible as a NASA astronaut, you also had to be American. It wouldn't have made a difference even if I had known. Although Valentina Tereshkova became the first woman in space in 1963, NASA didn't admit women into their astronaut program until 1978. In my own small way, like Wally, I was ahead of my time.

As a journalist, I have enjoyed a life in space by proxy ever since. I reported on space missions for television and radio during my time as a BBC science correspondent. I make space-related documentaries for BBC radio, produce short films on space missions for the European Space Agency, and interview astronauts and space scientists for the Space Boffins podcast.

In December 2017, I even experienced weightlessness during a series of thirty-one parabolic arcs aboard Novespace's Zero G plane, which is used by the European Space Agency to train astronauts to conduct scientific experiments in microgravity. Of course, Wally beat me to the experience. Her first taste of floating like an astronaut was in 2000. There is a fantastic picture of her upside down on the flight, arms wide and laughing. She was sixty-one years old.

In 2007, almost fifty years after their tests, the US Congress passed resolution 421 "honoring the trailblazing accomplishments of the 'Mercury 13' women, whose efforts in the early 1960s demonstrated the capabilities of American women to undertake the human exploration of space." The accolade, reported in the *Congressional Record* (no. 90, vol. 153, dated June 6), also "encourages young women to follow in the footsteps of those women and pursue careers of excellence in aviation and astronautics, as well as in engineering and science." For some people, though, recognition is simply not enough. There remains unfinished business to attend to.

In 2019, the same year as the fiftieth anniversary of the Moon landings, Wally will celebrate her eightieth birthday. During that year she hopes to finally cash in her ticket with Virgin Galactic for one of the first commercial flights into space. Understandably, she is eager for this new era of space tourism to begin. History, for Wally, will then have come full circle. Let's hope it isn't too long before her turn. She has literally been waiting a lifetime—and time is running out.

I Heard Her Through the Grapevine

May 2016. It was quite a welcome and also quite an outfit. Wally Funk, arms and smile outstretched, sported a cornflower-blue flight suit adorned with NASA mission patches and a US flag on her left shoulder. The effect was part pilot, part off-duty astronaut. Not far from the real thing even if, technically speaking, she was a pilot and *potential* astronaut. Present career combined with a long-held ambition.

Her hair hadn't changed and was as I'd remembered: short, like mine, but white enough to cause snow blindness. Like most Americans, she appeared to have more teeth than I did. Naturally they were whiter and straighter, too. Age had not changed her figure. Tall and slim, Wally moved with the vitality and easy nimbleness of someone much younger. Now seventy-seven years old, this was our first face-to-face meeting in nineteen years and it appeared only I had aged.

"Hey, Sue," she boomed, alerting everyone in reception to our presence. "I thought I'd surprise you. Did you have a good flight? What do you think of the weather? Is it cold in England? I hear you were waiting in the wrong spot. Are you coming round to my house? Grapevine is not far from here. Go and put your suitcase in your room and come to my house. You can meet the cows."

My brain imploded from the bombardment of questions. *Did she say cows?*

It was difficult to collect my thoughts. After departing a chilly English spring, the Texan heat had been a shock. Then I spent over an hour, standing without shade in the harsh sunlight after a trans-Atlantic flight, waiting for the motel shuttle bus. I had been at the right exit but the wrong level of Dallas Fort Worth airport terminal. The evening ahead had been deliberately unscheduled. My plan was to shower and have an early night to recover from jet lag, before meeting Wally, who would start presenting my BBC radio documentary, in the morning.

Wally stopped a random guest and handed over her digital camera. It resembled one from the 1990s. I checked the image afterward. Wally's right arm reached skyward in celebration. I appeared dazed and confused.

"Sorry. It's been a long journey so I thought I'd have an early night."

Wally's eyes widened in disappointment. "Oh," she said plaintively.

I dropped off my suitcase in the room. When I returned to reception Wally was no longer wearing the flight suit. She had changed into trousers and a blue T-shirt showing a Space Shuttle in mid-launch, rocket boosters firing, with the Moon in the background. It was topped by a matching blue satin bomber jacket. On the back, beneath an image of the Space Shuttle on a launch gantry, were the words "Kennedy Space Center." Alongside it was embroidered "STS-93 Columbia, Eileen M. Collins, First Woman Space Shuttle Commander."

Wally's minivan, outside in the parking lot, had definitely seen better days. It resembled the Mystery Machine from *Scooby-Doo*: battered but ready for adventure. Stickers on the windows read "Air Force Academy," "NASA," and "We Have Friends in High Places." She patted the hood. "Done me proud. Over a hundred thousand miles."

Before she reversed, I noticed she'd forgotten to put her seat belt on. When I pointed this out, she sniffed dismissively. "I don't like 'em," she replied.

Once the van was parked in her bungalow's garage, Wally headed for the back yard. Following her, I discovered that the house backed onto a field. A herd of cattle, alerted to her presence, ambled expectantly toward the wire fence as she began feeding them from a bag through the fencing.

"Do you want a picture of me feeding the cows? The TV cameras always like that. Come and film me feeding the cows. They come right up to the fence. Do you want to feed them? They'll take the food right out of your hands."

She seemed slightly manic, perhaps because my brain was on a mental slowdown and I struggled to stay awake.

"It's okay, thanks."

"Are you sure? People normally want to film me feeding the cows. I guess it makes a nice shot."

"I don't have a film camera. It's a radio program."

"Oh."

There was a brief puzzled silence, as if she was processing some huge misunderstanding. "Are you sure you don't want to take a picture?"

Beaten into submission, I rattled off a few photos on my iPhone and, once satisfied, she led me inside. Every surface, horizontal or vertical, was covered with memorabilia relating to either aviation or space. A propeller was nailed above the mantelpiece. There was another satin Space Shuttle jacket hung on the wall. A wooden Space Shuttle caught my eye, and there were stacks of books and framed photographs of astronauts everywhere. More worryingly, hundreds of loose photographs and highly flammable newspaper cuttings covered the electric rings on the oven.

"You'd better be careful cooking or we'll need to call 911."

"Ha!" Wally barked. "Open the door."

The oven shelves were packed with pots and pans.

"Check out the dishwasher."

I did. It was full of cleaning products.

"See—it's fine, honey," she stated cheerfully. "I don't cook."

"Not a problem. I cook but don't clean."

"Well that's perfect! We'll make a good team."

As I wandered around the living room, I noticed something else unusual. "Why do you have two televisions?"

"Because one is national and the other is permanently tuned to NASA. Never switch it off. I want to know what's going on all the time, the launches, the landings. I watch all the girls launch into space on there."

There was so much stuff it was hard to decide what to focus on next, but a miniature set of crystal glasses with matching decanter, inside a glass cabinet, seemed out of place. "They belonged to the Queen Mother."

"What?"

"I used to own her Rolls-Royce," she added matter-of-factly. "The set came with the car but I decided to keep the glasses when I sold it. There's a picture of the car in the hall."

Sure enough, a framed black-and-white photograph from the 1970s revealed Wally with a boyfriend, both dressed up to the nines, next to a vintage 1951 Rolls-Royce. She was wearing a long white gown. "It was my mother's wedding dress," she said.

The man's name was Michael. He had worked at IBM and they'd been together for about eighteen months. "Did you ever marry?"

"No," Wally responded promptly. "I'm married to my plane."

She was now beside a table searching among a pile of opened envelopes. "People write to me or send pictures asking for autographs. I've stopped signing them because people were selling them on Ebay. For $200!"

She eventually found what she was looking for. "I don't normally have everything out but I did it so you could see it." It was a pack of cards issued by the International Women's Air and Space Museum in Cleveland, Ohio. She opened the pack and fanned out the cards until she located one in particular. Wally was the seven of diamonds. The woman beside me, immortalized on a playing card, was gazing dreamily upward wearing a navy pilot's jacket under the title "America's first female Federal Aviation Administration inspector."

As I struggled to absorb it all, she picked up a medallion from another table covered with at least thirty more, as well as lapel pins, badges, and space-mission patches. This one was from a talk she had given to the military.

"Whenever you go to a military base they shake hands with you with a medallion in their hand," she explained, "to give to you. This one is the biggest I have. I needed to thank the commandant. Never got his card, never got his name but he gave me this wonderful coin. I got into the limousine and showed it to the driver and he said, 'You don't know who you've just met, do you?' And I said, 'No sir, I do not.' And he said: 'That's the man that killed bin Laden.'"

Welcome to Wally's world—colorful, slightly dizzying, and often totally unexpected.

"You want to film me talking about this, honey?"

"It's a radio program, Wally."

Although my intention had been to sleep within hours of arriving at the airport, I had portable equipment in my backpack and recorded her wandering around her living room commenting on the assorted fragments representing her life.

"See that pin?"

The memento was framed alongside a photograph I recognized instantly. It was from 1995 and showed seven members of the Mercury 13, including Wally in a NASA sweater, standing in front of a Cape Canaveral launch pad, gathered for a Space Shuttle launch. Wally was in between Gene Nora Stumbough Jessen and Jerrie Cobb, alongside Jerri Sloan Truhill, Sarah Gorelick Ratley, Myrtle Cagle, and Bernice Steadman. They were all the private guests of astronaut Eileen Collins.

Collins, mindful of their history, had invited the surviving female pilots from Lovelace's Woman in Space program to watch her become the first woman to pilot the Space Shuttle on February 3, 1995. It brought renewed attention to the Mercury 13 as their story, once again, resurfaced in newspapers across the United States. "After thirty-four years, the right stuff," reported the front page of the February 3 edition of the *Arizona Republic* via an Associated Press report.

"The sex barrier has been broken," declared Ratley.

"Finally!" said Truhill.

Inside the paper, Wally was shown lighting the long, thin candles of an enormous Space Shuttle-themed birthday cake belatedly celebrating her birthday with Jessen and Ratley. She had turned fifty-six just two days earlier. The launch must have been a bittersweet present.

Next to the framed photo, behind the glass, was a small metal brooch.

"That's my Ninety-Nines pin," she said, referring to the international organization of women pilots. "It's the only bit of me that went into space," she said wistfully. "It went up with Eileen."

Two years after Eileen Collins's launch, Wally and I met for the first time. It was March 1997 and I was recording interviews for my first BBC radio documentary, *Right Stuff Wrong Sex*. Computers and e-mail were not in widespread use at the time, so I had tracked down as many of the Mercury 13 women as possible, together with associated interviewees, the old-fashioned way via letters, phone calls, and contacts. Several of the women had already died by then. Jerrie Cobb, the first woman to pass the tests, was working and flying in the Amazon, performing missionary work. Luckily, four of the women located agreed to be interviewed: Geraldine "Jerri" Truhill (née Sloan), Sarah Ratley (née Gorelick), Irene Leverton, and the magnificently named Wally Funk.

Irene Leverton, the first female crop duster in the US and a competitive racing pilot, was one of the oldest of the Mercury 13. Age seventy in 1997, by then she had been flying for fifty-three years and continued to fly while working as a consultant for Aviation Resource Management at her local airport. She was often taken to air shows as a child and, like Wally, made model planes. Age nine, Leverton told anyone who would listen that she was going to be a pilot.

When the call came for the tests in 1961, Leverton was flying for a company in Los Angeles. They wouldn't give her the week off. "My boss indicated if I went on this trip I was out of a job." Leverton went anyway and, sure enough, lost her job. She signed the papers and showed up at the Lovelace clinic. As the chairman of NASA's Life Sciences Committee for Project Mercury, Dr. Lovelace had helped devise America's first astronaut tests. The physical tests were brutal, putting the astronaut candidates through extreme conditions in order to prepare them for the unknown environment of space. The men who took those tests were all pilots, like the women, and became known the world over as the Mercury 7.

"I was either very naive or very intelligent," she said, "I can't figure out which one. There are a couple of things I remember. One was the ice water squirted in the ears. What they were doing was testing our ability to recover from vertigo. And they time you as I'm staring at this bright light. The eyes are shifting back and forth rapidly, and they stop. Then you can focus and the vertigo is over. That hurt."

Leverton knew that the Lovelace tests wanted to see if women could meet the same standards as the Mercury 7 astronauts. "I felt this was another barrier to push on and there hadn't been a woman in space yet," she said. "I was so egotistical, I just felt my physical condition—which was good at the time—would prove to them that women belonged in space. And if one of us could get to go, fine."

She confessed to feeling "a little angry" when phase two was canceled. "I thought, so what else is new? I thought, *hmmm*. Some of the gals must have done too well on this test. I always believed I could do anything. That was like the door opening, the Sun shining in, the door closing, and it got dark and it was over. Of course it was a lost opportunity, but with the ultra-conservatism in the country at the time it's just amazing that that much got done. Thank God for Dr. Lovelace and Cochran's backing." The last comment referred to the woman who broke the sound barrier, Jackie Cochran, who was helping the tests financially.

As luck would have it, Truhill, Ratley, and Wally were all going to be in the same place at the same time, attending a Women in Aviation conference at the Hyatt Regency hotel at Dallas Fort Worth Airport. As a Texan, Truhill was on home turf and so, at her suggestion, we would record her and Ratley's interview at Truhill's home nearby. Wally was available in a separate location in the evening. Leverton's interview had necessitated a separate trip to Arizona, something I could justify while on a limited BBC budget by writing a few freelance print pieces for British newspapers along the way.

Despite the publicity of their presence at Collins's launch, the Mercury 13 remained relatively unknown in the late 1990s, and their interviews had a freshness to them. The women spoke clearly, simply, with heart and passion. Proud of their ambitions and flying careers, they were thoughtful about broken promises, indignant about the injustice of it all, and, in Truhill's case, tearful. I'd warmed to Truhill instantly. Feisty and outspoken, she—like all the women—had been ready to perform her patriotic duty and become an astronaut.

Geraldine "Jerri" Truhill showed me a typewritten and signed letter by W. Randolph Lovelace II, MD, from the Lovelace Foundation for Medical Education and Research in Albuquerque. It was dated September 14, 1960. "We have been informed that you may be interested in volunteering for the initial examinations for female astronaut candidates," the letter read. "These examination procedures take approximately one week and are done on a purely voluntary basis. They do not commit you to any further part in the Woman in Space Program unless you so desire."

At the time of her call-up, Truhill was part of several secret government programs. She was flight testing the first smart bomb and a military infrared system in B25s and B26s, both twin-engine bomber aircraft. When Cobb called her personally to ask if she could get away for a top-secret project, the answer was: "Sure." Nevertheless, she was surprised by Lovelace's letter when it mentioned astronaut training. "I was flabbergasted. I was taken aback because we weren't doing very well, mostly blowing up rockets on the launch pad. As far as people going into space, that seemed to me like it would be years away. But I figured if they could launch it, I wanted to fly it, whatever it was. I was hoping maybe it'd be a plane like the x-15 because women weren't allowed to fly jets at all. b25s and 26s were not to be sneezed at, but I wanted to get into jets if I could. So I volunteered."

Truhill gave me a copy of her confirmation letter too, dated March 24, 1961, asking her to come and take the tests nine days later, on April 2. By then Wally had already taken and passed her tests a few weeks earlier, but Truhill would not have known that. The first time they met was at Collins's launch over three decades later. Truhill recalled signing papers at a motel in Albuquerque. "I absolve the government from any responsibility for my death, being maimed, or losing a limb, and there's my name," she said. "I must have been out of my mind."

Truhill's father often took her on business flights as a child and she loved being in the cockpit pretending to fly. "My daddy said, 'Now if you grow up and be a registered nurse then maybe you can be a stewardess, Jerri, for an airline.' I said, 'I don't want to be a stewardess. I want to be a pilot.' I thought daddy was going to faint. He said: 'Women don't fly airplanes' and I said, 'I'm going to.' And I did."

Truhill was married with young children when the astronaut testing opportunity arose, and her husband, a decorated World War II pilot, despite originally encouraging her to fly, did not want her to take part. "We were having some other problems at the time and this rather escalated it." Her husband delivered an ultimatum: him or space. Truhill headed off for Albuquerque to take the tests.

"When I came back from the Lovelace Foundation, I was met at the airport by divorce papers. I think we all sacrificed a lot for that program. It changed our lives, all of us. We all made sacrifices and all we got for our efforts and our patriotism was very bad things said about us. Janey Hart, whose husband was

Senator Phil Hart, got hate mail saying, 'Why don't you stay at home with your children?' Ungentlemanly things. A lot of the girls lost jobs. I think I'm the only one that lost a husband."

She was also furious about a quote that she'd read in a newspaper, attributed to a NASA official who said he'd rather send a bunch of monkeys into space than women. Truhill believed it was from NASA flight director Chris Kraft. "That was one of the kinder things that was said."

Sarah Ratley had a degree in mathematics and was an accountant living in Kansas when we met. In the early 1960s, when the Lovelace invitation arrived, she was an electrical engineer for AT&T, had 1,500 flight hours and a commercial license, and had worked her way through college as a flight instructor. She, like many of the other Mercury 13, had taken part in the Powder Puff Derby—the colloquial name for the Women's Air Derby—a race across America for female pilots that began in 1947. Ratley remembered "the personnel at Lovelace being extremely affirmative saying, 'You can do it. We want you to pass.'" There was back up, support, just wanting us to accomplish this, to be in the program. I wanted more than anything else to pass and be a part of the program. I was young at the time, and when you're young, you think nothing can defeat you."

She described herself as "crushed" when the planned training in Pensacola was canceled. "The explanation I got was they were not quite ready for us," Ratley told me. "They felt it was more a man's field. The women were supposed to be in the home and protected and they didn't want them taking dangerous assignments. It was just the thinking at the time. It was like Camelot. Women were to be protected and stay at home and be more concerned with their families."

After our interviews, I asked whether they knew Wally. The conversation halted. It was as if neither of them wanted to utter anything incriminating. Truhill sniffed. "I found her a little overbearing."

Truhill's comment took me aback, especially when I found Wally gregarious, animated, and quick to laugh. Admittedly, Wally's energy levels were permanently on overload. Perhaps that was the issue.

Although in her late fifties then, Wally had a short shock of white hair. From afar she looked much older, but close up her clear skin, illuminated by a permasmile, knocked off at least a decade. There was also something about her I recognized from my own childhood after spending a large part of my youth climbing trees, riding bikes, learning how to throw stones correctly, and playing any sport possible. She was a fellow tomboy. But louder. Much louder. And more American.

Our interview took place later that day at a Dallas Fort Worth airport hotel. She had just given an aviation safety talk at the conference. "Is Wally short for anything," I asked while switching the microphone on. For a British audience, Wally was not only associated with a man's name, it was also a comical insult.

"No," she said firmly. "Just Wally."

And that was that. It took almost twenty years before she told me both her birth name and date of birth: Mary Wallace Funk, February 1, 1939. And that was under duress, because without those details I couldn't book her a flight. Wally's route into the Mercury 13 was different from everyone else's. The idea for women to take the tests was first mooted by Brigadier General Donald Flickinger from the Wright-Patterson Aeromedical Laboratory in Dayton, Ohio. His tentative "girl astronaut program," or Program Woman in Space Earliest (WISE), had been scrapped at the end of 1959. He wrote to Lovelace, asking him to take it forward. Lovelace agreed, renamed it the Woman in Space Program, and contacted the aviator Jerrie Cobb.

Cobb, then twenty-eight, had been flying since she was sixteen and was a perfect test subject. Her performance in February 1960 was described as "extraordinary" and ranked in the top 2 percent of all NASA's astronaut candidates. Lovelace, chairman of NASA's Life Sciences Committee for Project Mercury, revealed his "secret" testing of Cobb at the Space and Naval Medicine Congress in Stockholm, Sweden, in August.

None of America's first astronauts in waiting, the Mercury 7, had gone into space yet. In fact, no human being had. But seven American men had already shown they could pass the exhaustive tests devised by Lovelace and his colleagues. Could women do the same? Here was one women who most definitely could.

The media coverage didn't always match up to Cobb's achievement or treat it seriously. She was called a "Moon maid," an "astronette," and "a number one space gal who seems a little astronaughty." Some journalists mentioned her 36-27-36 figure. The day after Lovelace's revelation, the *Washington Post* reported from Stockholm via Associated Press on August 19, 1960, with a more measured and neutral response. The article was headlined "Woman Qualifies for Space Training" and opened with "America's first woman space pilot candidate is Jerrie Cobb, 28, of Oklahoma City, daughter of an Air Force Colonel and holder of several world records for women fliers."

To ensure that Cobb wasn't a one-off, Lovelace wanted other equally qualified women to take the tests, and his famous aviator friend, Jackie Cochran, became an advisor. All female astronaut candidates, like the men, had to be experienced pilots, so Cobb compiled a list for him. Wally was not on it. Not because she wasn't a good enough pilot. She was a great pilot. Wally wasn't on that list because she was too young. The minimum recommended age was twenty-five.

Instead, in 1960, a twenty-one-year-old Wally read the

August 29 edition of *Life* magazine. In it was the article, "A Lady Proves She's Fit for Space Flight." It featured twenty-nine-year-old Geraldyn "Jerrie" Cobb, US Aviation's Woman of the Year in 1959 and an advertising and sales promotion manager of the Aero Design & Engineering Company. Cobb was "the first prospective space pilot in a hitherto unannounced 12-woman testing program."

Wally read as it explained how Cobb had taken seventy-five tests and "complained less than the Mercury men had." Exclusive *Life* magazine photographs showed her on a bicycle taking fitness and endurance tests or breathing into a mask to test her pulmonary function. The designated "space lady" was also pictured playing tennis, swimming, and kneeling in prayer.

Cobb's achievement ignited a flame within Wally that remains alight today. She wanted to take these tests too and go into space. She even recognized the name Dr. William Randolph Lovelace II. Her father's doctor back in Albuquerque, New Mexico—the state where she grew up and where the Lovelace Foundation clinic was located—was also called Lovelace. Wally sent a letter immediately to Jerrie Cobb, but, when she didn't receive a reply, wrote directly to Lovelace on November 5, 1960, detailing her 600 flying hours, her bachelor of science in education, her commercial sea plane and instructors' licenses, how she'd won the "Ninety-Nine award for the top co-ed pilot of the Nation, two years in succession" at intercollegiate "airmeets," and her willingness to act as a test subject "to become an astronaut." He replied six days later:

Dear Miss Funk,
Thank you for your letter of November 5.
    Enclosed is a card listing the information we would like to have regarding your background. We would appreciate

your preparing a curriculum vitae following this outline. When we have had an opportunity to go over this, we will contact you further.

Under separate cover I am sending you a brochure which describes the Foundation and Clinic organization here.

Sincerely yours,

W. Randolph Lovelace II, M.D.

A couple of weeks later, at the end of November, Cobb wrote an apologetic letter on Aero Design & Engineering Co. headed notepaper.

Dear Wally,

Thanks for your letter of October 27, and I'm truly sorry for not having answered sooner, but the past three months I have been gone almost continuously on various flying trips.

I was so glad to hear that you are interested in the research program for women in space and you did the right thing by writing to Dr. Randolph Lovelace II in Albuquerque, since he is the one doing this research. There will a group of about twelve women pilots go through the examinations at the Lovelace Foundation within the next few months and I am sure you will be hearing from Dr. Lovelace on this.

Thanks again for your kind letter and if there's anything I can help you with please just let me know.

With best personal regards, I remain cordially yours,

(Miss) Jerrie Cobb, Manager

Advertising—Sales Promotion

Cobb had identified aviators for Lovelace's privately funded Woman in Space Program via the Ninety-Nines, a national organization for female pilots founded by—among others—Amelia Earhart. Candidates had to have a college degree, be under 5′ 11″—or they wouldn't fit inside the Mercury capsule—and have at least 1,500 flying hours (Cobb had 10,000). However, there was one important difference between the men and women when it came to recruitment. The Mercury 7 candidates were also jet pilot graduates from a military test pilot school. As these schools did not yet admit women, this requirement was understandably dropped. It made sense to bend the rules in this case, not least because the Mercury 7 selection process also broke the rules.

The college degree requirement was considered necessary because becoming an astronaut would involve more than great piloting skills. Astronauts would need to understand engineering too. John Glenn and Scott Carpenter did not have a college degree. Both men were obviously deemed literate enough in science and engineering to make an exception. Glenn, for instance, had been studying engineering at university but left before graduating to join the Marines. The education criteria did, however, exclude one of the best—if not the best—test pilots of that era: Charles "Chuck" Yeager, the first man to break the sound barrier.

The original age specification was, as with the men, for women over the age of twenty-five and under forty. Fortunately, Wally's experience was impressive enough for Lovelace to take notice. Even if she was four years underage, she had been flying since 1957 and was the only female flight instructor at an Army Ground Forces Air Training School on a US military base—as a civilian at Fort Sill, Oklahoma.

She had grown up at altitude in Taos, New Mexico, cycling, hunting, and fishing. She was also an expert markswoman, with a Distinguished Rifleman's award under her belt, and a competitive skier. Earlier that year she had trained for the 1960 US Olympic ski team in Squaw Valley, California, until a back injury put her out of contention. Potentially, there was no doubt she could have the right stuff to become an astronaut. In a letter dated February 2, 1961, when she had just turned twenty-two, Lovelace informed Wally that she was on the list.

Dear Miss Funk,
Examination of potential women astronauts is continuing. We have reviewed the credentials you have sent in and find that you are acceptable for these examinations. Miss Jacqueline Cochran, who has had extensive experience in high altitude, high speed flight, and was in charge of the WASP program in World War II, has been kind enough to review the entire program and has made a donation to the Foundation that will take care of the expenses for room and food up to $100 during the approximately six days you would be here. She will serve as special consultant in this program . . .

Cochran was the record-breaking pilot who founded the Women Airforce Service Pilots (WASPs), where female civilian pilots were trained to fly military planes to release the men for combat duty in World War II. Now in her mid-fifties, Cochran was too old to take the tests. Brought up in poverty, working in a cotton mill at age six, she was now married to Floyd Odlum, one of the wealthiest businessmen in America. The couple lived on a vast ranch in California and were generous in their financial assistance for Lovelace's program. Wally's letter continued:

We would like you to plan to arrive in Albuquerque on Sunday, February 26, and report to the Clinic Monday at 8:00

AM, without anything to eat, drink, smoke, or chew (i.e., gum) after midnight Sunday. You should be through the examinations by Saturday noon.

Lovelace concluded by saying:

Only the names of those that pass the entire examination will be released. It is hoped to have the candidates that pass the examinations meet together late this spring.

A few weeks later Wally headed further west from Oklahoma to her home state of New Mexico. She arrived at her parents' house in Taos in the red Vauxhall car they had bought for her graduation. As she was under Lovelace's official age limit, her mother drove them to Albuquerque and signed Wally in, giving written permission for her daughter to take part in the tests. Wally then checked into the Bird of Paradise motel across the street from the clinic in Albuquerque. That evening the clinic collected the first of what would become numerous stool samples "in a container provided for that purpose." Wally didn't understand the instruction. She told me that until that point she had thought a stool was something you sat on to milk a cow.

When the Mercury 7 took their astronaut tests they did so as a group and bonded together in the face of extreme physical intrusion and exertion. It was different for the women. They mostly took their tests paired in twos. Wally met the woman who was to be her testing partner at the clinic, and together they began a series of eighty-seven different tests over a period of five and a half days. They would be exactly the same as the Mercury 7 tests, but with additional gynecological examinations.

Wally's testing partner dropped out within a few hours. Wally never saw her again and can't even recall her name. The other seventeen women who completed the week—making nineteen in total including Cobb—all took their tests at different times and, for the most part, no one knew who else was taking them. Two of the women were twins, however, and Wally had told another pilot, Gene Nora Stumbough, to write to Lovelace and offer to take the tests too. The departure of her test partner meant that Wally underwent the rest of the week's tests by herself. Wally shared her schedule with me.

Day 1, on February 27, 1961, began with nothing to eat, drink, or smoke and a stool specimen "if not previously collected Sunday evening." Wally reported to the Laboratory Appointment Desk on the first floor of the clinic's Lassetter building at 7 AM. She was then allowed to have breakfast before Master 2-Step tests at 8 AM. This was an exercise test named after a Dr. Arthur Master to assess cardiovascular fitness. Walking on and off some steps would also reveal any hidden heart conditions, since it was feared that space flight might cause the heart to explode.

At 9 AM, Wally reported to Audiology in the basement for an ear examination, then at 10 AM it was up to the third floor for cold presser tests. Wally had to place her hand in water, at 39°F, for three minutes while a member of the clinic's staff measured her blood pressure and heart rate every sixty seconds. The same experiment was conducted with her feet. Half an hour later, further tests continued, followed by lunch at noon and a proctoscopic (rectal) examination at 1:30 PM. Considering this must have been a shock to a relatively sheltered woman from an all-girls' private school, she was surprisingly matter-of-fact and dismissive about the intrusive nature of it all, even the tests which required ingesting a radioactive material. "We ate barium. We had barium enemas. We had enemas all the time, so no big deal, we knew we had to be tested."

Sinus X-rays were at 2 PM, then further tests at 3 PM, and

pulmonary function testing in Physiology on the first floor starting at 3:30 PM. In the evening there were "no restrictions on eating, drinking, or smoking," but a stool sample was taken either then or first thing Tuesday morning. This pace continued for the rest of the week. During that time, on her own, Wally did everything she was asked to do. She had also agreed to be stuck with needles here, there and everywhere for constant blood tests and, as instructed, swallowed three feet of rubber hose tube to examine the gastric juices in her stomach. Was it uncomfortable? "Oh heavens yes," she said. "It was kind of a shock. I swallowed so many tubes. And I had so many tubes up me. But I could take it."

But how did she manage three feet of rubber tubing? "You just sat there and went . . ." Wally made a loud turkey gobbling noise until her own laughter forced her to stop. ". . . and swallowed it."

Wally's gung-ho approach toward being jabbed and prodded, providing nonstop stool samples and being given barium enemas, provided an insight into her strength of mind. During the cycle ergometer test, for instance, electrodes were attached to her body as she rode an exercise bike. These measured her oxygen consumption and lung capacity. "They were stuck in our bodies, not the kind that are plastered on today, they were sort of painful. But pain was not a situation with me. I would do anything," she said. "The clock was right in front of you. It was a psychological factor, I'm sure, and you would pedal to the speed of a metronome. It was ticking, going back and forth, in a room full of doctors and nurses."

The aim was to cycle until physically exhausted. "I wanted to break the barrier on that test and go for eleven minutes because ten was all they expected. It was pretty easy going until nine and a half, ten minutes, so I grit my teeth, closed my eyes, and felt my second wind coming, and I did it. All the electrodes were taken off me and they said, 'Wally. I think we better help you.' And I said, 'No, I'm fine' and then I went . . ." She clapped her hands loudly. "And fell right off."

The tests pushed both the men and women to their physical limits to ensure that any hidden or unforeseen health issues were identified before a space mission. Bodies would undergo G forces on launch and then the unknown environment of space. These G forces, or G, represent the force acting on a body resulting from acceleration or gravity. We may not feel any such force going about our daily lives on Earth, but our gravity has a force of 1G. A sharp, prolonged acceleration toward space, however? Your body will definitely feel the pressure of increased G forces. Heart rates would race. Blood pressure might rise. "We could not afford to overlook any tests that might catch even a minor heart defect," wrote Lovelace in the April 20, 1959, edition of *Life* magazine. "There might, for example, be tiny congenital openings between the right and left sides of a candidate's heart. Normally a man so afflicted might never show a sign of heart trouble, but under extreme circumstances—like sudden decompression at high altitudes—such a defect could mean death." The tests therefore covered every aspect of the body including liver function and thyroid efficiency, while daily urine tests checked for the excretion of hormones.

Lovelace described one test as resembling a dunking stool because the astronaut candidate was seated in a chair that was lowered into a tank of water. This gave a measurement of the body's specific gravity, which could then go on to determine the total amount of body fat.

On Thursday, March 2, Wally reported to Carco Air Service at the Municipal Airport and flew to Los Alamos. She drank radioactive water for a total radiation body count and that evening was instructed to shampoo her hair but not to "reapply any hair dressing until after EEG testing on Friday morning." This was so that any oil or lotion didn't interfere with the readings.

Friday started differently. "You may eat breakfast." After that, it was an electroencephalogram to measure brain activity at 8:30 AM, more tests until lunch, then finishing with tilt-table examinations in the Cardiology department in the afternoon to detect any cardiovascular defects. Wally had seen a picture of Cobb undergoing the tilt-table test in *Life* magazine. Wally's blood pressure and heart rate were measured every minute as she lay on a table that moved from a horizontal position through to a steep sixty-five degree angle for twenty-five minutes at a time and back again to see if her body could cope with being in this position.

Despite having no one to compete against, Wally completed every one of those tests without complaint; she was determined to do her best. Lovelace's letter to Wally, dated May 17, revealed that those efforts were rewarded:

Dear Miss Funk,

By sometime in June we hope that all of you that passed the examinations here will be able to go in a group to a service laboratory where further test procedures will be carried out. Just as soon as a definite date is picked, I will let you know immediately. We also hope that funds will be available for your transportation to this service laboratory and your expenses while here.

Meanwhile I would like for you to achieve the best possible physical condition that you can as the forthcoming tests are going to require considerable physical stamina. I would recommend walking, swimming, and bicycle riding as well as calisthenics.

I am happy to say that you were one of those that were

successful in passing the examination.
Sincerely yours,
W. Randolph Lovelace II, M.D.

Cobb also wrote to the twelve women who had successfully matched her physical feats on May 29, 1961:

Dear FLAT (fellow lady astronaut trainee),
It is with pleasure that I send my sincere congratulations to you upon passing the astronaut examinations at the Lovelace Foundation.

The US Navy has arranged for us to take a series of tests at their school of Aviation Medicine in Pensacola, Florida. These tests consist of physical fitness, endurance, low pressure chamber, acceleration, clinical examinations, airborne EEG, etc. I have just completed these tests and am sure you will find them interesting as well as informative . . .

It is of utmost importance that you do not mention this to any press.
Cordially,
Jerrie Cobb

Wally's typewritten reply to Lovelace on May 31 revealed her eagerness to take part and "can do" attitude.

Dear Dr. Lovelace,
I was most happy when I received your exciting letter saying that I had passed all the examinations. In fact I immediately started to work on your recommendations for the forthcoming tests as: I ride my bicycle eight miles a day, to and from work; try to prop as many airplanes as needed: calisthenics and running. These tests in the coming [months] mean

quite a bit to me to help you out in your research for the program and, in the future, I hope our nation.

She offered to attend meetings, tests, or functions:

to help the program or to better myself in learning in this magnificent field I am at your command to do so anywhere in the US at any time. As my job can be arranged to be very flexible. If in time that funds would not be available, I would like to help out in my own personal way [sic].

Wally ended by describing a photograph attached to the letter.

Enclosed picture was taken about a month ago when I flew to Shepard AFB to see about a jet orientation ride and also fly an F-86 simulator. I am happy to say that I have just about gotten up to 1,300 flying hours.

The simulator prepared pilots for the F-86, a single-seat Sabre Jet airplane built by the North American Aviation Company. It had proved invaluable against the Russian MiGs during the Korean War. Wally had not only showed initiative in terms of obtaining this experience, even though flying jets was officially denied to women in the military; it was immediately clear that she was prepared to do whatever it took to go all the way and qualify as an astronaut candidate.

This wasn't Wally's first time in a jet cockpit, however, simulator or not. She had flown in a T-33 jet at Fort Sill. "I had an instructor when I was flying that one," she told me. "It was fantastic because it was so fast. Taking off and landing it was a faster speed, honey, but control-wise it was just the same. But jets today probably can't compare as T-33 was a trainer. It flew like a general aviation aircraft, just a little faster. It had more power, it was slicker, and I could do my maneuvers, take-off and landing, a 360, turns, stalls . . ."

The next phase of testing would be as a group at the US Naval School of Aviation Medicine in Florida, where Wally would finally get to meet the other successful women. They would undergo ten days of physical training, high-altitude chamber tests, experience G forces, get their brain activity measured during jet maneuvers, and practice escaping from a cockpit under water. Cobb took these space-flight simulation tests in May and equaled the scores of experienced Navy pilots.

The twelve successful women were to do the same phase as Cobb and were due to be tested in July. By this stage, Cobb had been appointed as a part-time special consultant to NASA but retained a key role in Lovelace's plans. These plans were heavily dependent on funding from Cochran and her husband, but Cochran was unhappy that she'd not been kept informed of the next stage of testing. She made it known to Lovelace that she wanted more involvement and more of a leadership role within the program. Lovelace hastily rescheduled the tests for when Cochran was free, which meant delaying the women's tests by several months.

The Western Union telegram to Wally, dated June 29, 1961, read:

Testing has been rescheduled for September by Dr. Lovelace. If this is not convenient notify Dr. Lovelace or me immediately. Regards Jerrie Cobb.

It was a tactful telegram since it was Cochran, not Lovelace, who had forced the delay. A few weeks later a letter arrived from Lovelace:

July 8, 1961

Dear Miss Funk,

As you know, further tests have been arranged for the girls in the Woman-in-Space program who passed the initial examinations here at the Foundation. Originally these tests were set for July 18. It has been necessary to change the testing date to begin on Monday, September 18.

These tests will be conducted at the US Naval School of Aviation Medicine at Pensacola, Florida. You should arrive in Pensacola on Sunday, September 17 and plan to spend two weeks there. Further details of the testing are being worked out at present and we will keep you informed as the time draws nearer.

There is to be no publicity whatsoever about these tests or your trip to Pensacola. Any and all news releases will be made only after the testing is completed and then only with the permission of the US Navy and the girls participating in the Program.

For someone like Wally—single and with a job as a flight instructor that she could leave fairly easily—moving the phase two tests in Pensacola, Florida, from July to September was a workable inconvenience. For those women who were married with families and jobs to juggle, however, it was logistically much more difficult. Yet the twelve female candidates made the necessary preparations.

It must have been a delicate balance for Lovelace to tread, both professionally and privately. He needed the funding and had been friends with the famous Jackie Cochran for over twenty years. Jerrie Cobb had been his first female test success and the embodiment of his medical program: proof that physiologically there was nothing to stop women becoming astronauts and going into space. But, as a medical scientist, he had to have more test subjects to prove the case that Cobb wasn't simply a one-off success.

A letter from Lovelace dated July 12, written just a few days later, revealed that his decision to fit in with Cochran's schedule had produced the financial reward of further funding from the couple. This was essential because, although the Mercury 7 astronauts did exactly the same tests as the women, theirs had been government-funded via NASA.

Dear Miss Funk,

This is a follow-up of my letter to you of July 8 with respect to the scheduled time for the tests at Pensacola.

Miss Jacqueline Cochran has agreed to provide the funds for transportation to and from Pensacola and the maintenance costs while there for any candidate who needs and desires such financial assistance. She will provide much needed funds through donations to the Lovelace Foundation for Medical Education and Research . . .

As Miss Cochran will be in Pensacola for a few days during the tests, you can thank her in person.

In case that wasn't a hint enough, the letter had been copied via Cochran. All letters up until this point insisted on secrecy. This one finished with a prediction as to how the future might unfold for the women.

Immediately after the final selection is made of those of you that pass the tests at Pensacola it is suggested that you have a meeting as a group to decide on a group policy for any publicity. As you know, the male astronauts have acted as a group on all matters concerning publicity every [*sic*] their initial selection and I would like to strongly urge that the results of their group acting in this field be considered very seriously.

Jackie Cochran sent a letter to all the successful women on the same day. Apart from reiterating her role as a financial donor, it also clarified the reasons for her support:

> As you probably know I am not a participant in these medical checks and tests. They were set up for women under forty years of age. Some of you may therefore wonder why my great interest and my assistance.
>
> There is no astronaut program for women as yet. The medical checks at Albuquerque and the further tests to be made at Pensacola are purely experimental and in the nature of research, fostered by some of the doctors and their associates interested in aerospace medicine. No program for women has been officially adopted as yet by any of the governmental agencies. As a result you were under no commitment to carry forward as a result of successfully passing your tests at Albuquerque and you will be under no commitment as to the future if you pass the tests at Pensacola.
>
> But I think a properly organized astronaut program for women would be a fine thing. I would like to help see it come about.

Jerrie Cobb also wrote to Wally and the other members of the Mercury 13 in July 1961. Before their expected September arrival in Florida for phase two, she offered the women the chance of optional additional testing in Oklahoma City for psychological and evaluated stress response. Two women arranged to do just that. No prizes for guessing the name of one of those women.

Dear Wally,

Sorry I missed your call, but Bonnie said that you prefer the dates August 3 through 5th, to undergo the psychological and sensory deprivation (isolation) tests here in Oklahoma City. Arrangements have been made with Dr. Jay T. Shurley, chief psychiatric services division, Veterans Administration Hospital, for you to begin your testing Thursday morning August 3rd at 8:00 AM and you will be completed sometime Saturday afternoon.

Rhea Hurrle of Houston, Texas, is coming this Sunday and will start the tests on Monday morning, finishing up Wednesday afternoon. I do not know exactly when she plans to leave, but if you arrive Wednesday afternoon or evening, perhaps you two will have a chance to get acquainted.

I would be delighted to have you as a guest in my home, during the days you are here, and if you will let me know approximately when you will be arriving, I will meet you. Or if you are driving I'll give you instructions on how to find my house. It was good seeing you in California and I'll look forward to seeing you again Wednesday, August 2. If there is anything at all I can help you with, please don't hesitate to call me collect.

With best wishes, I remain

Cordially,

Jerrie Cobb

The isolation test differed significantly from the Mercury 7 test. For the men, isolation meant being in a dark soundproofed room for up to three hours. John Glenn, for instance, was seated at a desk and found a pen, writing poetry in the darkness to while away the time. For the women, the test required float-ing in a circular flotation tank in a dark soundproofed room instead. Test subjects couldn't see, hear, taste, or smell anything. By keeping the water at body temperature, people would also find it difficult to experience the sensation of being touched. Most people hallucinated during this test. Not Wally. She spent ten hours and thirty-five minutes in the tank in complete silence before the test was forcibly stopped. Dr. Shurley informed her that she had broken the record. She prepared for the next stage of astronaut tests by doing everything she had to and more, taking charge of her destiny. Unfortunately, what happened next was beyond her control.

Despite Lovelace having NASA credentials, the privately funded program had no official NASA involvement. He had entered an informal arrangement with the Naval School of Aviation Medicine for the Pensacola tests. Jackie Cochran then did something inexplicable. This aviation trailblazer for women aired concerns about the Woman in Space Program to Admiral Robert Pirie, since his military facility was hosting the women. It resulted in the Naval School clarifying the situation with NASA. The space agency confirmed that the women's phase two testing was not an official request, and the tests were canceled.

Wally received a Western Union telegram from Jerrie Cobb. It was in block capitals, dated September 11, 1961, and had been sent by a colleague of hers, Bonnie Doyle, at the company where she worked.

MISS COBB HAS JUST INFORMED ME FROM WASHINGTON THAT SHE HAS BEEN UNABLE TO REVERSE DECISION POSTPONING FLORIDA TESTING AGAIN. LOVELACE WILL CONTACT YOU SHORTLY BUT JERRIE WANTED YOU TO KNOW IMMEDIATELY SO YOU WOULD NOT PLAN TRIP THIS WEEKEND. VERY SORRY FOR SUCH SHORT NOTICE BUT IT IS UNAVOIDABLE.

A day later Wally received another Western Union telegram at Fort Sill Oklahoma, again in block capitals, but this time from Lovelace and without punctuation. It was dated September 12, 1961, just six days before the women were due to start phase two testing after passing the toughest physical tests on Earth:

REGRET TO ADVISE ARRANGEMENTS AT PENSACOLA CANCELED PROBABLY WILL NOT BE POSSIBLE TO CARRY OUT THIS PART OF PROGRAM YOU MAY RETURN EXPENSES ADVANCE ALLOTMENT TO LOVELACE FOUNDATION C/O ME LETTER WILL ADVISE OF ADDITIONAL DEVELOPMENTS WHEN MATTER CLEARED FURTHER.
W. RANDOLPH LOVELACE II, M.D.

Considering what Wally and all the other women had been through, it was a cruel and shocking blow. Some of the women had lost jobs in order to take the next phase of tests. Others, like Truhill, paid a more personal price. Becoming an astronaut, at least in the United States, was to remain a man's job for the next seventeen years.

The Mercury 13's chances ended officially in July 1962. Two of the women—Jerrie Cobb and Janey Hart—had instigated a three-day congressional hearing before the House Science and Astronautics subcommittee with the aim of representing and highlighting the Mercury 13's achievements and getting women onto NASA's official astronaut training program. The names of all the Mercury 13 were made public for the first time: Geraldyne "Jerrie" Cobb, Jane "Janey" Hart (née Briggs), Geraldine "Jerri" Sloan (later Truhill), Sarah Ratley (née Gorelick), Bernice "Bea" Steadman, Irene Leverton, Jean Hixson, twins Janet "Jan" and Marion Dietrich, Rhea Hurrle, Gene Nora Stumbough, Myrtle Cagle, and the youngest, Mary Wallace Funk.

Hart, as reported in the *Washington Post*, was forthright making their case: "I am not arguing that women be admitted to space merely so that they won't feel discriminated against. I am arguing that they be admitted because they have a very real contribution to make. Let's face it: for many women the PTA just isn't enough." That last comment was probably heartfelt, since Hart had eight children. She also stated that it was "inconceivable that the world of outer space should be restricted to men only, like some sort of stag club."

Cobb gave several press interviews at the time of the hearings, but journalists reported her achievements with little respect or seriousness, asking questions about her makeup or marriage. For some of the women, the exposure resulted in hate mail, telling them to stay at home with their children.

"Women are eventually going into space," Cobb told the House space subcommittee. "There is no question about it. Why not begin now?" Later, she was reported saying, "They won't let me take the actual training course, but I see they have a female chimpanzee named Glenda who is being trained to take it."

NASA had three men testifying against the women, including astronauts John Glenn and Scott Carpenter. "I think this gets back to the way our social order is organized, really," said Glenn. "It is just a fact. The men go off and fight the wars and fly the airplanes and come back and help design and build and test them. The fact that women are not in this field is a fact of our social order. It may be undesirable."

The Mercury 13's third witness for their case was Jackie Cochran. When she became the first woman to break the sound barrier, the feat was witnessed in the air by her chase pilot Chuck Yeager. Cochran had been too old to take the Mercury 13 tests and surprisingly, despite helping to fund Lovelace's project from her private wealth, did not take a sisterly approach to the women's aspirations.

After Hart and Cobb's powerful arguments, and considering she was supposed to be on their side, Cochran's words were damaging. "With regards to racing with the Russians," Cochran said, "sure it's nice to be first, but it's nice to be sure. There is no doubt in the world that women will go into space and I think they will be just as good as men . . ." The sting was yet to come: "I don't want to see a woman fall flat on her face."

Despite the Mercury 13's success in proving themselves fit for an astronaut squad, Cochran suggested that, when it came to women, more research and testing was needed. For many of the Mercury 13, Cochran's public testimony was a complete betrayal. The next day, before the hearings were scheduled to be concluded, procedures were brought to a close. Women, it was concluded, couldn't join NASA since they couldn't join the military and obtain the required jet experience.

A year later, on June 16, 1963, history would record the first woman in space. To the United States' dismay, as with the first man in space, the woman wasn't an American. Her name was Valentina Tereshkova and, to add insult to injury for the Mercury 13, Russia's record-breaking cosmonaut wasn't even a pilot.

"She orbits over the sex barrier," *Life* magazine proclaimed, before describing the achievement of the first woman in space as "blue-eyed blonde with a new hairdo stars in a Russian space spectacular." It was an odd choice of words because, as the accompanying photographs clearly showed, Tereshkova was a brunette. But this was an era, in the early 1960s, when only one in four women in the US worked and the greater expectation was to be a wife, a mother, or an adornment. Even so, the magazine also noted: "Much better qualified than Valentina were 13 American women. But for a variety of reasons, including

NASA's outstanding lack of enthusiasm, their woman-in-space program has never been able to get off the ground."

After Lovelace's program was canceled, Wally took matters into her own hands. She traveled around the United States to take further tests, including those that Jerrie Cobb had completed the year before and that they had been due to take in Florida. She did this by writing letters to military bases or using her connections, including flying students, to find institutions that would allow her to do the same tests as for phases two and three of the astronaut tests. She underwent a centrifuge test at the University of Southern California and, at El Toro Marine Corps Air Station, California, in August 1962, Wally took a Martin-Baker seat-ejection test, which involved sitting in a chair and being flung up a pole at high speed.

There was an audience for her high-altitude chamber test, which gradually reduces the amount of oxygen, helping a pilot recognize the symptoms of hypoxia (low oxygen). Wally began by breathing pure oxygen through a mask. This purges nitrogen from the blood and removes the risk of decompression sickness when atmospheric pressure is reduced in the chamber to simulate the conditions at high altitudes.

"The guys were looking at me through the windows. They took me up to 40,000 feet and I was writing on paper," Wally explained. "Then they said, 'Wally take your mask off' and I did and didn't think anything of it as I'd flown a Stearman at 12 and 14,000 feet with no oxygen and my stomach could take it. Doing all those acrobatics made me tough. Then at 40,000 feet you take your mask off and I'm supposed to do different tasks, writing, push out the blue button, push out the red button, push out the yellow button. Then they yelled at me, 'Wally put your mask on. Wally put your mask on. Wally put your mask on!' I didn't feel giddy, I didn't feel sick, and then the doctor came in and put my mask on. Honey," she said, "it's like I saw you and everyone else in beautiful colors. It really didn't dawn on me until much later when I was giving a speech, that in those last couple of minutes, without oxygen, you only see grey."

She also hadn't realized that her writing had deteriorated into a mess of scribbles. "That's when you get in trouble and people have accidents. You should have seen the guys' noses pressed up against the window as if to say, what was this girl going to do? Were they expecting my body to blow up? I'm no different than a guy. I did just as well."

During the centrifuge test, Wally had shown initiative. She knew that, as a civilian, she would not be given a G suit—the tight-fitting pressurized flight suit worn by pilots when certain maneuvers caused them to experience G forces. These suits stopped blood pooling in the legs and feet and prevented the loss of blood, and therefore oxygen, to the brain, reducing the chances of blacking out.

"So I called Mother and said: 'I need your worst Merry Widow and a couple of girdles.'" The Merry Widow was a firm, strapless, form-fitting piece of underwear, popular in the 1950s, rather like a basque or a corset. "I made my own G suit. When I walked in all stiff, they didn't know what I had done, so I never blacked out."

By the time I first interviewed Wally in 1997, she had applied to NASA's astronaut program several times but, without the requisite engineering or science qualifications, hadn't succeeded. She wasn't taking no for an answer even then. We parted and exchanged addresses so I could mail her a cassette of the completed radio program. Over the years, I exchanged occasional letters with Wally, Jerri Truhill, and Irene Leverton. Truhill had given me a magnificent black-and-white photograph, which I framed, of her standing on the wing of a plane modeling a flight suit. Leverton wrote considered missives about her life in Arizona. Wally sent photographs with short, breezy notes, usually accompanied by smiley faces. I assumed that I would never see her again.

🚀

By 2016 the world had improved for women, but for decades they had had to overcome barriers, including sexism, to pursue careers within the space industry. I wanted to tell this updated story and sold a documentary to BBC World Service radio on the history of women in space. After making *Right Stuff, Wrong Sex* nineteen years earlier, the title chose itself: *Women with the Right Stuff.*

At a meeting at BBC Broadcasting House in London to discuss the program's content, I listed potential interviewees who represented the different roles and achievements of women. They included Wally for the historical Mercury 13 perspective. I suggested Sarah Cruddas, a female space journalist and broadcaster like myself, as presenter. The commissioning editor, Steve Titherington, stopped me mid-pitch.

"I know who the presenter should be."

To be honest I was flattered but not totally surprised. As a former BBC science correspondent, I had reported on TV news bulletins for almost a decade and presented BBC radio programs on and off for over twenty years. After a few seconds considering how best to let him down gently, I said apologetically, "I'm afraid I want to produce."

"Not you," he replied, as if talking to an idiot. "Wally Funk."

There was a long silence. Not out of embarrassment but because I was blindsided. Frankly, it was impossible to picture harnessing Wally's manic energy into a controlled interview situation, with her asking questions instead of answering them. Neither could I imagine her voice reduced to that of a BBC-style radio presenter. A few years earlier, I had interviewed Wally for Radio 4's *Woman's Hour* about her plans to go into space with Virgin Galactic. Her voice was louder than I'd remembered; the answers longer and looser. This made interviewing and editing difficult. Reducing a ten-minute interview to six minutes was a cinch. Cutting a forty-minute interview to six was a nightmare. But it brought a renewed audience, yet again, to the story of the Mercury 13. It was as if history had collective amnesia every ten years.

The other obstacle to Wally presenting was her distinctive speaking style. She emphasizes CERTAIN words at unusual PARTS of a sentence and at a sound level ten decibels ABOVE one of the planes she flies.

Clearly the commissioner had never heard Wally speak. As these thoughts ricocheted around my brain, I realized he was still waiting for a response. I stalled. "What made you suggest Wally?"

His reply was unexpected. "I saw the way you smiled every time you mentioned her name."

Titherington was right. After meeting Wally it is impossible to think about her without smiling. But I also recalled that Wally belongs in the category of women, described in the film *When Harry Met Sally*, who are high maintenance, but think they are low maintenance. I recognize the traits, though mostly in hindsight. During the 1980s three boyfriends bought me David Plante's book about the lives of Jean Rhys, Sonia Orwell, and Germaine Greer titled *Difficult Women*.

Much as I liked Wally, I knew that working together would be challenging. Wally is a fiercely independent woman who has that protective sheen of a much-loved only child used to getting her own way. I am also a fiercely independent woman, but the eldest of six who grew up constantly in charge, often with responsibilities way beyond my age range. I knew even at that point that my patience would be put under immense stress producing a show with Wally as presenter.

Sitting at the BBC, mulling over what the commissioner had proposed, I realized that he had made an inspired choice. Producing an eccentric seventy-seven-year-old's first radio documentary could potentially turn a good program into an unforgettable one. Or it would be a disaster. Either way, my workload had just doubled.

Months later, sitting in Wally's home in Grapevine, Texas, it was time to put that fear to the test. Since she had so much energy, I gave Wally a couple of the radio documentary links to read. These were the cues or introductions to our interviews that I'd already written before leaving the UK. Doing this now would at least give me an early indication of how recording the program would work, and I could hear her read a script. Wally was a great interviewee, but not everyone can read a script, and I'd not yet heard her do this.

Wally peered at the piece of paper I handed her, deliberately printed in large type. She took a deep breath and began. "Two . . . "—there was a long pause—". . . of the Mercury 13, Jerrie Cobb and Jane Hart wrote to President John Kennedy. It resulted in a public hearing two YEARS before the civil rights ACT . . . MADE . . . sex discrimination illegal. Astronauts Scott Carpenter and John Glenn were among those REPRESENT-ING . . ." Another pause.

". . . NASA . . . speaking against having women ASTRO-NAUTS. There were several *appeals*, but it took ANOTHER sixteen years before women . . . could be . . . come . . . part of America's ASTRONAUT selection process in 1978."

Wally ended the link with a coughing fit and I tried not to panic. It wasn't just the idiosyncratic delivery. Was she fit enough for our flight to the NASA Johnson Space Center in Houston the next day? We were scheduled to meet a number of inspirational women, the modern versions of Wally in different areas of the space industry. But once she had cleared her throat, she bounced around the room again, searching for something.

"Here it is." In an age where streaming was making my DVD collection obsolete, Wally held up a video cassette and inserted it into a large black machine.

It was a Travel Channel cable TV report of her trip to Star City and the Yuri Gagarin Cosmonaut Training Center in Kazakhstan in 2000. The producers had paid the fee for her to experience a weeklong program of cosmonaut training experiences. She wanted me to watch it. I put the recorder on pause.

According to the commentary, Wally, or the "woman of steel" as they referred to her, was being strapped into a centrifuge. "There's no going back now," the disembodied voice said. "Any last words?"

"I just hope I don't swallow my tongue," Wally responded.

"Speaking of tongues," the voice-over continued, in a commentary as cheesy as the accompanying music soundtrack, "keep in mind that all of the controls are in Russian. One wrong button and it's *do svidaniya*, Wally!"

Wally emerged from the centrifuge as calm and confident as a woman who had looped the loop and barnstormed in planes since she was a teenager. "Hi guys. It was fantastic," she said. "I want to do more!"

Wally then underwent weightlessness inside a Russian cargo plane as it performed a series of parabolic arcs, from 35,000 feet to

10,000 feet and back again. There's a reason these planes are nick-named "vomit comets." Wally was dismissive. "I never got sick."

As if in homage to the sexism women astronauts have experienced over history, the voice-over announced: "Wally is not complaining about a little air turbulence. After all, how often does one lose weight after their vacation? But unfortunately those pounds don't stay off by themselves and all too soon it's time for reentry."

At the end of the report, Wally stated her aim to go into space and be in orbit in 2003. Thirteen years later, and over fifty years since her secret astronaut tests, she was still waiting. I asked her to stop the tape. It was now 2016 and she still hadn't gone up. It was too painful for words.

The joy on her face, upside down and attempting somersaults in microgravity, had been plain to see. "The parabolic flight was one of the greatest things I've ever done," she said. "And I knew to practice in a swimming pool here to propel myself in a loop, in a roll, and swim so that I could do it in the aircraft as the aircraft is diving down toward the Earth. They showed about three times but we did about twenty. This was a chance for me to go back to Russia and see Star City as I couldn't get in there on prior vacations."

It was clear that Wally's preparations for space had never stopped. I couldn't take her to space but at least, by presenting my radio program, she would meet some interesting people in the space industry. I handed her another piece of paper to rehearse a different interview link and advised her to slow down this time and to try and make it more conversational.

She cleared her throat again and concentrated. "The first WOMAN in space was a RUSSIAN! Valentina Tereshkova." She rolled her "r" in "Tereshkova" so long it made the word at least two seconds longer.

"It was on June 16, nineteen . . . sixty . . . THREE. And she spent TWO DAYS and TWENTY-TWO HOURS on board Voshtok 6."

I interjected with "Vostok 6," and she repeated it correctly. "When Valentina came to London for the opening of the COS-MONAUT exposition . . ."

"Exhibition."

"Oh. When Valentina came to London for the opening of the COSMONAUT expedition . . ."

"Exhibition."

"Didn't I just say that?"

"No."

"You know I met her?"

I hadn't. Wally leapt across the room and searched through some photo albums. There she was in the Soviet Union in 1988, in full aviation uniform talking to Tereshkova through an interpreter. She had been part of an international women pilots' delegation with the Ninety-Nines.

Before I left for the motel and a much-needed sleep, we tried another link. This one was an introduction to one of our first interviewees at NASA in Houston. We had a busy schedule ahead and it had taken months of negotiation, but our interviewees would include a female flight director, an astronaut, and a flight surgeon. I hoped. The flight surgeon was confirmed and the link covered her work retrieving and checking the NASA astronauts who returned from the Space Station in a Russian Soyuz spacecraft. An experience that has been described by NASA astronaut Scott Kelly as like "going over Niagara Falls in a barrel—that's on fire."

On scanning the words, I realized that the script mentioned that the flight surgeon's role took her out to Kazakhstan. This could be trouble.

Wally practiced her first question. "When you go to KachaSTAN to check ASTRONAUTS in the . . ."

I stopped her for a correction. "Kazakhstan."

"That's what I said."

"No. You said Kachastan. It's Kazakhstan."

"Okay . . ." She took a deep breath. "When you go to KachaSTAN to . . ."

"KaZAKhstan."

"When you go to KACHAstan to check ASTRO-NAUTS . . ."

"KaZAKhstan."

"Kacha . . ."

"KaZAK . . ."

"When you go to KachaSTAN to check ASTRONAUTS . . ."

Eight minutes later we were still recording that one line. We had only four days to get our interviews and record all the other US-based material and links. This was not a promising start.

"KaCHASTAN . . ."

"KaZAKhstan."

"Kazakchan."

"KazakhSTAN. Can't I just say Russia?'

2

Houston, We Have a Problem

"Okay, see the slats on the wing. They're down ... that helps slow us up a little bit. Well, let's see now, there's a river ..."

It was more monologue than conversation. Probably because I wore headphones and was listening to Wally's recollections and the program links we recorded at her home in Dallas the night before. Yet, despite the aircraft noise, and her voice in the headphones, Wally remained audible in the next seat.

"Didn't they have some flooding down here not so long ago? Maybe that's not the right town? The name will come to me eventually ..."

During the descent it took a while to realize that the commentary had stopped. Wally's head was arched backward, face to the ceiling, eyes shut, mouth open. Totally still. For an awful moment I thought she had died in her sleep. Then a small ripple of air escaped from her throat and caused her to start. She peered across my lap out of the window and picked up where she'd left off. "We're at 2,000 feet right now ..."

Since the running commentary might be useful material for the radio program, I searched for the recording machine in the bag under my seat. If I got the levels right, we could hear Wally clearly above the engine. I asked her to explain where we were, where we were going, and why. Her response, as befitted a pilot, was extraordinarily precise.

"We're on flight 5849 from DFW to Houston and we are about 1,500 feet above the ground, landing south at Houston, and in a few minutes you're going to hear the gear make its contact with the runway. We'll have three gears, one on each side and the nose gear. Now we're about 1,000 feet and we're coming down at around 400 feet per minute, and now we're about 600 feet."

Time for a prompt. Why were we coming to Houston?

"So Sue and I can have a good time at NASA with the important people we're going to meet!"

Wally snorted with laughter and I felt slightly guilty. I hadn't told her that, despite several months of negotiations, NASA had only confirmed an interview with the flight surgeon the day before, and was yet to confirm which of my other requests had been granted, including an astronaut from the class of 2013 and a flight director. All women. From past experience, the US space agency always came through, but not knowing exactly who we would get had been extraordinarily stressful. I'd had to go ahead and book flights on past experience and a prayer. Hopefully some e-mails would be waiting for me when we arrived in Houston. She didn't need to know about the sleepless nights.

"Now we're about 100 feet and the runway's in sight, and we're going to be having a wonderful time, and the runway is ten feet, five feet . . . on . . ." She paused. "Right now . . ."

On cue, the wheels hit the runway and the plane shook briefly from side to side. "And the brakes are being put on." There was a wrenching screech. "Sounds like he's got rough brakes . . . and we're turning on the taxi way . . ."

At an airport rental company Wally and I collided shoulders beside the car like two NFL footballers. Both of us had tried to get into the driver's seat at the same time. A perfect metaphor for our situation. Once we'd ascertained roles—no discussion allowed, as mine was the only name on the rental agreement—

we headed toward downtown Houston accompanied by an annoying and persistent beeping sound. Unable to locate the cause, we had almost reached our hotel before I realized what was going on. "Can you put your seat belt on, Wally?"

"It's okay. I never wear one."

"It's not okay to me, I'm afraid. Can you put your seat belt on, please?"

"Why? It's not bothering you."

"What if I have to brake suddenly? You'll go through the window."

"Well, honey," she said, in a voice that betrayed a touch of irritation, a smidgen of sweetness, and a large dose of bloody-mindedness, "that's my problem."

Two could play at that game. "I'm not driving if you don't put it on."

A disgruntled mumbling accompanied the familiar clank of a metal seat belt clasp. The beeps stopped. At the hotel, Wally ordered some short, hard pillows and stated that something important needed to be sorted out first. "I need cranberry juice. I can't do anything without my cranberry juice."

"Have you tried reception?"

"They don't have any."

"Have you tried the drinks machine?"

"That's no good. It has to be a certain strength, honey, and there's only one brand I like that's good enough. I need to go to the mall. I asked them where it was and it's real close by."

"Okay. I can drive there in the morning."

"I need it tonight, but you don't need to drive me. I can go by myself."

"You're not insured on the car."

"It's okay, honey."

"No, it's not."

Stalemate. Someone had to cave in. I would drive her to the mall. We'd meet back downstairs in fifteen minutes. "Sure," she said, and mumbled about having left something in the car. I gave her the keys so she could fetch it. Fifteen minutes later, outside the hotel, I headed toward the parking space and realized the rental car was missing.

"Over here, honey." Both Wally and the rental car were parked, to my right, outside reception.

"You shouldn't have done that," I scolded.

Wally had the grace to look slightly shamefaced. "I only wanted to do something nice."

It was indeed a short drive, and the seat belt warning was blissfully silent. A small victory. At the mall I drove slowly around the storefronts as Wally staked out the restaurants, nail bars, and clothing stores. There didn't seem to be anywhere that might sell cranberry juice. Eventually we rounded a corner and spotted a supermarket. As I began to turn the rental car off the main drive to the right, toward a row of parking spaces, I got a shock. Wally's seat was empty and I was driving with the passenger-side car door wide open.

A disturbing thud reverberated from the front of the car and my foot automatically hit the brake. *I must have hit a pedestrian.* Except there wasn't a passerby on the other side of the windshield. It was Wally, in the middle of the road, and very much alive.

The thump had been her hand, slammed on the hood to stop the car from hitting her. I was too shocked to say a word. She stretched out her other hand in a policeman-style halt position and, as my mouth remained open and silent, Wally strode forcefully toward the supermarket entrance, shouting over her shoulder: "I'll be right back!"

Once parked, slightly shaken after almost running over

my presenter, I noticed that her seat belt was tightly fastened and flat across the passenger seat. It was as if she'd performed a Houdini trick and escaped from her bonds without unlocking the shackles. She'd obviously buckled it up and simply sat on the locked seat belt after our dispute. This explained why the car's seat belt alarm hadn't been triggered. Beneath the irritation, I was curious how the hell a seventy-seven-year-old had moved from her seat to the front of a moving car so quickly. And, to be honest, more than a little impressed.

The next morning we headed first to Space Center Houston. The Official Visitor Center for the NASA Johnson Space Center was just across the road, where our interviews—now all confirmed—would take place in the afternoon. The idea was to record Wally offering some impromptu observations at the museum whenever something relevant triggered a memory. The British-born American journalist Alistair Cooke, whose *Letter from America* radio broadcasts ran from 1946 to 2004, famously reported that, during a school survey after World War II, when television was relatively new, a seven-year-old boy said he preferred radio "because the pictures were better." It was true. Location recording and its sounds allowed people to envisage the scene in their minds.

After showing our tickets at the main gate, Wally issued a range of instructions as I drove into the parking lot. "I like to back up into a space and make sure you find somewhere in the shade. Mother told me that." It was good advice, considering the heat. Then Wally began shouting. "Wow. Oh wow."

Wow indeed. To our right, by the museum entrance, a Space Shuttle appeared to float above a huge plane, piggybacking on a modified Boeing 747. This was known as the NASA shuttle carrier aircraft 905, and there was nowhere else in the world where you could see this configuration of shuttle and shuttle carrier up close. "Just wait until I've stopped the car before you get out," I warned.

Too late. A draft of warm air wafted across my lap. Wally's distinctive brisk and rolling gait, caused by a hip operation that left one leg slightly shorter than the other, hastened her across the parking lot into the best position to take a photo of the plane–shuttle combo. Wally's two favorite things in the world, aviation and space travel, were in the same shot.

The museum was fun and exhausting in equal measure. Wally's enthusiasm for everything around us was totally uplifting; she was so uncool in expressing her enjoyment that it became cool. Full of energy, she asked a stream of questions, although many of them could have been answered if she'd stood still long enough to read the exhibit displays. After a while, I responded to any questions by simply telling her to read the signs. It didn't seem to offend her in any way.

We entered Skylab, the cylindrical space station from the 1970s, and it was so well done that it took a while for us to realize that the man somersaulting in microgravity wasn't real. Wally had addressed the mannequin. "How does it feel up there, mister? Wow, I would love to go sailing through there like the guys did."

A lift inside took us to the entrance of Space Shuttle Independence. When we emerged several stories higher, we were outside and the sunlight dazzled us. There was the black-and-white tiled spaceplane. "You didn't say when we were parking we were going in a shuttle," Wally said happily.

While the carrier aircraft beneath it had carried real space shuttles 223 times, the spaceplane on its back was not one of them.

"It's a replica, but full scale, so it's going to feel like the real thing. I'm taking you to space, Wally."

"That's okay, honey. I wouldn't want to go with anybody else but you."

It was an outrageous act of flattery. Sure, we'd kept in touch on and off for years, but we hardly knew each other. If I hadn't sent a recent photograph to her, as requested, she wouldn't have recognized me in the motel reception. Wally quickly had second thoughts about her space trip. "Maybe Eileen."

While staff validated our tickets, she then went into full exuberant Wally mode. "Hi! You guys must have a good time here. How many employees are here? I guess you're loving it, huh? Hi, how are you?"

Wally addressed the young man who scanned our tickets. "Are you going to be our pilot today?"

"The last time I took it for a spin," he replied drily, "I took it through a Wendy's parking lot and the city didn't like it."

Inside the payload bay, Wally examined the instrumentation. "Now the brown and white is your artificial horizon, the other one is your compass . . ."

"Similar to an aircraft?"

"Yes."

A video streamed on a display near the Canadian robotic arm, and she spotted a familiar face. "There's Eileen Collins."

When we left the payload bay to appreciate the view of the shuttle again from outside, Wally sighed. "My gosh, we got in the shuttle." We leaned against the top of a wall above the aircraft and across from the shuttle. How did she feel watching Collins's launch?

"I was so excited. I'd seen her months before, and just knowing she was up in the vehicle in her seat. When they blasted off I said: 'Go Eileen, go for all of us . . .' We were all crying. It was wonderful she got the chance to go up."

She recalled being taken aside for TV interviews. "They seemed to just want me. I don't know why that was . . ." I knew exactly why. "I think I sought Eileen out before anyone else did. We became friends."

Recalling Truhill's unflattering description of Wally in 1997 as being overbearing, I asked what she thought of the other six members of the Mercury 13 when she met them for the first time at Collins's launch. "They were nice," she said, "although I thought Jerri Truhill was a little overbearing."

In the main museum hall, I called Wally over to a piece of black shiny rock. It had been brought back from the edge of the Sea of Serenity by the Apollo 17 mission in December 1972. It was 3.8 billion years old.

"Hey, Wally. I'm touching the Moon. Come and touch the Moon. It's really smooth."

She cackled. "You gonna bring it home?"

"No, they've glued it down."

When we met up again, Wally was sitting in a replica of a Space Shuttle cockpit. "Here's where Eileen sits. That is so great. They got the rudder and joy sticks, just like airplanes . . . all the hydraulics. Wow, look at all the buttons up here. Certain buttons do certain things that I'm not smart enough to know. With all that heavy suit on, you wouldn't think they'd fit in here."

I had been thinking the same. "You can see why they'd think being a woman might be an advantage, being generally smaller."

"Affirmative."

In the next room we encountered an unexpected sight. There, hanging from the ceiling against a backdrop of night sky and stars, was a genuine Mercury capsule, on loan from the National Air and Space Museum in Washington, DC. All the

Mercury capsules' names contained the number 7, because there were seven Mercury astronauts. This one was Faith 7.

"I was going to go up in that if my time ever came," she sighed.

Due to their small size, the Mercury spacecraft were all called capsules. "It was a one-man cockpit," Wally declared. After peering into Faith 7's cockpit from behind the barrier, she slammed her hand on the rail in delight. "It's got round dials!"

"1960s technology."

"They didn't have to have any rudders either. This is so nice to see. Who would have thought?"

"You could get in there," I joked.

"I've tried in many museums," Wally replied seriously, "but they wouldn't let me."

She continued to examine the control panel. "The left hand is probably on a thruster of some sort. Wow. What a neat panel. So easy to read."

"So you would have no problem flying this?"

"No, I wouldn't have thought so."

A museum sign related that astronaut Gordon Cooper had flown this particular Mercury capsule on May 15–16, 1963. "Gordo," she acknowledged. "Glad I got to meet him."

She read the rest of the signage out loud. "Faith 7—around the Earth 22 times in 34 hours, 19 minutes, and 49 seconds. WOW. That is so incredible."

"When you met him, did he know what you'd done?"

"Yes. He had written a book, *Into That Silent Sea*, that is only about the Mercury guys, and there's a chapter: 'Wally and Wally.' Wally Schirra and Wally Funk."

Schirra was one of the original Mercury 7 astronauts. "He did an excellent job. He was just very gracious, very wonderful, and said, 'I wish you could have made it' and what a great time he'd had."

Wally gazed at the Mercury capsule. "And now being here and seeing this, against the stars, makes me feel like I want to jump in it and go. You couldn't have picked a better one for us to see."

As it happens, although she met Cooper, he did not write that book. The authors were Francis French and Colin Burgess. There was a copy in the gift shop on the way out. "My goodness, all the books they have!" Wally exclaimed, and began reading out the titles: "*Stages to Saturn, The Man on the Moon, The Countdown, Moon Launch, Before This Decade Is Out, The First Man on the Moon, The Last Man on the Moon, Rocket Men, Apollo 13 . . .*"

"What about the women?"

"I don't see any. There are no books here on the Mercury 13," she said. "Isn't that interesting? It's all about the guys."

Even though I have visited NASA's Johnson Space Center in Houston before, it remained a thrill to pull up outside Mission Control, also known as Building 30 or, as it's been known since 2011, the Christopher C. Kraft Jr. Mission Control Center. It was named after America's first flight director, Dr. Chris Kraft, one of the original members of the Space Task Group for Project Mercury and flight director for the Mercury missions.

Kraft was a smart, visionary, disciplined, and pure NASA alpha male during the glorious era of the Apollo missions, later Skylab, and the Apollo-Soyuz test program. Like many of those in the control room during the 1960s, he wore a suit, white shirt, and black glasses. Unlike the rest of the team, there was no doubt that Kraft was in total control, after having led and implemented the rules, operations, and contingency plans required for a space mission. In Kraft's heyday, flight director was undoubtedly a man's job, and he had a formidable reputation. When I'd met him at his home in Houston in 1997, he'd been retired from NASA for fifteen years after spending a decade as director of the NASA Johnson Space Center. But it was clear, even then, that you'd think twice about questioning or disobeying this man.

Kraft was not involved in the selection of America's first astronauts, but he was unapologetic about the fact that NASA selected men and did not open up opportunities to women. "The qualifications were very straightforward, and very simply stated that we wanted men or women who had flown in high-performance airplanes who, frankly, were willing or had put their lives on the line in these kinds of planes on a continuous basis, so that the fear of the new environment that we were going to put them in would not be something that they had to deal with. It would be natural to them," he said.

"The requirement that they had a certain number of hours in a high-performance airplane eliminated any women at that time, because there weren't any women in this country who had that qualification. They just simply didn't meet the qualifications. Frankly, I don't know whether we were right or wrong at the time. The men we chose and the men we flew were excellent pilots, and they all did a fine job."

Later in the interview, however, he singled out Scott Carpenter as one of the Mercury 7 astronauts who had not, in his opinion, done "a fine job."

"Carpenter did not have a test pilot's training and, to be perfectly blunt about it, he shouldn't have flown in space. But he got there, and fortunately he lived." There was an angry pause before his final words emerged, almost as a growl, through gritted teeth. "Damned fortunate."

The Mercury 13 women who had wanted to be considered, I suggested, would be disappointed to hear that one of the men wasn't up to the job. Kraft's judgment about the women's Russian counterpart, Valentina Tereshkova, was harsh: "Their first woman was an absolute basket case when she was in orbit, and they were damned lucky to get her back. She was nothing but hysterical while she flew. How do you know we wouldn't have gotten into that situation as well?"

Rumors undermining Tereshkova's achievements had continued for several decades. Many of them were from Soviet scientists who reported that Tereshkova had had last-minute nerves and that she vomited in space—as if that was a sign of weakness, even though it is commonplace for astronauts to be space-sick. Hysteria, the word that the Soviet space scientists had used, is also a commonly used term for denigrating women. If sexism within the United States was endemic in the early 1960s, Russia was no better, either then or later.

The woman, who was often disregarded as a parachutist by some, had graduated from the Zhukovsky Air Force Academy as a cosmonaut engineer in 1969. Seven years later, after a doctorate in engineering, the former factory worker became Professor Tereshkova. Despite this, Tereshkova's earlier lack of qualifications was always quoted in space history, rather than her later academic achievements. It wasn't until 2004 that a true insight into Tereshkova's conduct was revealed. She had noticed on entering orbit that her spacecraft, Vostok 6, was pointing in the wrong direction. There had been an error in Vostok 6's automatic orientation system. She had been instructed on returning to Earth to fire the retrorockets. Facing the wrong way, this would have meant being propelled into a higher orbit instead. The result would have been the world's first—and dead—female astronaut, orbiting the Earth until her slow demise from starvation. She informed ground control and, when her prognosis had been confirmed, they sent new commands to correct the problem. Her clearheaded actions were not exactly those of a "basket case."

Years later, I heard Tereshkova speak about this near-death experience in person. She was at London's Science Museum in September 2015 for the opening of their Cosmonauts exhibition. Tereshkova's spacecraft, Vostok 6, was one of the exhibits. She had, it transpired, not wanted the engineer responsible for the error to be punished. So she had kept it a secret. For thirty years. "Cosmonauts can keep their word like men and women," she said, "particularly women." Tereshkova also revealed that the ground crew had forgotten to pack her toothbrush. When I asked if she was disappointed about the nineteen-year gap after her flight and that so few female cosmonauts had flown into space since, Tereshkova responded, "I think the attitude to women will change." She then addressed the Russian dignitaries on the front row of the audience with a pointed and feisty, "Do you hear me?"

I mentioned to Kraft the quote that Truhill had brought up—"I'd rather send a monkey into space than a bunch of women"—allegedly said by him. He had no knowledge of it, but was prepared to comment. "The feminist movement had not happened yet, and although Ms. Cochran made some noise about not being selected and not even being considered, that was a nit as far as the public aspects of the program were concerned, so that thinking at the time wouldn't have even been considered."

He admitted that, in light of the world now being politically correct, in a later era women would have been selected. "Women would be trained to be [jet] pilots because the PC situation has demanded that that happen and I think they would have done very well. Then again, I think it would have been a burden on us in the Mercury program." He mentioned urination as one reason—I'd written *"urination?"* which means I must have thought his explanation ridiculous. But my transcription ended there, because what he said next must not have been usable for the radio program. Even so, it was a glimpse into what it must have been like trying to forge a career in an era when men and women both were desperately trying to rise above the expectations and perceived limitations of their sex.

Nineteen years after that interview, Wally and I were meeting one of NASA's newest flight directors, Mary Lawrence—the thirteenth female flight director to qualify at NASA and one of six women currently active in the position. We were in a viewing area above a control room. Its consoles were empty and without operators, because it was being upgraded. Just a few weeks earlier, it had been in action as a control center for the International Space Station. Once the work was completed, that role would continue again.

This was to be Wally's first-ever interview as a reporter. She was great at being interviewed, but asking the questions required a different skillset. Questions must not lead to "yes" or "no" answers, other than "Did you murder your wife?" Interviewers must listen and mentally reorder future questions if an earlier answer includes a response to a later question. Interviewers must also clarify answers that are complicated or assume too much prior knowledge. It was a big ask for a first-time presenter. Wally glanced down at her questions and immediately went off script. "You get to talk to some of the astronauts?"

Lawrence was an engineer. Good school teachers had influenced her decision to study math, science, and engineering. The film *Apollo 13* had inspired her to work for NASA. It showcased the incredible job that Kraft and his team had done in 1970 to enable the safe return of three astronauts from their damaged spacecraft after it encountered "a problem." After we got back on track, Lawrence outlined her career path to flight director.

"First I became a flight controller, studying how systems work and undergoing a series of simulations where you're dealing with malfunctions and normal operations. Once you make it through that training, you get to sit in this room and gain years of experience. I was lucky to be flight controller during the assembly phase of the space station, so spent a lot of time building technical knowledge."

Lawrence expanded that knowledge further as a flight director, learning what the crew would need to do in an emergency as well as the ground team's role in supporting them. The training used control room mock-ups and ran through scenarios such as a fire in a module.

Wally's response was pure Bogart. "Wow, that's a plateful for you, kiddo."

Lawrence explained the layout through the glass window below. "Each console is built of a bank of computers showing data or telemetry coming from the Space Station," said Lawrence. "It's manned by one flight controller who reports to the flight director who makes any of the final decisions for operations." The consoles are dedicated to different ISS systems. "Communications systems, attitude control systems—so we have control moment gyros on the station that keep us in attitude (orientation) and flying straight; power systems, thermal systems . . ." Wally's eyes widened.

"We have people that manage the time lines and day-to-day activities of the crew. Of course we have the Capcom console that talks directly with the crew and several others that make up an entire team of people to keep this thing flying. And this is just the Houston team," Lawrence added. "There are teams in

Europe, Russia, and Japan covering their systems to drive their particular modules, but we're all united in the same mission."

Cameras are permanently pointed at the astronauts and Earth. "We see it as they see it 250 miles above," Lawrence said. "Do you want to go up? You've got to make that happen."

Her home, Lawrence insisted, was in mission operations on the ground. "I've actually fallen in love with the work I'm doing here and am happy supporting and making sure astronauts are safe, and doing that as part of a team."

"You're very humble," Wally responded. "For me, I'd wind up there in a heartbeat."

When asked about how she felt at being an inspiration in such a visible role, Lawrence's answer was unexpected. "I'm proud to be a woman as part of the flight director office in a leadership role. I'm also a mom, so I'm demonstrating it is possible to do it all. That's one of those things close to my heart. You can raise small children but also have a successful career in whatever you want to do."

If they'd heard Lawrence, the members of the Mercury 13 who had children themselves would no doubt have cheered. When Wally asked about the future, Lawrence didn't hesitate. "As far as NASA goes, everyone dreams about a human mission to Mars, so I feel people who are here now are the foundation. Don't know if I'm going to be here, but know I'll be part of that because of the work that we're doing today."

Unlike the rest of her interview, this was a rote answer. It was NASA's focus at the time. Mars, Mars, Mars. And if there's one thing NASA PR does well, it is ensuring that everyone reads from the same script. Personally, I doubted NASA would reach its stated goals within their intended time frame. Returning to the Moon seemed a more achievable goal, and one to build on, in terms of learning how to live off-planet with the available resources and surviving the radiation. After a change of president, that would indeed happen.

Andy Weir's science fiction novel *The Martian*, self-published in 2011 and rereleased in 2014, resulted in an equally popular film in 2015. Most of the content was rooted in solid science and engineering—the only real flight of fancy was allowing the stranded astronaut to survive for so long. In reality, the radiation on Mars is unforgiving, with a thinner atmosphere than Earth and no protective magnetosphere (the area of space around our planet that is controlled by its magnetic field).

The Mars rover, Curiosity, has a radiation assessment detector, and while a "short" long-term mission was possible, even the 180-day outward journey would expose an astronaut to radiation the equivalent of twenty-four CAT scans—fifteen times the annual limit for someone who works in a nuclear power plant. Assuming 500 days on the surface, followed by the 180 day return journey, an astronaut would just exceed a lifetime limit of 1.01 sieverts. This is associated with a 5 percent increase in the chance of contracting a fatal cancer.

Theoretically, one of NASA's class of 2013, then their most recent astronaut selection intake, could make history. "They will be the youngest and the closest to go to Mars," said Lawrence. For the first time, the astronaut candidates contained a 50:50 split of men and women, the highest percentage of women in the space agency's history. The first footprint on Mars could be from a woman's boot. A lot more had to be done, however, to make that happen. The most powerful rocket ever built, NASA's new Space Launch System (SLS), was still in a test phase, with the eventual aim of exploring deep space, launching its Orion spacecraft, and taking a crewed mission to Mars. Meanwhile, with the Space Shuttle retired and commercial companies racing to fill the gap, the Russian Soyuz rocket and capsule remained the only way for astronauts to travel and return from the International Space Station. But whereas the Shuttle glided like a plane onto the runway, the Soyuz capsule returns via parachute onto the ground and makes a notoriously hard landing. NASA astronaut Tracy Caldwell Dyson had heard it described as "a train wreck followed by a car crash followed by falling off your bike" before she returned to Earth in 2010, after six months on the Space Station.

When an astronaut returns to Earth this way, NASA flight surgeon Dr. Shannan Moynihan is often one of the first faces that they see when the hatch opens. Like Wally, Moynihan has aimed high from an early age. But whereas there were no women astronauts as role models in 1960, Moynihan had someone to emulate.

"I have a note from when I was four years old in kindergarten," she said. "I had written to Shannon Lucid."

Lucid was a biochemist and one of America's first female astronauts. Her classmate Sally Ride just beat her to that post. Lucid had been working at the Oklahoma Medical Research Foundation when NASA finally opened the astronaut candidate training program to women in 1978. She was selected and went into space as a mission specialist on STS-51G on June 17, 1985. By the time she retired, in 2012, Lucid had logged 5,354 hours (223 days) in space, held the record for the most hours in orbit by any woman in the world until June 2007, and before that, in 2002–03, served as NASA's Chief Scientist in Washington, DC.

"I didn't know she was a doctor then," said Moynihan. "I had the great honor of working with her in Star City while we were both there. So that was just a dream come true for me."

Moynihan, a tall, smiley woman with a halo of curly hair, must be a welcome sight for astronauts after a rough ride home. "Some astronauts are feeling very well, others might be having some symptoms due to gravity, sort of like a bad case of vertigo, dizziness, off-balance, nauseated. They might want to vomit. Some are weak and dizzy, and have difficulty walking in a straight line."

"Does space affect a woman's body differently than a man's?"

"The answer is no. We haven't seen any definite differences between women and men in orbit. The same physiological effects from being in that environment seem to affect both men and women," she said. "It's an interesting question, but, to date, no."

According to Dr. Donald "Don" Kilgore, however, who had worked with Lovelace on the astronaut tests for the Mercury 13, "The results were impressive in that the women very frequently performed at least as well as the men did, and in some cases they performed better. The tests then were rather primitive compared to what we can do nowadays. To test balance, we rotated the patients in a chair while we measured eyeball movements in response to those stimulations. We also irrigated the ears with water at zero degrees centigrade, which causes vertigo. That was the unpleasant test that all of the candidates, both male and female, remembered for years afterward. The presence of ice water in the ears is not a pleasant experience."

Wally agreed. "That test made me lose control of my body."

A pilot himself, Kilgore became the chief executive officer of the Lovelace Medical Center until his retirement in 1987. Ten years later, we had discussed the issue of performance for the male and female pilots. "The women utilized less oxygen, they were lighter in weight, they endured things like the sensory deprivation experience with greater strength than the men did," said Kilgore.

"Some of the men didn't last very long in the sensory deprivation experiment, which had to do with floating in water in total darkness with no sensory stimulation—no light, no hearing, no smell," he said. "The women routinely did better than the men in that particular test. Dr. Lovelace early on delivered a paper in Sweden in which he suggested that women were perhaps more suitable space candidates than men, but there was considerable objection to that for many reasons."

In 2014, the *Journal of Women's Health* published manuscripts that summarized the latest published and unpublished research into human spaceflight. Six work groups, put together by NASA and the National Space Biomedical Research Institute, examined the work and investigated whether being a man or a woman made a difference physiologically, psychologically, or behaviorally in space. No evidence was found of psychological or behavioral differences, but small differences were recorded between male and female bodies. Female astronauts were more likely to report space motion sickness after arriving at the International Space Station, for instance, while more male astronauts were sick on returning to Earth. Men had a higher risk of a visual impairment after space travel and, since women are more susceptible to cancers induced by radiation, women required lower exposure levels. In certain mental tests women were slower but more accurate; men chose speed over accuracy. In other words, more modern tests showed a case of six of one, half a dozen of the other. However, the pool of eligible results for women compared to those for men was small, since eight times as many men had flown into space at the time of the studies. One of the recommendations was, therefore, to select more female astronauts for space missions.

As Wally's interview with the NASA flight surgeon progressed, Wally poured through my list of questions and brought up the practical issue of being a fertile woman in microgravity. "Women nowadays have the opportunity to suppress their period while on orbit by taking hormone pills," said Moynihan.

"That's something that's done on the ground very routinely for people, and it can make training and logistics easier for them. If a woman chooses—and it's all a woman's choice—to menstruate while in orbit, that is certainly something we can accommodate, and we have in the past."

For older women, like Wally, bone loss during prolonged stays in space is more of an issue. "Having a crew member who is post-menopausal is something we work with," said Moynihan. "We're always concerned with bone loss in microgravity. Post-menopausal becomes a bigger risk. We have several different ways to deal with that, and we work with group of experts to tailor a specific program for each woman who is going to fly." This could involve a course of hormone-replacement therapy or a different category of medication to help protect bones.

Moynihan was warm and encouraging, putting my near-octogenarian interviewer totally at ease. "What are the advantages for women in space? Do we have any advantages?"

Before Moynihan could respond, Wally answered the question for her: "I would think so! How do today's physical requirements compare with those needed when I did tests in the 1960s?"

"I would guess a little bit gentler and a little bit more focused than what you dealt with back then," Moynihan said fondly. "We've learned a lot over the years. We do a good deal of screening, obviously, when people are selected and before they're assigned, to make sure they're healthy and ready to go fly. It'd be interesting to hear your experience."

Out it poured, spoken quickly with barely time for a breath, but interspersed with delighted laughter from Moynihan: "Jerrie Cobb called and said, 'Wally, do you want to go to space?' and I said, 'Absolutely!' She said, 'Get a hold of Dr. Lovelace.' Okay, the name Funk rang a bell with Dr. Lovelace because his uncle took care of my father, who was ill, and brought him to New Mexico. That's where I was born and raised, in Taos, New Mexico, at 7,000 feet. I am used to altitude. I skied at 13,000. So, as a youngster, I was able to do anything I wanted to do: bike, shoot, ride, ski. I was never told no. If I hurt myself, I licked my wounds and went about my business. I was totally brought up differently from most girls. Made model airplanes and liked space. I wanted to go so bad, so when Jerrie [Cobb] said, get to Lovelace, and I did, Lovelace said, "You be here on Monday." I had a week of tests that I could not believe. I don't hurt. I don't have pain. I've learned how to deal with pain. Of course they wanted to x-ray every bone, every tooth, every part of my body. First, they strapped me in the Dennis chair and injected 10-degree water into one ear, and what do you think happens to your body?"

Moynihan, the medical doctor, knew immediately. "You get a little dizzy."

Wally shook her head rapidly and lolled her tongue from side to side like a horse neighing. I lowered the recording level on the sound recorder.

"You go crazy!" Wally added.

In between laughs, Moynihan responded with an "absolutely."

"You cannot control yourself," Wally continued. "They make you go out the room, and they bring you inside in an hour and do the other ear. Well, yeah, that one pierced a little bit, but I got over it. Then we were taken into an area where they wanted to see if we would hallucinate."

Then, like a needle skipping over a track on a vinyl record, Wally jumped ahead to a memory from when she had met the first American woman in space. "Sally Ride said, 'Wally, thank you for taking all those tests. They barracked you with needles and prongs.' And it didn't bother me. I was so normal that I beat the girls and I beat the Mercury 7 guys."

Moynihan mumbled, "That's impressive."

Inwardly, I winced a little. Wally had done extremely well in the tests, and had surpassed both the men and women in at least one of them. But she hadn't beaten all of the men in all of the tests, as her wording might have implied, and reports from newspapers in the 1960s state that she had come fourth out of the women overall. Also, as the telegrams showed, the time frame between being called to the clinic was weeks rather than days. But, to be fair to Wally, it is easy to forget exact timings as you get older.

"Then they took us into the tank to see if we would hallucinate or get strange."

It was another mental jump. We had gone from discussing phase one of the tests, which were taken by all the women, to the phase two isolation-tank test, which just Jerrie Cobb, Rhea Hurrle, and Wally had taken. It consisted of a circular container of warm water in darkness, to mimic conditions of sensory deprivation and simulate weightlessness, in a soundproofed room.

"When I got into the pool, the first thing I recognized was, as I slapped my face, I couldn't feel anything. I couldn't feel the water. They had the temperature exactly to my temperature and all aspects of the room to my temperature. So this was their way of saying this is what it's going to be like in space. Jerrie had a whole flotation deal around herself. I had something around the size of a brick. I had foam rubber behind the back of my neck and my back, and I was to lay on that body of water. The lights came down, my ears were plugged, and they said, 'Wally, talk or tell stories, do anything you want, stay in as long as can.' In those days I didn't talk, so I've come a long way." Moynihan grinned.

"Anyway, I stayed there, and after a while they said, 'Wally, how do you feel?' I said, 'I feel fantastic!' Then they said, we're going to turn the lights on and take your ear plugs out, and I came out. I knew there was a clock by the door, and I was real anxious to see how I did. Those guys were so smart—they'd covered the clock. Anyway, I went out, I did my debriefing and got a lot of the same questions I'd had three days before about my parents, my animals, my studies, the Bible, and so forth. They asked me everything about my life. Everything was the same!" Wally was indignant. "I didn't change my mind on anything just because I was in a tank with water the same as my temperature. So then they said, 'You stayed in 10 hours and 35 minutes . . .'"

Moynihan took a large breath.

"'. . . and you broke the record.'"

"Wow." For once, this "wow" was not from Wally. There was not much more to be said, to be honest, when you've heard it in more detail instead of just a number. It was an incredible feat.

"So," said Wally, "I don't know if this kind of a test goes on in today's time or not?"

"No ma'am, no ma'am. What an amazing story. Thank you for sharing that. I'd heard pieces along the way, but I've never heard a firsthand report."

Wally laughed and said, "You're welcome." It was a wonderfully engaging exchange between a twenty-first-century female NASA flight surgeon and a woman who, fifty-five years earlier, in the last century, had been a medical guinea pig for female human space travel.

"Dr. Lovelace was ahead of his time in just about every area in which his interests took him," his colleague Dr. Don Kilgore told me. "He understood that women had an equal place in history that was being made in those days and he did his best to convince other people. He was only partially successful in that, but his attitudes in the 1950s were refreshingly different to those of the average person, and certainly very different to what we found in the media coverage of what we were trying to do."

The headlines from Michigan's *Lansing State Journal*, September 4, 1960, were a case in point. "To Space in High Heels? First Lady Astronaut Is First a Woman. Pretty Jerrie Cobb Puts Femininity Right Up There With Flying."

The article on "America's first lady astronaut"—written by a woman—was, like many of the day, focused on Cobb's appearance, reassuring readers that the aviator remained a woman first and foremost. Cobb was "a pretty 29-year old miss who probably would take high heels along on her first space flight if given the chance."

It later told the reader that Cobb was "equally at ease in a fashionable dress and hat or bulky space suit and helmet." She "maintains her femininity with deliberate aplomb." And, in case that was too subtle: "There's nothing masculine about her 121 pounds attractively arranged over 5 feet, 7 inches."

"The fact that we had these wonderful women who were wonderfully well qualified and tremendously motivated was an interesting phenomenon," said Kilgore, "but it couldn't change fact—and the fact was the world wasn't ready for women astronauts on this side of the Atlantic."

Although that attitude certainly changed in the United States, it took longer than many women expected. However, by 1997, when I'd spoken to Kilgore, female astronauts within NASA were the norm. Linda Godwin, for instance, whom I had met at the NASA Johnson Space Center, had been an astronaut for eleven years and completed three missions. Her fourth and final spaceflight, in 2001, was yet to take place. Godwin combined impressive science qualifications with being a pilot, as many astronauts routinely do now. "The women in the past paved the road for this to make it better today," she said. "Those were the women that bucked the system and took a lot of the curves out of the road for the rest of us."

I'd also interviewed a relatively newly qualified female astronaut, mission specialist Dr. Janet Kavandi. She was from the class of "95, which consisted of nineteen astronauts. Kavandi was one of five women on the team. Two of them were pilots. The rest, like her, were scientists. "Personally I have not experienced a situation where it was a disadvantage to be female," Kavandi said. "I know that's probably changed over the years, but honestly, today, I feel the equivalent of all the male and female members on the team. From my perspective, I get treated like everybody else in the astronaut corps."

At that time, Kavandi had two young children and a supportive husband, and was waiting to fly into space. Today, she is a veteran of three spaceflights between 1998 and 2001, the earliest being the final Space Shuttle mission to the Russian space station, Mir. She spent thirty-three days in space and made 535 orbits of the Earth. In 2016 she was appointed director of the NASA John H. Glenn Research Center in Cleveland, Ohio.

Nowadays, the tests for male and female astronauts take the form of a less invasive but more extensive form of medical screening over several weeks, including a psychiatric and physical component. Due to the collaborative nature of the International Space Station, the ability to speak another language has become an additional required skill. When Wally made her first bid to become an astronaut, America and Russia were rivals. Decades later, American and European astronauts learned Russian for joint missions on board their communal home, orbiting our planet at 17,500 miles per hour.

So far, despite my reservations, Wally had done a great job with her first two interviews as reporter. While she drank a glass of water, I decided to get thirty seconds of "room atmos," since it was useful for editing, and explained the need for silence. There was just one problem. Wally couldn't keep quiet. Within ten seconds she started whispering to Moynihan. Audible, ludicrously loud stage-style whispers.

"You do know that me recording the room in silence means you not giggling?"

More sniggering followed. This time from both of them. My producer's poker face faltered. "I'll record the room afterward."

When we continued, Wally showed Moynihan a photocopy of her schedule for several days of her tests at the Lovelace Clinic. "This is amazing," said Moynihan. She read it out loud, skipping the odd word. "Monday, February 27th, 1961: stool sample . . . Report to the lab. Audiology . . . we do that as well . . . cold presser . . . proctology exam . . ."

Proctology was an anal examination or, as Moynihan put it, "that's looking from down below." There then followed, "sinus . . . that's to see if you're able to equalize . . . pulmonary tests . . ."

Wally was astonished. "It's interesting you're recognizing this when it was so many years ago."

"Hmm," said Moynihan. "A lot of barium and a lot of stool samples . . . ENT, very important with pressure changes. EET . . . Brain and procedural activity. Oh, tilt table. We still do that."

"Bet you're not putting zero-degree water in their ears."

It was ten degrees, but we knew what she meant. It was ice cold. Moyhinan laughed. Both the women were united, doctor and test subject, separated by over fifty years, but comfortable with each other in mutual recognition of their roles within the US space industry. When the interview was over, Moynihan thanked Wally effusively. "It was so great to meet you—a member of the Mercury 13."

"And I'm the only one of them alive," Wally replied.

"No, you're not," I said.

Wally turned around to look at me, surprised, and said: "Oh."

Jessica Meir was a recently qualified astronaut candidate from the class of 2013. NASA's astronaut selection that year had made worldwide news. For the first time, it was an even split—four of the eight astronaut trainees were women. Meir appeared far younger than her mid-thirties and was obviously eager to get into space. The reality was, as she knew, that it could take years on the waiting list, and every astronaut has to be patient. Like Wally's, her ambition had started young. "I wanted to be an astronaut when I was five years old," she said. "My first distinct memory was when I drew an astronaut on the surface of the Moon."

Meir spoke fast. It was clear that Wally was struggling to understand what she was saying, as was I. Every so often, we asked her to slow down. The NASA line about the Orion spacecraft and the new Space Launch System (SLS) rocket—part of the Agency's "journey to Mars"—featured heavily and repeatedly in her answers. She came across as a slick, on-message NASAbot, and sounded as if she'd said it all before hundreds of times—which she probably had. Astronauts are always in demand by the media. The appearance of automation was a shame because, like the flight surgeon and the flight director, Meir was phenomenally impressive.

An assistant professor of anesthesia at Harvard Medical School, Meir was a biologist with a doctorate from Scripps Institution of Oceanography, specializing in how animals adapted to extreme environments, and a master's in space studies from the International Space University. Her background included working for Lockheed Martin's Human Research Facility and serving as an aquanaut crew member in the Aquarius underwater habitat for Extreme Environment Mission Operations, or

NEEMO mission. She dived, climbed mountains, cycled, and skied. Meir was also a pilot. So far, so Wally. Meir's first trip into space will be to the International Space Station, but in the future this woman could, theoretically, also become the first woman on the red planet. Wally asked Meir if she wanted to go to Mars.

"Sure, once NASA designs a program, I'd be happy to go delve into the spirit of exploration and get us back safely," said Meir chirpily.

"Has any woman inspired you?"

"No, not really."

It was an honest answer but a disconcerting one. When Meir admitted she didn't know anything about the Mercury 13 either, I was disappointed, especially as she appeared uninterested in learning about them too. Wally went uncharacteristically quiet. Afterward, instead of the usual elation that often accompanied meeting an astronaut, regardless of whether they'd been in space yet or not, our spirits were somewhat dampened. Meir represented the future and, perhaps due to living in an era with greater opportunities for women, seemed not to have considered the sacrifices made by women within her field in the past. Women who had pushed hard to make the opportunities that had come Meir's way possible. Women like Wally.

A few years after our interview, Meir learned how to fly jets—something Wally and the Mercury 13 were desperate to do (officially) over fifty years ago. Meir's experience at this point sounded almost superhuman, but that's because, compared to you or me, she *is*. If entry requirements into the exclusive astronauts' club were high in the 1950s and 1960s, they are even higher now. Twenty-first-century astronauts are overwhelmingly qualified. Today it is no longer enough to be a great pilot.

It was touch-and-go whether we'd make it to the airport. North West Regional was only a few miles away from Grapevine, Dallas, but we were heading there in Wally's camper van: a vehicle close to retirement, with a driver long-past retirement. As usual, Wally refused to wear a seat belt.

Wally was taking me flying. She leaned behind my seat to check if she'd brought a second pair of headphones for the flight, and every so often the van swerved gently across the road.

"It's okay," she reassured me after I objected. "I'm not crossing the line."

The sooner we got to the airfield, the better.

I was not a complete novice in a small aircraft, thanks to an assignment from the *Sunday Times*' travel section to spend a week learning to fly in La Rochelle, France. Despite the beautiful location, it was a surprisingly tough week. There was a huge amount to learn and absorb, and as the runway approached on my first landing attempt, I panicked, lifted my hands from the control wheel and used them to cover my eyes. By the end of the week I could pilot the Cessna from La Rochelle to Nantes with the instructor beside me. It was an incredible experience. I loved flying, and still do; but even so, it was clear that even twenty years ago I had not been a natural pilot, and preferred being served a glass of wine and some nuts as a passenger instead.

To my delight, the blue-and-white airplane Wally led me to was a familiar one. The only type, in fact, I could recognize. "This is a Cessna 172," said Wally. "It's a 1972 model, which is quite old."

The old part was not reassuring.

Wally spotted a guy, Eddie, in the distance. She pointed to me and shouted: "She's going to be filming part of this."

Even after all the audio interviews we'd done, and despite my reminders, Wally still defaulted to television instead of radio. She used a small ladder to climb onto the wing to check the gas. "This is the Wally stick," she said holding up what looked like a drum stick. "I'm putting it in the tank to see how much gas is there. Seven inches. That tells me the tank is full. Then I check the oil . . ."

Back on the ground, Wally checked the flaps at the edge of the wings and examined the top of the wings and the ailerons at the tips. She then tapped the elevators and the rudders. Eddie wandered over after hearing me chatting with Wally.

"Your accent doesn't sound like you're from Alabama," he said.

"She's the head BBC girl," said Wally.

This wasn't the first time I'd been promoted, and I didn't want to explain about being an independent supplier for the BBC either. "No, I'm one of the minions."

"Can we hear you on the BBC?"

"Occasionally. Very occasionally . . ."

"I've met a lot of journalists through knowing Wally," he said. "I've flown a cameraman once for CBS News, filming Wally."

After Wally checked the ailerons and the elevators "to see that they go up and down smoothly," she asked me to give her a hand getting the aircraft wheels out of the muddy ground from under its shelter. The three of us got into position around the plane. "Push on that strut, honey."

The idea, from my viewpoint, was to record the actuality of Wally flying. This meant sitting there working and recording. Her idea was for me to do the flying. She explained it to Eddie. "Maybe I'll do a couple of takeoffs and landings at Alliance airport's runway. Maybe I'll have her do a couple of turns. She wants me to talk, but I want her to talk to the Tower."

"There's a bit of a power struggle going on, as you can tell," I informed Eddie.

"If you don't want to do it, then you don't do it," Wally responded. Eddie left.

"I don't mind having a go, but I want to hear you. Which side does the pilot normally sit?"

"Always to the left."

"Shouldn't you go in the left seat?"

"I'm right here. I'm always to the right." She handed me a cushion. "I want you to sit down and see if this is comfortable, and you see over the nose of the plane."

"But you'll be able to fly it as well, won't you?"

"No. You're going to fly."

"I can't operate this," I said pointing to the audio equipment, "and fly at the same time."

"I'm kidding you."

"I'm feeling quite nervous."

"Stop it," she snapped. "You don't get nervous with me. I'm the boss here. You were the boss earlier." Wally grinned.

Inside the plane, I got comfortable. "Now there's a lever under here somewhere," said Wally. "I want you to get just so your toes are on the rudders. Keep your heels on the floor. Just relax. Atta girl. Alright. Here's your full call sign. November Seven Four Seven Victor Hotel, ten o'clock, and it's overcast and windy."

Wally began scrabbling under her seat. "I can't find them."

"Find what?"

"I have a pair of underpants."

What?

"A clean pair of underpants. They help me keep my headset clean. I put it around the headset so I don't hurt the wire."

"I got a bit nervous there when you said you had a spare pair of pants."

There was a pause. "I didn't understand what you just said."

"It's just as well."

Unfortunately for Wally, my aircraft headphones weren't working. It didn't bother me because I needed to wear my own headphones to monitor the recording levels. But it bothered Wally.

"Now to start an aircraft. The first thing we have to do is push the mixture control all the way rich so we have gas going all the way to the carburetor. You're going to prime it."

We taxied to the runway and were almost ready to fly. "Gas is on, trim set . . . that's off. Okay, we're going to turn the master switch on. Atta girl. Both of them. Now I'm going to put my feet up on the brakes. Let's try and get this thing started," and Wally yelled a throaty, "Yeah! We got it started . . ."

This was, I realized, a potential start to the program. What better way to begin when the presenter was a pilot who had once aimed at flying even higher? When the airplane lifted off the ground I experienced a wonderful sensation of freedom. No wonder Wally had chosen a career in aviation. Flying is quite a rush.

We circled above Texas at 2,000 feet. "Now we're over Cowtown," she announced, giving the local name for Fort Worth. "There's the stadium . . . All those buildings down there belong to Ross Perot. He's a wealthy man. Now I'm going to take you in for a landing . . ."

That night, as usual, I made backup copies of all our recordings. It was clear by then that people would either love Wally's enthusiastic, idiosyncratic but somewhat shouty delivery, or that the program would be a complete disaster.

3

Cape Canaveral

There were more brands of cranberry juice on the supermarket shelf than expected. I reread Wally's e-mail. Unusually, it was not in block capitals. On request, I typed using block capitals for her e-mails too. It felt as if I was permanently shouting. The irony.

"Okay, the cranberry deal is R.W. Knudsen cranberry juice concentrate, eight fluid ounces," she instructed. "You might not find it. A regular bottle is okay, just watered down."

Juice located, I read on. "I cannot pack my cookies. I like a box or package of chocolate-chip cookies. I dip them in hot water before I go to sleep."

It was March 2017, almost a year after our trip to Houston, and not much had changed. Wally was my anxious, controlling, easily bored presenter. I was her anxious, controlling, easily stressed producer.

The food shopping was in preparation for Wally's arrival in Orlando, Florida, that afternoon. Wally's nutritional requirements tended toward "meat and two veg"—providing those two vegetables were sweet potatoes, green beans, or spinach. I added a pack of pork chops alongside the chocolate-chip cookies, potatoes, eggs, oatmeal, bacon, sausages, spinach, and green beans in the basket. Compared to British prices, steaks in America were a bargain at twice the size. Wally loved steak.

And I loved steak at twice the size. Four steaks went into the basket. During the 1970s, I had grown up in a family where tomato ketchup was considered "too spicy." Since then my food tastes had expanded considerably. Unsure whether I could survive a week with Wally eating food that resembled British food at its plainest, I added fresh garlic and a handful of red chilies to cook for myself.

Hotels had been surprisingly expensive on Florida's Space Coast, but I'd found a suite at Cocoa Beach with two bedrooms, a living room, and kitchen/diner. Wally was excited at the idea of sharing, and the arrangement would help yet another lean radio budget stretch a lot further, especially as we also had a trip to Europe ahead. Since Wally's oven in Dallas was stacked with pans, I knew her meals were often fruit or a flatbread with lots of beef and spinach from her local Subway. "Mother asked me if I wanted to learn how to cook," Wally told me, "and I said no."

The only potential problem was that the rooms surrounded a long, enclosed courtyard. There was a small pool, barbecue pits, and areas to sit or play deck quoits. Most people were in family groups, wearing shorts or swimsuits, drinking sodas and beers. The noise was considerable. We were there to work. Everyone else was on holiday. Wally, I worried, might not like it.

We were in Cape Canaveral to make another BBC World Service radio program. Wally's distinctive delivery on our *Women with the Right Stuff* radio documentary made listeners gasp in astonishment—fortunately in a good way. People had not only enjoyed hearing about the history of women in space, they had loved Wally's tremendous enthusiasm, natural warmth, and odd, shouty delivery. The program had almost brought me to my knees during the making and editing, but it had been a success. In the week that the documentary went online, it was the BBC World Service's second-most-downloaded podcast, with millions of listeners. As a result, the same commissioning editor had wanted to pair us up again, provided the subject matter was right. It didn't take long to come up with an idea.

The world was approaching the fiftieth anniversary of the Moon landings. Six Apollo missions touched down on the lunar surface, starting with Apollo 11 in July 1969, and ending with Apollo 17 in December 1972. Although there was still much to learn, the Moon was considered a "been there, done that" destination by many within the space community. Lately, however, there had been a resurgence in the idea of returning to the Moon. China had landed a robotic rover on the lunar surface in December 2013—the first one since the Russian Luna 24 rover in 1976—and was now preparing for further missions, including landing people. The European Space Agency's director general, Jan Woerner, had publicly put forward his hopes for the construction of a "Moon village" and, although no one knew in which direction the new Trump administration would steer NASA, several US companies already had their sights set on the Moon.

There had been an increasing realization that the Moon was more than a source of scientific wonder, exploration, and artistic inspiration. It was also prime real estate, and represented a potential business opportunity. As government space agencies thought seriously about returning to our nearest astronomical neighbor and the technologies required to facilitate a potential base, a new frontier had opened up for the private sector. Commercial spaceflight companies wanted to open up the experience of space to people like Wally, but others were thinking much bigger than flying above the Earth's atmosphere and back again.

The Google Lunar X-Prize had kick-started a commercial race for the lunar surface by offering $30 million in prize money, challenging companies to put a robotic spacecraft on the Moon that could travel 500 meters and transmit high-definition images and video back to Earth. Registrations closed at the end of 2010. The deadline to land, like real space missions, kept being extended, but five teams from around the world had reached the shortlist.

The combination of government-funded and commercial interest across the world in returning to the Moon also offered an opportunity for women on several levels. Apart from behind-the-scenes careers in science, engineering, and mission operations, one side-effect of all these exciting plans would be that, at some stage in the near future, history would celebrate the first woman on the Moon. That was my angle for covering this renewed race. The title was easy: *The First Woman on the Moon*. Who better to present it than a woman who, if history had been more enlightened, could have been the first woman on the lunar surface herself in the late 1960s or early 1970s: Wally Funk.

In an alternate universe, Wally had already succeeded in going to space. One of the novellas that makes up Ian Sales's Apollo Quartet had reimagined America's space history. In the novelist's world, Dr. Lovelace's Woman in Space program hadn't been canceled. Women were needed because many American pilots were still fighting a fictionally prolonged Korean war. It resulted in "Commander Funk" and other women from the Mercury 13 realizing their dreams.

At one of Orlando's airport gates—our agreed meeting place—everyone came through except Wally. I waited. And waited, until an announcement from the airport speakers requested: "Would Sue Nelson please meet Wally at the baggage carousel?"

There she stood, arms outstretched as usual, shouting my name. She wore a dark green shirt with a Space Shuttle monogram on one side and Wally on the other, her diamond-studded plane brooch, a red scarf around her neck, and a Mars Science Lab mission patch on the right-hand back pocket of her cargo pants. As usual, she had traveled light: hand luggage including a small black suitcase and a red carryall, both labeled with "Wally Funk" embroidered patches. At Cocoa Beach, she scrutinized the hotel's small check-in area and addressed the receptionist. "Do you have *US Today*?"

They didn't. "Oh." The disappointment was clear. This was not a good start. "I like reading *US Today*. Most hotels have them in reception for free."

"The hotel across the street has them," said the receptionist. Like me, and everyone else it seemed, here was someone eager to please Wally. "They do free tea and coffee too."

"I don't drink tea or coffee. But thank you."

Inside the apartment, she did a recon of the rooms. "You've put the chocolate-chip cookies on my pillow. I love that!"

Wally removed several pressed cotton shirts from her suitcase. Each one was folded with military precision. Bottles of vitamins and health pills were lined up neatly by the bathroom sink, and her toothbrush was placed carefully on a washcloth. My cosmetics were haphazardly scattered across the rest of the shelf. She glanced into my bedroom. Admittedly, it looked as if it had been ransacked. She appraised the clothes, papers, notebooks, microphones, batteries, and recording equipment scattered across the two twin beds, bedside table, and chest of drawers . . . and said nothing.

She disappeared outside to explore while I packed the fridge and cupboards with my food supplies. Her distinctive high-decibel voice traveled far enough that I was always aware whenever she was shooting the breeze with strangers. No one remained a stranger for long with Wally. It was one of the things I admired about her. She returned with a copy of *USA Today* and a cup of free coffee for me, from a hotel neither of us were staying at. I appreciated the gesture.

Even though it was evening, the air was warm, and children played and screeched happily outside our room. It was especially loud because Wally had wedged the door open with a chair. She went to the doorway and I prepared for a complaint. To be fair, as I know from experience as a broadcaster myself, most presenters and producers preferred their own space.

One of the few times I shared a room with a BBC radio producer, in Cambridge, Massachusetts, was also for budgetary reasons. We were making a documentary in 2004 on the Harvard Computers—the poorly paid women who measured the brightness of stars on photographic glass plates at the Harvard Observatory from the end of the nineteenth century onward. Many of these women, including a maid and former school teacher from Scotland, became important astronomers in their own right. It was a great story. In fact, I had recently reviewed Dava Sobel's superb bestselling book, *The Glass Universe,* about these women for the scientific journal *Nature*. Over ten years earlier I had tried to sell the same book to a publisher in the UK, but was told "nobody buys women's history." Like Wally's attempt to become an astronaut in 1960, it was a case of right idea, wrong time.

Sharing a room, however, was a test of everybody's relationship. It worked for me and my producer, and we became friends. Since working with Wally the previous year, our professional relationship had also morphed into a friendship, but I was unsure how she'd react to the accommodation. There was not much I could do if she didn't like it, either. The hotel was full.

If a shared apartment surrounded by noisy, vacationing families was a mistake, we were in trouble.

"This is great, honey," she beamed. "Did you ask for this room or did we just luck out? We're right here with people and that's what I needed."

"You're okay with the noise?"

"If we were looking out somewhere else I wouldn't have liked it. I like to be with people. That's why I'm having a hard time in Grapevine."

Her home in Grapevine, Texas, was in a pleasant residential area, but her closest companions physically, I realized, were probably the cows. "The churches," she said, "the people I try to help. Some of them know who I am and that I'm there to help them. I don't bathe them, but I take them places. One girl has a walker . . ."

She trailed off. "Now who are we meeting again tomorrow, honey? I want to go over those notes you gave me and do my homework. I want to do my best."

She was incredible: a seventy-eight-year-old single woman who helped the elderly, enjoyed being around people, and took researching and making a radio program seriously. I could have kissed her. Instead, I informed her we'd be heading for Moon Express in the morning so that she could read up on our first interviewee, practice her radio links, and go through the questions. She sat in front of the TV repeating her introduction: "Bob Richards is the CEO of the American company Moon Express," each time with a different emphasis on a different word.

Moon Express was the first private company granted permission by the United States to go to the Moon. Founded by entrepreneurs from Silicon Valley and the space industry, it was formed in 2010 with the intention to "reopen the lunar frontier." The Florida office, close to the entrance of a US naval base, overlooked the launch pad facilities that took the Apollo missions to the Moon. That was where its ambition lay.

Next door to Moon Express, another commercially minded company had its sights set off-planet. It belonged to Space X and was their launch and landing control center. Space X's Dragon spacecraft had already made multiple return trips delivering cargo to and from the International Space Station for NASA. Naturally, I had requested an interview with Elon Musk, who, after founding the company that became PayPal and selling it for around $180 million to eBay, had gone on to launch the private space company Space X in 2002. Equally naturally, as most journalists have discovered, he turned that bid down. I spotted a Cadillac in the car park with the registration NO1 KING above the Space X company logo. *Could that belong to him?* Probably. It wasn't a Tesla, though, which is the electric car another of his start-up companies produced. Who knows? It could have been anyone who worked there because, in order to succeed, commercial space companies were not modest in advertising their ambitions.

We set up by a picnic table in a secluded grassy area behind the Moon Express building and beneath some trees for shade. This way we could see the Cape Canaveral launch pads in the distance and hear the buzz of air traffic in the background, to give the interview a sense of location. A few miles away, at Moon Express's new campus at Launch Complex 17 and 18, they were building robotic lunar landers. I could not secure access to those as I was a foreign national. Wally, as a US citizen, was free to visit, but she would not reveal her social security number to NASA or Moon Express. I tried to persuade Wally to take this opportunity and at least see the rovers for herself, even if I couldn't. "You must never give anyone your social security number ever," Wally told me firmly. "It's not safe. I've seen it on TV."

While I unpacked the recording equipment, the PR woman, Julie, kept tabs on Wally's movements. "I'm very curious," Wally yelled as she headed off, "and I want to know what these buildings are."

When Wally returned, she asked for Julie's phone number. The local area code was a reminder that we were among the world of space and rocket launches. It was three, two, one.

Dr. Robert (Bob) Richards had an impressive academic background within space science from several institutions, which included being special assistant to Carl Sagan—the inspirational astronomer, writer, and science popularizer at Cornell University. Born in Canada, Richards had cofounded the International Space University and Students for the Exploration and Development of Space. In 2008, while director of Optech's Space Division, the company's technology inside instruments onboard NASA's Phoenix lander discovered falling snow on Mars.

Richards is a visionary. A visionary who knows his space history. "I am so honored," he exclaimed on meeting Wally, hurrying toward her. He gave Wally an enormous hug and declared excitedly, "I should be interviewing you."

"Well, I feel honored to meet you."

"Likewise," Bob responded. "I'll tell you that."

Wally offered her business card. "You don't ever get to Dallas, do you? To Forth Worth?"

"Sometimes."

"Okay, well, you've got my card. I'm right there at DFW." Locations for Wally were almost invariably defined by their airport letter codes.

"I'll have to remember that."

"Yes, sir."

"We'll go dancing."

I wasn't sure where this conversation was headed. Neither, it seemed, was Wally.

"Oh, well no," she said hesitantly. "I want to know more about space and what you're doing."

Both of them laughed. Wally, a little nervously.

"Okay," said Bob and then, keeping a straight face, added: "Coffee and then dancing."

It was an unusual start to an interview. But both were enjoying each other's company. She read her introduction, and while the emphasis was still not exactly how I'd have preferred, both the link and her interview were the most relaxed I'd heard her do.

"We are a company that's concentrating on building spacecraft," explained Richards, "basically robots that can fly through space and land on other worlds, including the Moon. Not launching, we're hitching a ride to go into space."

Once separated from the launcher, the robotic spacecraft would then light its own rockets for the rest of the journey. Wally was transfixed.

"That is absolutely mindboggling because I'm not around this information, so thank you for that."

Okay, so it wasn't the usual reporter response either, but she was doing great.

"I want to be interviewing you," he replied.

Richards was a charismatic speaker. He had a vision and was generous in referencing others with a similar outlook: Space X, Blue Origin, and Virgin Galactic. The new era of entrepreneurs brought "democratized access to space."

As a boy in Toronto, Richards visited the Space Coast and the Kennedy Space Center for family holidays. "I was a child of Apollo. I grew up watching people walk on the Moon, turning channels on the TV and seeing Captain Kirk rocket through the galaxy on the Starship Enterprise, going to the movie theater and watching *2001: A Space Odyssey* and what it must be like meeting an intelligence so much vaster than ours that they appear godlike. This was my boyhood. I believed in that dream. But in 1972, with the cancellation of the Apollo program, I became an orphan of Apollo. Me and an entire generation. So what we're seeing now is that generation of believers doing it for themselves."

He described where we were standing, overlooking the Cape Canaveral launch pads, as "hallowed ground" and saw this historic location as the new future for space and business. "We will go to space to stay and to move the economic sphere of Earth outward so we can live on the Moon and go to Mars," he declared, "and the human species will expand as a multiworld species. The miracle today is that small teams of entrepreneurs driven with a vision can do what superpowers could only do before. That's how technology is accelerating to allow you and I to go into space."

Here was a man, alongside Richard Branson, Elon Musk, Jeff Bezos, and others, who was working to make his dreams, Wally's, and mine come true. And—let's not forget—make money along the way. The Moon contains minerals, rare-earth metals, helium-3, water, nickel, gold, silver, and platinum group metals. According to Richards, it was a "gas station in the sky," which Richards saw as an opportunity for exploration and exploitation but also as a way to stop plundering the Earth. He wanted to help create a permanent "space-faring species" with Moon Express at the beginning of that era. Richards, like Wally and his fellow space entrepreneurs, had a dream where mankind routinely went into space.

A few weeks earlier, Elon Musk had announced that he was going to take two unnamed private citizens on a paid trip to the vicinity of the Moon and back in the SpaceX Dragon 2 capsule. No one knew the ticket price, but news reports had speculated that the weeklong trip would cost somewhere between $35 million and $90 million.

So far, most paying customers into space have been male, accurately reflecting the gender divide for the richest people in the world. The first ever space tourist was US millionaire and former NASA engineer Dennis Tito. He signed a deal in 2000 for a reported $20 million to get on board the Russian space station Mir. But a year later, before his planned mission, the aging Mir was removed from orbit to burn up in the Earth's atmosphere. The remaining pieces fell into the South Pacific.

Fortunately for Tito, a US company called Space Adventures brokered another deal. After eight months of training in Star City, outside Moscow, Tito flew up to the International Space Station on a Russian Soyuz rocket on April 28, 2001, and spent six days in space. A few years later, in 2004, the Iranian-born American engineer and entrepreneur, Anousheh Ansari, became the first female space tourist.

After Tito's flight, from 2001 onward, commercial space tourism was open for business. There would be some major differences, however, in the experience that these early space tourists had on board the International Space Station and what would be offered by companies such as Virgin Galactic in a spaceplane. In this case, the time spent in space on a commercial flight would be measured in minutes rather than days. The upside was that tickets were more affordable. More affordable compared with the millions paid by Tito. Wally had paid $200,000 to Virgin Galactic for a taste of space. If she was to buy her ticket today, it would cost an extra $50,000. By comparison to the early space tourists and the effects of inflation, Wally appears to have got herself a bargain.

Before dinner that night, we rode a free hotel shuttle bus to Cocoa Beach pier. A notice instructed people not to walk through the Pelican Bar & Grill to reach the pier's drinking area, but somehow, while I took the detour, Wally had quietly navigated the diners and was waiting for me at the last remaining free table. As I took photographs of the sunset, Wally threw discarded potato chips into the air in order to get close up shots of seagulls swooping in to feed. I overheard her chatting with a couple who had inquired about her space-related outfit.

"I'm an astronaut, honey."

Had I misheard? Usually she used the phrase "astronaut candidate." On the way back to our room, Wally expressed a sudden desire for chocolate. Out of all the supplies on her e-mail, a bar of chocolate wasn't one of them. "I need chocolate, honey."

I drove to a Public's and, since it was a large supermarket, we split up to find the candy aisle. Unfortunately, the couple of decent brands of chocolate she later spotted in my basket didn't pass muster. "No. I don't like any of those. I like Hershey's."

Once the Hershey's was located and in the basket, she ripped off the packaging and began eating it, prompting a flashback to when my son was a toddler. "We've not paid for it yet," I said primly.

"It's okay. We'll pay for it. And we need to get more spinach."

Dinner was steak, potatoes, and fresh spinach leaves for me, cooked spinach for Wally. "I've not had steak in ages," she enthused. "This is delicious. Cooked just the way I like it. Thank you, sweetheart. I don't bother too much with meals at home. Sometimes I get my food from a soup kitchen."

I was shocked and unsure whether this was through frugality or a shortage of funds after retirement, though I suspect it might be because she enjoyed the company.

During the rest of the week, plans changed here and there. One of our space journalists had a stomach bug, but we met Ken Kremer from *Universe Today* at the Mercury Memorial Space Park in Titusville, on Florida's coast. This was where locals could gather to watch a launch from one of the NASA launch pads on Merritt Island. We stood beside a monument honoring the Mercury 7 astronauts and those from the later Gemini missions. Another reminder, for Wally, of what could have been.

Kremer had been recommended via a friend of a NASA volunteer I'd met in Houston. The community of former NASA employees is an enjoyable one to be around, as they are so helpful and keen to share their knowledge, expertise, and advice in associated museums or on NASA sites. I'd witnessed this at a NASA Social in Cape Canaveral in December 2014. NASA runs these events for people with a space-related social media following. Sometimes they were to a NASA facility, sometimes to a launch. Either way, they provided behind-the-scenes access to space scientists and astronauts. The launch I went to as part of the NASA Social was important because it was considered a "stepping stone to Mars": the test flight for the new Orion spacecraft on a Delta IV Heavy rocket. Orion was the first NASA spacecraft since Apollo that was built to carry human beings into deep space. The design was similar but larger, with the ability to send four astronauts into Low Earth Orbit or beyond.

My NASA volunteer contact, Herb Baker, had worked in business and accounting and was a former manager at the Johnson Space Center before his retirement. Through supporting NASA's Flight Operations Directorate, he had enjoyed access to the Mission Control Center and the Space Vehicle Mockup Facility. It was pretty clear that, for him, loving space was inevitable. He had gone to school with the children of the Mercury 7 astronauts, and a love of space ran in the family. His mother Aylene had sewn and repaired the fabric heat shield that saved NASA's Skylab in 1973. On contacting one of Baker's friends via Facebook, Jean Wright had suggested a number of potential interviewees. After we'd connected, I later discovered that she had been a seamstress for the Space Shuttle and had hand-sewn the thermal protection between the spaceplane's tiles.

At the Kennedy Space Center, Wally and I met the delightful Hugh Harris, a former radio broadcaster who had been known as the voice of Space Shuttle launch control. The first Space Shuttle launch, in 1981, marked the start of hundreds of human beings eventually going into space. But during the 1960s, Harris had worked in the NASA Johnson Center press office during the Moon landings, and so had witnessed the excitement first-hand—perfect for our program. However, it turned out NASA had recommended Harris because they would not provide a spokesperson. For the first time in my twenty years of BBC radio programs, the space agency had been uncharacteristically unhelpful with a straightforward media request. A few months into the Trump presidency, no one at NASA was prepared to discuss a possible return to the Moon.

This was purely political. It had been almost four months since President Trump's inauguration, but no one had yet been nominated as the new head of NASA. This left the space agency unwilling to speculate on an unknown future and rudderless in terms of not knowing what its direction would be under a new administration: a continued long-term path toward Mars with the Orion program, or a shorter-term return to the Moon? Harris had retired, so was free to air his own views. Interestingly, his opinion chimed with the European Space Agency's planned direction.

"We should be going back to the Moon," he said, "and make use of it to go out and colonize other worlds. The big advantage to the Moon is learning how to live on a hostile world."

Harris had recommended that we drop in to see John Tribe, a former Apollo propulsion engineer. He lived in a stunning lake-side house filled with space memorabilia, vintage clocks, and a model train that, in one room, ran above our heads on tracks connected to the walls. Tribe had been the chief engineer for the Boeing-Rockwell Company, but he was born in the UK and began his career with an apprenticeship at the British aviation company De Havilland. He had also worked on Britain's Blue Streak rocket during the 1950s before he was offered a job at Cape Canaveral, joining the US Atlas rocket program. He bought a ticket for passage on the HMS *Queen Mary* and arrived in the United States on February 1, 1961. Tribe went on to work for Project Mercury and sat beside Werner von Braun for some of the Ranger launches. "This was in 1962. In 1944 we got hit by a V1 rocket when I lived in Portsmouth." He paused to laugh, "and here's one of the founding fathers of the German rocket program right next to me!" Apparently, the relationship between the German scientists and the few British-born engineers was extremely cordial. "We would kid each other about the war."

I noticed a grey panel mounted on wood. The words "engine control" are above a number of switches and buttons labeled with names like "ready," "start," "engine lox tanks pressurized," and "ignition." On the left-hand side there's a key in a slot, and on the right-hand side a worrying big red button. "This is the engine control panel for an Atlas rocket," explained Tribe. "It's the panel from the block house in complex 36, and it's the same panel we had for John Glenn's flight."

When the building was being torn down, Tribe rescued the panel and used the original schematics to wire it up. "The key is the engine ground power, and then as you go through the various engine controls you would arm the system."

He asked me to push the start button, and when I did there was a crackly recording. "That's John Glenn's voice." Someone else said, "Godspeed, John Glenn." Tribe informed me that this was Scott Carpenter. Then we heard a countdown to the launch.

It was a strange feeling listening to the two men who testified against the Mercury 13 while watching a member of the Mercury 13 through the window walking outside in the garden adjoining the lake with Tribe's wife.

Tribe eventually moved from Project Mercury to the Apollo program, and at the end of 1972, when Apollo 17 became the final manned Moon landing mission, he was reassigned to NASA's new spaceplane—the Space Shuttle. There he met Melinda, another Shuttle engineer who would later become his wife. One of their windows in their home overlooked an outdoor miniature train track and was decorated with colorful stained glass. Naturally, considering their history, the design was of a Space Shuttle.

Women may not always have been visible in the US space program but, as the book and film *Hidden Figures* testified, they had been present in many aspects of the space industry for a long time—from engineers and seamstresses to mathematicians.

As usual, during our drives back to our hotel after a full day of interviews, Wally was on her phone leaving voice mails for friends. Most were upbeat, some were occasional reprimands—"You didn't call"—and there were plenty of questions and non-stop commentary for me. Whenever we went over a bridge across the Indian River, she assessed the conditions from looking at windsocks, the bending of the trees, or the waves hitting the shoreline.

"Wind speed ten knots. Twenty knots on the water. How full's your tank?"

"Half."

"It must be a very economical car. I wonder how many cylinders it's got. Four or six I guess." There was a brief silence as she opened the glove compartment to read the driver's manual.

"Do you want to get a tattoo?"

"No."

"I almost had DNR put on my chest. Sometimes I write it on there."

"Do not resuscitate?"

"Yeah. In pen. You know I don't want any of that stuff, honey."

I often learned something new—she'd once co-owned a restaurant in Hermosa Beach—or gained an unexpected insight into Wally's fearless approach to life. Once, while stationary at a red traffic light, she spotted a typical Florida tourist attraction. "There's a gator park," she said. "I stood on a gator once. You stand on his back and cover his eyes with your fingers. By the way, I've not talked to you about my ballooning..."

On one of those evenings, back at the suite after a day's work, she realized that her diamond-studded airplane brooch, a gift from her beloved dead mother, was no longer pinned on her shirt. It could have been anywhere on the ground thirty miles away in Titusville's Memorial Park or by the lake near John Tribe's house, where Wally had gone for a short stroll with his wife. This was assuming no one had pocketed the distinctive brooch, because by now five or six hours had passed since our first stop at the park. Understandably, Wally was distressed. Then I recalled admiring her brooch when we stopped off to eat lunch inside the Moon Light drive-in diner and looked up their phone number.

"You mustn't have noticed it wasn't on straight."

The diner not only had the brooch, it was already securely locked away in a safe. It was a huge relief for all concerned. As the restaurant was about to close, we arranged to collect it in the morning. It would mean an earlier start, but we could pick it up on the way to Embry-Riddle Aeronautical University up the coast in Daytona Beach. Wally switched back into her normal happy mode, and I celebrated averting a potential drama by opening a nicely chilled bottle of Sauvignon Blanc, for one.

Perhaps because of the potential loss of the brooch from her mother, our discussion over dinner turned to family. Her father's name was Lozier. I got her to spell it out since I'd never heard that name before. "I haven't either. First time I've said it in a bunch of years. Lozier, L-O-Z-I-E-R, Ray Funk, and Mother was Virginia Shy Funk."

"Shy? You are the opposite of shy."

"Oh no. Shy was the family name." We both cackled. "No, I'm not shy at all."

Her father owned several five-and-dime stores in New Mexico, including one in Taos. "Funk's 5 and 10 on the Plaza. Five and dime. It had everything you would ever want from candy to soda, to linen to toys, to women's dresses, men's clothing," said Wally. "I suppose it would be like a Walmart today because Walmart did put Father out of business."

Wally was always making pocket money. "I brought up rabbits and would take them in front of the store and sell them to the tourists. I'd also take my shoe shine stuff and shine shoes for a dime. Father said, 'What are you doing with your nickels and dimes?' I said, 'I'm gonna put 'em away.' He taught me how to save and invest."

He also advised: "Don't ever borrow and never lend. And the same with clothes." According to Wally, that was "the greatest thing he could ever say to me."

Her father was born in Indiana in 1897. Before running the shop, he had been a math teacher. "He was quite a bright boy because he owned a car back in the 1920s and 1930s, and most people didn't have cars back then. He was in the 5 and 10 business when he met Mother. The story went that Father was trimming the shop window. Mother was looking at him and slipped and fell on the sidewalk. He went out and picked her up. This was at the 5 and 10 in Olney, Illinois—that's where Mother was born and raised. They obviously dated and fell in love and married."

When Lozier Funk contracted tuberculosis, his doctor suggested a move to a better climate in Taos, New Mexico, to be treated by the doctor's nephew, another medical professional. Taos was north of Santa Fe, 2,120 meters (7,000 feet) above sea level in the high desert, surrounded by mountains. "Father was cured in the high mountains and the pure air."

The physician's nephew turned out to be Dr. William Randolph Lovelace. The man who treated Wally's father would later devise the astronaut tests for the Mercury 7 that were also used for the Mercury 13. The man who would push Wally to her physical limits to see if women also had what it took to go into space. It was a fortuitous move on several levels. By relocating to the mountains, Wally was able to grow up skiing, cycling, running, and performing all sorts of other sports at high altitude. She was in no doubt that it was these experiences that had made her physically strong enough to make the grade.

The 5 and 10 in Taos was particularly popular with artists, since it sold brushes made from squirrel hair, and her parents enjoyed company. "They ENTERTAINED a lot," she said. "Mother had beautiful china—Limoges crystal from Europe and jewelery made by Indians with turquoise that you can't find today."

Wally's memories are of a happy childhood filtered through the unconditional love of her parents. She had one brother, nine years older, who later entered the military. This surprised me, as she had the self-possession of an only child. "I grew up feeling like an only child," she said.

"At two, Daddy said I was very investigative. I was always curious as to how things were wrapped up. Mother had a picture of me trying to figure out how to open one of Daddy's packages at the store. Then later I saw Father shaving one time and, when he left the razor, I got up on a stool. Mother said, 'What are you doing?' And I said, 'I'm shaving like Daddy.'"

Considering the razor in those days was of the open cut-throat variety, Wally's mother responded calmly: "You don't want to do that right now." Voices were never raised.

"Never was I ever put down. Never: 'You can't do that.' 'No' was not a part of it."

Never being told no must have played a formative part in shaping Wally's character. It could have made her spoiled or precious. Instead, it gave her unlimited confidence in her own abilities. For someone so keen to try out new experiences, this was a tremendous asset. She viewed the world—as she still does now—as a place with limitless potential. Her parents, unlike many others in the 1940s and 1950s, did nothing to prevent their only daughter from learning to shoot or hunt or run or ski. They imposed no limits on her aspirations. Wally grew up thinking she could do anything.

In Taos Wally ran to school and back, morning and afternoon. "Mother would say, 'Honey, you make sure that when you have to go to the bathroom you do it at home. You don't do it at school.'"

I was confused. "Mother said it was not clean." Her voice became almost inaudible. "She said, 'You're with the Spanish and other people.'" Wally sounded apologetic for her mother's views. "So I always ran home after school to the bathroom. To this day I put toilet paper on the john because that's the way I was taught." She laughed. "Do you?"

"No."

"You don't put toilet paper down?"

"No!"

"Do you sit?"

"Yes."

"All those germs on your bottom?"

"I have a shower every day." She didn't look convinced. "It's fine," I said. "You need a certain amount of germs to survive."

"Well, I don't think I have those."

A slice of bread I was cutting shot off the table. I picked it up from the floor and put it back on my plate. "You never saw that," I said. Wally nodded in collusion. My germs were just fine.

There was only one occasion when her Mother's poise faltered. "At four, Daddy was bringing me balsa wood to make planes. I was given a razor blade and everything you'd need to cut out the balsa wood to make the ribs, wings, fuselage, and glue to put everything together. I put the wings on the fuselage and then realized you had to put tissue paper over the fuselage so that I could eventually paint it. I got the tissue paper around the wings and glued it, but it wasn't taut enough. I needed something to spray on it and I had watched Mother spray herself with her perfume. So I dumped out all of her perfume, which was quite expensive, put water in it, and sprayed the wings and it came out perfect. That's the only time she said: 'You shouldn't have done that. This was expensive perfume. Ask before you use my stuff.'"

What did you say? "Okay ma'am." She then informed me, as if this had been the purpose of the story: "You dope it. You don't use that word anymore." (She was right. I had to look it up. At the early part of the last century, "dope" meant adding varnish to the cloth surface of airplane parts to make them taut.)

Wally described herself as a "happy-go-lucky kid." She had a palomino horse called Victor and often wore a Wild West costume. She was jokingly called the Taos Kid. "Mother said, when I had Victor, 'If you fall off your horse or your bike, you lick your wounds. Don't come back running home crying.'"

I found that a little harsh, but not Wally. "They taught me to look after myself!"

Were her parents proud of what she did with the Mercury 13? "I guess they were, but they never really told me about it," she said. "The hugs and things were all there. But there were times that I was doing very well but they weren't there."

Wally also related an often-repeated story about being given a superman cape for her fourth birthday. "I got out on the barn with some hay down below and . . . ," her voice became sing-song, ". . . jumped off the barn trying to fly. You've heard that story many times. I did it again and thought, oh, it's because my nose didn't have a propeller. And then it wasn't until later that I learned you had to have lift. I had no lift off my wings. But I would be making all these wonderful planes and, to this day, after I went to college, I never saw another one. They must have got destroyed. I don't know why they got destroyed or where they went. I hope they went to some kid because I made hundreds of them."

Wally didn't finish high school. "I went to Stephens at fifteen." This was in 1954. "It's a girls' college in Columbia, Missouri. I was not doing very well at school, so my parents sent me there."

At first glance, Stephens College was not a natural fit for a tomboy. Founded in 1833, the second-oldest girls' college in the United States turned out well-dressed young ladies with a view, some critics have said, to producing acceptable wife material. Parents and family friends were even interviewed "to see what kind of a girl you were" before acceptance into the school.

"Mother had to get me all new Neiman Marcus clothes, all dresses. Including one fancy white one for church on Sundays." Since it was around 800 miles away, Wally boarded "the Stephens Susies train" at Lamy, New Mexico, with her trunk.

It sounded like something out of Harry Potter, but it was the name given to the train that went to Columbia, Missouri. "Before my time the College president could never remember the girls" names. Susie, would you get this for me. Susie, would you take care of that situation over there. They were all Susies. So we were the Stephens Susies."

When she arrived at Stephens, it was a complete culture shock for a girl used to wearing chaps, riding a horse, and shooting her gun. "The girls had long fingernails, and their fingernails were colored." Before that, the only person Wally had ever seen with painted nails was her mother. "The girls had long hair and I had a short haircut. I was dressed well but I didn't fit. I didn't fit IN." She almost shouted the last word.

"I wasn't sure I was going to like it. I unpacked my clothes and my trunk—you had to have sheets, washcloth, linen. About the second day I called home and said, 'I don't know if this is the right place for me.' And Mother said: 'Why don't you just stick it out for about a week and you can come home when you want to.' Brilliant. As I got to know people I enjoyed it more because I've always been out there . . . What's the word I want to use?"

"Gregarious?"

"Yeah. But you see these older girls kinda overtook me. Their makeup, their dresses, their fingernails. Some of them had little drinks. They were all frou-frou. I don't like frou-frou. I loved going to the gym. But I got into my courses and started getting along with people and met other people who weren't as frou-frou. I called Mother and said, 'I think it's gonna be okay.' I was meeting more people that were interested in things that I did as a kid. I was a tomboy. I did mostly sports, and what's funny is the sports we did then were basketball and baseball. I did some skating. Skiing I was good at because I was going to go to the Olympics. I had no fears. I'd do anything. I wasn't going to break anything. I had a lot of confidence in myself. The spirit of the Taos Mountain . . ."

About six months after arriving at Stephens, Dr. Bates, Wally's advisor, called her parents. He informed them that their daughter was not doing as well as she could in her class work. Wally's mother asked him if they had an airport. In the 1940s, Stephens College had started an aviation program based nearby in Columbia Municipal Airport. Wally's mother told him to get her daughter out there, and Wally started flying. All those years of studying how aircraft fly, making balsa wood planes, and hanging them from her bedroom ceiling became a reality.

"Did your grades improve?"

"I don't remember because I was either at the gym or the airport."

I took that as a no. But there was another unexpected bonus to flying for Wally. "I could wear pants! Every night you had to have heels, hose, and dress. In school, frou-frou stuff and a skirt. If I was going flying I could wear pants. Not Levi's but pants."

In the time I'd known Wally, she'd always worn trousers. Did she ever wear a skirt? Wally was indignant. "Of course. I have skirts in my closet now, but I can't wear them as I don't have the heels. Oh yeah. Mother always had me decked out. I had multiple dresses, honey, and heels, hose that I had to wear. It just wasn't my thing, and they understood it. Anyway, I got through. I didn't have the best grades, but you know what? I had more fun with my flying instructors, and I was very ANIMATED. I didn't know much. Daddy helped me with my math. Mother helped me with my spelling which, to this day, is bad." More laughter. "Anyway, I'm flying, flying, flying thanks to my father for letting me do this."

Did she date? "No. Just flying. Got my license at Stephens. Graduated on my second year. Mother wanted to give me a coming-out party in New York. I said no. I'd rather be out shooting my gun."

Calamity Jane, eat your heart out.

During her time at Stephens College, Wally flew for the Stephens Susies flight team. "My last year I was super qualified to go to NIFA [National Intercollegiate Flying Association] air meets in the United States. I'd have a copilot and she would navigate and I'd fly the airplane. We'd come home and I'd have done very well. One time we won. That was about the time I graduated in 1958 and saw what Oklahoma State University had done. They had won EVERYTHING."

Armed with her private pilot's license, Wally knew exactly where she wanted to go next: Oklahoma State University (OSU) in Stillwater, Oklahoma. Although it was not what her parents had planned, Wally was there for one reason only: its aviation club.

OSU had a student flying team renowned for winning. They were called the Flying Aggies. "I had a ball. Got the rest of my flight ratings. It was a big, big part of my life."

These ratings included qualifications to fly a seaplane and a glider, and later becoming an instructor herself. Not surprisingly, when not talking about space, Wally talks aviation. Earlier that day in the car, she had recalled watching the Thunderbirds and the Blue Angels, the air demonstration teams for the US Air Force and Navy respectively, from air traffic control towers. When down on the ground, she would hang out at the Ninety-Nines booth belonging to the women-only pilots' organization. Former students would often approach her and say hello. Recently she recognized one of them but couldn't recall from where or when until he said: "You gave me my private license in 1963 in Hawthorne, California."

At that point in her life, age twenty-four, Wally was a chief pilot at a flight school. I asked her how many people she had taught to fly since then. When she answered, it was my turn to shout: "Three thousand? Wow!"

"But you know everything about me, honey," she said. "What about you?"

She knew about my husband and teenage son, so I gave her the short version of the rest: eldest of six, parents divorced, estranged from my mother for the best part of twenty-five years. Considering Wally's closeness to her own mother, that last fact visibly shocked her. But I considered myself lucky. My mother-in-law Penny, a wonderful woman, had been a mother in all but name for twenty years. I did not lack motherly love.

"What about your house?"

Wally was staying with me the following week in England. I pulled up an old Google Maps image of our black-and-white mock-Tudor house, typical of 1930s English suburbs, on my laptop. "That's a big house," she said.

"Ah, no, only half of that is ours. It's semidetached."

"Oh, they put two houses together. What about the noise? Is that common in England? That's kinda how my apartment is—but what happens if you both want the fire going and there's only one chimney? Do you have people or kids living next door to you? Do you hear crying?"

Once reassured about the noise levels, I showed her the village online. "I don't think I lived with anybody in England," she said. "I was always camping."

She cooed over photographs of Richard and our son Matthew. "Oh, look at how cute! Boy, is he looking dandy. Very royal. That's a good shot of you too . . . I like that one. You have a good smile." A video cropped up. Matthew was playing water polo.

"How many to a team? How are they trying to get the ball away from each other? He's about to shoot. Good job!"

She knew I still enjoyed playing tennis but wanted to know what other sports I had done when younger. Like Wally, I had been active and was in the school tennis, netball, gymnastics, lacrosse, and trampolining teams. It wasn't easy describing lacrosse. "It's a stick with some netting on the end and you catch the ball in it and run."

"Doesn't it fall out?"

"You move your arms back and forth." I tucked my elbows into my ribs and waved my arms as if holding an invisible lacrosse stick. It didn't help. Then, as if on cue, a boy walked by our hotel window carrying a lacrosse stick. "There's one." Wally ran outside and the boy let her inspect it more closely.

I showed her some of the photos I had taken that day. "I didn't realize my hair was so stupid . . . That one's okay. Not that one, I'm okay but you're frowning. You've got your eyes shut, so delete that one. That's nice. Nah, that's not so hot. God. I hate my wrinkles."

That was the first time I'd heard her remark on her personal appearance. It was unexpectedly negative considering how young and vital she looked. It was now or never. "Have you ever had any work done?"

"No. And I should have done that about two years ago because mother's face looked fabulous."

To be honest, it was harder to tell in America, as plastic surgery was much more common than in the UK.

"Everybody has their boobs done, their eyes, their nose," Wally lamented. "Then there's rehab. I have good insurance."

And good genes? "Oh yeah, I have good genes, but I think being out in the Sun and everything my eyes have got a little more wrinkly than I anticipated. I wish I were fifty years younger. Time goes by so quickly. It would have been fun if you had met me in my twenties. I did everything."

She ascribed her confidence to her mother and the spirit of the Taos Mountain. I'd heard her mention the spirit of the Taos Mountain a lot, and it bothered me. It was too hippie. And airy. Like the power of crystals or astrology. A bit . . . unscientific. What was this spirit? Was it related to the Native Americans she grew up around in the Taos pueblos?

"No. Can you get Taos on that thing?" She meant my laptop. I scrolled through the numerous images that came up.

"There's the mountain," said Wally excitedly. "There it is. Stop it! See, you can kind of make out the hair and the two eyes looking this way with his white collar, and that's George Washington."

I couldn't make out a thing.

"That's the spirit of Taos Mountain right there. It gave me . . ." she patted her heart, ". . . the knowledge to do everything I wanted to do. Nobody taught me how to work on a model T Ford or how to crank it or how to drive a tractor when I was about ten. I got in and did it. It was second nature. When I was growing up. I just did things. How did I know how to build my house? It just came to me. So I've been very, very lucky in that respect. The spirit. I know it's hard for people. People say, 'Are you praying to it?' and I say, 'No,' but I suppose some people do. Some people say, 'If the spirit doesn't like you—you will never come back . . .'"

She pointed to the snowy peaks. "That's where I skied at 12,000 feet. This picture is at 14,000. Many times, I had to take ashes and scatter them over the mountain."

"Whose ashes?"

"The people. They were cremated, and people wanted their ashes to be flown over Taos Mountain. I'd get the ashes. They came in a box like a shoe would come in with a little door, and I was taught exactly how to let the ashes out little-by-little out the door. I'd make a circle around Taos Mountain and get all the ashes out of the box, and I'd do it about five or six, seven times."

It didn't always go as planned. "One time the wife wanted to take her husband's ashes out, and she was sitting in the back seat in their airplane. I said, you have to open the door and only have it opened about an inch, and you have to pinch out the ashes. She didn't understand this, and before you knew it, you had whatever his name was all over the cockpit."

Did she want to go back to Taos? "I thought eventually I was gonna go back there, but I don't have any friends left. Everywhere I've lived, maybe they've died or moved somewhere else. I was thinking about Palm Springs, but my friends are gone. I'd like to go back to New Mexico, but I've sold the house. My friend Mary has gone from Albuquerque, and everybody's a husband-and-wife thing and I can't ask for help."

Although Wally spent a good part of the evening speaking to friends on the telephone, it sounded like a lonely existence for someone who loved being surrounded by people. No wonder Wally traveled so much. By now, she'd almost finished her dinner. "Are you enjoying that?"

"Very much," she replied. "I'm not going to leave a drop on this plate."

Afterward Wally washed the dishes and wiped every surface spotless. "That was a nice pork chop," she said happily. "Tomorrow we can have steak again."

4

The Waiting List

"This is great. I like your home, honey. How is it plumbed? Where do you get your water from? Where does the power come in? That's a big back yard. How many feet to the bottom?"

Wally paced around the kitchen, bubbling over with energy. Things were not working out as planned. I had hoped we would both be napping by now. But within hours of arriving from Orlando into the UK at six in the morning, it was clear that the only person suffering from jet lag was me.

Wary of the effect an overnight trans-Atlantic flight would have on Wally's stamina and health, I had scheduled a break at my house. The idea was to rest for a few days and ease through the transition before taking a Eurostar train to mainland Europe to continue collecting material for *The First Woman on the Moon*. The first stop would be Cologne, and then on to Paris for interviews with various members of the European Space Agency.

"Where are your pipes, honey? You know I like to know these things. I like to know how things work. Do they come in under here? How old is this house?"

That one I could answer. "It was built around 1930 . . ."

My brain was on slowdown and couldn't keep up. Richard, my husband, took over. Wally had greeted him and our sixteen-year-old son, Matthew, like long-lost friends. Her natural warmth and friendliness toward them thawed my sleep-deprived irritation.

"When can we see the town, honey? Shall we go now?" All plans for a nap disappeared.

According to the road signs, I live in a "pre-Roman riverside village." It's a picturesque part of Hertfordshire, and the River Lea, which runs through the village, is practically a stream at this point before it joins the Thames in London around thirty miles away. There is a narrow main street consisting of a church, a couple of pubs, a few shops, and a Women's Institute, plus some pretty good Chinese, Indian, and Thai restaurants. Wally doesn't like spicy food so, before leaving Florida, I'd created and ordered an online shop filled with her favorite food: steak, pork chops, sweet potatoes, green vegetables, plenty of spinach, and cranberry juice.

Due to its proximity to the capital, the village contains a lot of commuters. The train station, however, which playwright George Bernard Shaw once cycled to for his own commute, closed after the Beeching Report, officially known as the Reshaping of British Railways, in 1965. A small section of track and a platform remain, restored by a local heritage society. An oak carving of Shaw now sits permanently on a bench, legs crossed, waiting for a train that will never arrive. "That's neat," said Wally.

We visited the tombstone of another famous local resident, the Antarctic explorer Aspley Cherry Garrard, a survivor of Captain Scott's doomed expedition to the South Pole. Wally was appreciative, asked questions I couldn't always answer, and soaked in everything. Within thirty minutes I'd run out of things to show her in the village. Plus I was exhausted after the journey from the States. *Why wasn't she tired?*

Back at our house, it didn't take long before Wally became visibly bored. An English friend of hers was due to join us for dinner—his girlfriend was a US pilot who Wally had taught to fly—but I had nothing planned during the day. I had mistakenly assumed that, as I normally did after an overnight flight, a seventy-eight-year-old would want to rest. As someone who requires at least eight hours' sleep, I became increasingly tetchy. After another barrage of questions about the inner construction of the house's power supply, my voice hardened dangerously, and I marched out of the kitchen mid-conversation to avoid losing my temper. Richard was left to pick up the slack. Again.

I know from experience that many producers fawn over presenters or treat them as if they are special and require constant coddling. Presenters are the "talent." A phrase I loathe because any production—be it in radio, TV, or film—cannot happen without a team of equally talented people. My first job after university was as what many people in commercial radio called a "sound engineer." In the BBC, it's known as a "studio manager." I operated mixing desks, played sound effects from records on "gram machines," edited tape with a razor blade, and rattled tea cups and clashed swords for radio dramas. Later I went into production, reporting, and presenting. But from that moment on, I knew it took a studio manager, PA, producer, and editor as well as a presenter or actors, to make a program. The presenter–producer relationship was never, for me, master and servant. No matter what side of the microphone I was on, working alongside a presenter or a producer was always a collaboration. But somehow—and it was a failing that I reflected upon with shame—I had got that balance wrong with Wally.

Sugar-coating words was a skill I had yet to acquire but, with Wally, I realized I was often too blunt, too impatient, bossy and intolerant. Upstairs, lying on my bed, I reflected upon my inability to cut my presenter some slack. I calmed down, took several deep breaths, and atoned for my sins by finding my laptop and reaching out to a good contact at an Airbus Defence and Space site nearby. No matter my own mental and physical limitations, I needed to up my game and show Wally a better time.

The following day my space contacts got back to me. It was on. I wouldn't tell Wally where we were headed in the car, and it was worth fending off all the questions as she was so excited at the prospect of a surprise. And boy was it a surprise. While I couldn't arrange for Wally to go into space, I could at least take Wally to another planet.

In Stevenage.

Inside a brick building in the UK's first "new town," there was a thirty by thirteen-meter indoor simulation of the planet Mars. Located at Airbus's Stevenage site, the Mars Yard consisted of 300 tons of red sand with the same grain size as the material covering the planet's surface, littered with the occasional rock. The Mars Yard's backdrop was a montage of real images of the red planet taken by NASA rovers over 30 million miles (50 million kilometers) away. A glass-paneled control room overlooked one end of the facility. Our shoes sank into the fine sand.

"I'm walking on Mars," yelled Wally. "This is fantastic!"

The Mars Yard was built to test prototype robotic rovers for what will become Europe's first Mars rover. This rover, which will carry a drill and search for signs of life, was due to fly on board the European Space Agency's ExoMars mission in 2020. Or, to put it another way, this was a giant Martian sand pit with robots. Our guide was the ExoMars rover's lead spacecraft structure engineer, Abigail "Abbie" Hutty.

Hutty received the Institute of Electrical Engineering's Young Woman Engineer of the Year award in 2013 and, like Wally, is a role model for women. Her eyes were opened to a career within the space industry by reading about Britain's Beagle 2 Mars lander, which reached the Martian surface on Christmas Day 2003. It didn't matter that it failed to return a signal after one of its solar panels didn't open. The mission showed that engineers could work on spacecraft and robotic rovers. Hutty graduated first in her class with a master's degree in mechanical engineering from the University of Surrey. Now she led the team that was creating the Mars rover's chassis, as well as managing its development, design, and testing to ensure that the structure could withstand the launch, journey, and landing on Mars. This meant she was the perfect Mars Yard guide for Wally.

There were several prototype rovers on the red sand, and each one looked different. One resembled a rover's metallic skeleton and was solely to test the electrical systems. "This rover is Bryan. We're developing the autonomous navigation for the rover," Hutty explained, "so it's about what the rover sees, what obstacles and rocks it climbs over, and whether it can make the right kind of decision and plan a path through the terrain."

"This is great. What about this one?" Wally pointed to the biggest rover, which was topped with solar panels and most resembled the NASA rovers that are currently on Mars. This one was called Bruno. "Will this go on Mars? Can I ride it? What's going on . . . I love the engineering. Can you tell me what you're doing?"

It was a match made in heaven. Hutty could not only answer Wally's questions, she provided the technical specifications as well. Driving home afterward, Wally was thrilled, and kept repeating: "That was so great!"

The entertainment continued into the evening, although potentially it had less chance of success since it was not space-related. Six months earlier I had joined a community choir, and once a week went to Rock Choir to sing. Tonight was an end-of-term social for friends and family.

Musically, Wally preferred opera, classical music, and church choir. Opera most of all. When she was a child, her parents took her to the Santa Fe opera house. Verdi was her favorite. Our harmonized versions of Beyonce's "Halo" and Queen's "Don't Stop Me Now" might not have the same effect. I took a punt.

Inside the hall of a local school, Wally brightened at the sight of so many people. There was never a need to worry about Wally in a social situation because she never waited for an introduction. She simply marched up to someone and simply said, "Hi. I'm Wally!" and the conversation would begin. Several hundred people were in the room enjoying snacks and drinks. Once Wally had settled in, I appreciated her personality and sheer exuberance once more. As she made new friends, and members of the choir gathered on stage to showcase several of our new numbers, I spoke to our conductor, Pippa, and briefly explained Wally's presence and background.

While I sang with the choir, I spotted Wally dancing joyfully and appreciatively at the side of the hall. Before our final song, Pippa addressed the audience: "I'd just like to say that one of our choir members has brought a very special friend. She's called Wally Funk—an incredible name by the way—and she's from America. And back in 1961, Wally took secret tests to become an astronaut. And she passed. But while she never made it, she's hoping to go into space soon. So we're thrilled to have you here. Where are you, Wally?"

Wally raised her hand. To my surprise, she appeared embarrassed. Modest, even. Pippa addressed her directly: "Are you enjoying the singing?"

"I love it!" she shouted.

The room fizzed with goodwill.

The next day, before our train to Cologne, there was something important to do. Wally wanted to meet her contacts at Virgin Galactic's new headquarters in London. Virgin Galactic is one of a number of commercial companies offering future space-flights. These companies allowed anyone with enough money to become an astronaut. Not for a long mission, but to briefly experience life above the Earth as a space tourist. NASA and the Russian Space Agency preferred the term "spaceflight partici-pant" to "space tourist," but it had never really caught on.

Wally had bought her $200,000 Virgin Galactic ticket in 2010, using money from her parents' inheritance. "They came to the house here three times to make sure that was what I wanted to do." Like the actions of all pioneers, it was a leap of faith. But that wasn't the only ticket she had bought. "I bought several from other companies but don't remember the names. They didn't return the money, and that was the end of that."

After checking some newspaper archives, I discovered reports saying she had bought tickets from the Sierra Nevada Corporation, the Interorbital Systems Corporation, and one in the 1990s from Zegrahm Space Voyagers, who later in 1999 merged with Space Adventures. At that time, these were the only two companies that offered private trips into space. "That's not true, honey."

In fact, Space Voyagers had helped Dennis Tito become the world's first space tourist. Space Voyagers continues to act as a facilitator for those who want to undergo astronaut training—and have deep pockets—but the main three companies that intend to offer shorter tastes of space are: Blue Origin, set up by Amazon founder Jeff Bezos; Elon Musk's Space-X; and Richard Branson's Virgin Galactic.

Most planned commercial flights are to the bottom range of Low Earth Orbit, a designation which covers orbits up to 1,200 miles (2,000 kilometers) above sea level. The International Space Station, for instance, orbits the Earth at around 250 miles (400 kilometers). Most scientific satellites also operate in Low Earth Orbit. The spaceplanes are usually suborbital, too, meaning they will fly outside the Earth's atmosphere, up into space, switch off the engines for a period of weightlessness, and then fall back down again for a controlled return flight, rather than going into an orbit around the Earth.

NASA and the US Air Force define space as 50 miles (80.5 kilometers) to award astronaut status. The USAF, for instance, assigned some of the pilots of its experimental X-15 planes official astronaut status for surpassing this altitude. The officially adopted boundary beyond Earth to cross into space, however, is 62 miles (100 kilometers) above sea level, and is known as the Karman Line, after the Hungarian-American aeronautical engineer Theodore Von Kármán.

Newspapers in the 1950s and 1960s often referred to Von Kármán as the "father of the supersonic age" and the "Einstein of aviation." After gaining an international reputation in Europe for his research, Von Kármán became head of the new Guggenheim Aeronautical Laboratory at the California Institute of Technology in 1929. He founded the US Institute of Aeronautical Sciences three years later and, in 1936, helped students set up a rocket test facility a few miles away. This area eventually became the NASA Jet Propulsion Laboratory. Later President Kennedy would award him the country's first National Medal of Science.

Based on his calculations, the Karman Line was an altitude where the atmosphere became too thin to support flight, since any aircraft would have to fly faster than orbital velocity—the minimum velocity required to go into orbit—to get enough aerodynamic lift to stay airborne. The Fédération Aéronautique Internationale adopted this definition in the 1950s, although, ironically considering Von Kármán became a US citizen, the US did not adopt the definition, and uses its own definitions of space. Nevertheless, it is considered a benchmark by many commercial spaceflight companies.

On June 21, 2004, a spaceplane called SpaceShipOne made history when it became the first privately developed vehicle to fly into space, 124 meters above the Karman Line. Built by aerospace designer Burt Rutan's company Scaled Composites, and backed by Microsoft cofounder Paul Allen, SpaceShipOne seated one pilot and two passengers. When it repeated this feat within two weeks, the spaceplane officially won the Ansari X Prize competition, which had offered $10 million to the first non-government vehicle to fly into space. It was funded by brothers Amir and Hamid Ansari and the latter's wife Anousheh, who was the first female space tourist.

Five years later, Virgin Galactic backed Rutan's next development: SpaceShipTwo—which Wally will fly on. It has been designed to take two pilots and six passengers above the Karman Line of 62 miles (100 kilometers) and is a reusable spaceplane, like the retired Space Shuttle. Unlike the Space Shuttle it will be suborbital. It will not go into orbit around the Earth and will not require a rocket to launch it into space either. A four-engine aircraft called WhiteKnightTwo, whose dual-fuselage design resembles two planes connected together by a central shared wing, will carry SpaceShipTwo to an altitude of nine miles (fifteen kilometers).

After SpaceShipTwo is released, the spaceplane will then fire its rocket engines, producing an acceleration of 3.5 Gs. All those on board will then experience G forces that make them feel three-and-a-half times their body weight. Once in space, passengers can unbuckle their seat belts—assuming Wally has fastened hers in the first place—and will experience several minutes of weightlessness. They can also enjoy the beauty of space through one of its seventeen windows, before the spaceplane returns to Earth using the shuttlecock "feathering" system. The rudders are "feathered" by turning ninety degrees to give the spaceplane better control through the atmosphere. They then reconfigure into a glide position to land on a runway at Spaceport America in southern New Mexico.

Wally was insistent that we visit the Future Astronauts' PR team in London, since she had already met some of them on trips either at the spaceplane's hangar in Mojave, California, where the spaceplane was built, or at the Spaceport in New Mexico where her spaceflight will begin.

These visits had several purposes. They kept ticket holders updated and informed about progress, and also maintained interest in the project for some extremely patient people. Richard Branson—always ambitious both in outlook and business— had been promising flights for a long time. In 1999, quoted in the *Cedar Rapids Gazette* from an Internet chat, he said: "I hope in five years a reusable rocket will have been developed which can take up to ten people at a time to stay at the Virgin Hotel for two weeks."

Almost two decades later, the idea of a space hotel remains purely on the drawing board. Virgin Galactic's commercial spaceflight program also suffered a serious setback during a fourth powered test flight on October 31, 2014. The mothership WhiteKnightTwo released SpaceShipTwo, as planned, but thirteen seconds later the spaceplane began to disintegrate. The wreckage was scattered across a five-mile (eight-kilometer) area near Mojave Desert's Koehn Dry Lake, California. The pilot,

Peter Siebold, director of Flight Operations for Scaled Composites, which built the spaceplane, survived with extensive injuries because his seat ejected from the vehicle and he could descend using an emergency parachute. When the spaceplane broke up, his copilot, Michael Alsbury, was not so fortunate, and the experienced thirty-nine-year-old test pilot died.

"From my eyes and my ears, I detected nothing that appeared abnormal," said the chief executive of the Mojave Air and Space Port, Stuart Witt. This observation turned out to be right. An investigation by the National Transportation Safety Board, Wally's former employer, found that the crash had resulted from human error. The copilot prematurely unlocked the spaceplane's two tail wings at Mach 0.92 instead of 1.4. This action placed too much strain on the fuselage, and the G forces caused the spaceplane to break up. Since this action had not been predicted, there were no safety procedures in place.

It was a serious setback for commercial spaceflight since, three days beforehand, on October 28, an Antares rocket belonging to another private company, Orbital Sciences Corporation, had malfunctioned shortly after liftoff. NASA destroyed the rocket with a kill signal. The explosion could be seen for miles along the coast of Virginia. The rocket was flying supplies to the International Space Station as part of a contract with NASA.

The two accidents caused many media pundits to discuss the future of commercial spaceflight, but many concluded that it was here to stay. Earlier that year Orbital Sciences had entered into an agreement with Alliant Techsystems. The result was a new company, Orbital ATK Inc. Today NASA has two partners in its ISS commercial cargo program: Space X and Orbital ATK.

Virgin Galactic's program also got back on track with its second version of SpaceShipTwo. The first six seats for its first official flight, as before, belong to Branson and his family—a public show of his faith in its viability and safety. Over 650 people have bought tickets. Although the press has reported various celebrities as ticket holders—from actor Ashton Kutcher to singers Justin Bieber and Katy Perry—the list is a secret. While Wally bought her ticket early, others are probably ahead of her on the waiting list, and SpaceShipTwo carries just six passengers at a time. This means there could be a long wait if there are monthly flights, though not so long if extra spaceplanes are in service and flights take place every two weeks.

Wally was sure that some people on the waiting list had either dropped out, as a result of the crash, or simply died while waiting to fly. There had been unconfirmed reports in the British press, for instance, that Princess Beatrice had a ticket, but after the accident no longer planned to fly. Why hadn't Wally's number gone up? Wally had also heard rumors about some line-jumping. This was an opportunity for her to address those concerns directly to the team.

Virgin Galactic had recently moved their offices to join others at London's main HQ, "The Battleship," an appropriately named grey concrete building under an overpass near Paddington station. Wally was both excited and anxious. She was especially disappointed that one of the team she'd met in America—Gemma (which she pronounced with a hard G)—was in New Mexico.

Inside the Battleship we found staff, none of whom looked over thirty, working at computers in an open-plan area surrounding a kitchen/bar area. There were plenty of windows, natural light, and glass doors leading to meeting rooms called things like Hub 1. In the communal bar area, topped by a candelabra, were four wooden stools, an impressive coffee machine and snacks (chocolate and protein bars, packets of quinoa or hummus-flavored chips). On a glass shelf above the self-serve area stood bottles of beer and a model of SpaceShipOne.

It was fun and funky, but Wally's enthusiasm dampened on realizing that the Virgin Galactic team was also part of this open-plan office. "There are no pictures of space."

"That's because there aren't many walls."

There was, however, a standing bookshelf filled with Branson's various publications, including his autobiography *Losing My Virginity*; *Like A Virgin: Secrets They Won't Teach You At Business School*; and multiple copies of *Screw Business As Usual*. Wally wrinkled her nose. I suspected the language wasn't to her taste since, other than "bloody" and "bugger," I'd never heard her swear. "Is this what he's doing? Writing books? Is this why we're not going up?"

One of the Virgin Galactic team arrived and, surveying her workspace, asked, "What do you think? Cool, isn't it?"

Wally switched immediately into Wally mode. "It's better than cool, it's fantastic! You guys—are you really stoked about working here? Don't you want to go there? To space? I would go in a heartbeat."

Clare seemed very fond of Wally. She apologized that not all the team were present and gave us a quick tour. There was a bumper car and bowler hats that doubled as light shades, and we posed for photographs beside a cardboard cutout of Branson in an astronaut suit. The inner walls were covered in Branson's images, as if it was a family home rather than an office. There were pictures of young Branson, an older, greyer Branson, black-and-white Branson, technicolor Branson. His famous toothy grin and goatee beard were often next to people whose names I probably should have known. I recognized three framed images of astronaut Buzz Aldrin, each one autographed for members of the Branson family: for his son Sam, daughter Holly, and, of course, for Richard himself.

None of this impressed Wally. In fact, she was visibly impatient. She wrinkled her nose at the sign on the wall that said: "Screw it, just do it."

Clare introduced Wally to the other employees. One staff member was clutching a US book on the Mercury 13. Uh oh. It was *that* one. The book that, according to Wally, had repeated familiar mistakes. The woman pulled me to one side and asked quietly if I thought Wally would sign it. "Of course," I replied, "but be prepared for a negative comment, because Wally doesn't like that particular version of events."

Clare sat us down and explained the situation so far, reminding Wally gently, "It's all in the e-mails, too." At that stage, they had just done a 50,000-foot glide, with a "feather flight"—where the tail fins unlocked and moved ninety degrees—planned for the following month. Powered test flights, we were informed, would take place toward the back end of the following year. "Richard isn't going up until the end of 2018 at the earliest."

Wally was almost speechless. Almost. "I thought he was going up in 2017!"

"We never had plans to fly this year," Clare said gently.

The problem in managing Wally's expectations partly arose because newspapers had been reporting the company's readiness to take space tourists for almost a decade by now. In 2012, for example, several newspapers quoted Branson stating he intended to fly into space by the end of the following year.

I brought up Wally's fear about line-jumping and mentioned the auctions. In 2014, for instance, someone had bought a Virgin Galactic ticket at an auction for close to $1 million to be on the same flight as the actor Leonardo DiCaprio. Would this put the successful bidder on an earlier flight than Wally?

Clare reassured Wally that any new tickets took people to the bottom of the list and that, although places might free themselves up, they remained empty on their list so Wally may well have fewer people ahead of her. But as the list was kept secret, we didn't know for sure, and Wally was none the wiser.

"Stephen Hawking is our only free ticket," said Clare.

Once flights were underway, they would happen every couple of weeks. This was an astonishing thought. Several spacecraft were currently being built, and there would be three in total. Clare related that Branson liked to say, "We're not building a spaceship; we're building a space line."

The Mercury 13 book was produced for Wally to sign. As expected, she was not impressed. "I don't like this one." She signed it in red pen anyway, with the usual smiley face, and did the same with the black-and-white photos inside. On seeing Jackie Cochran's image, Wally grumbled loudly: "It was all her fault we didn't go up. Her and Johnson. Jackie Cochran was a son of a gun."

When he was vice president of the United States, Lyndon B. Johnson sent a typed letter to NASA administrator James Webb, dated March 15, 1962. It had been drafted by Johnson's assistant Liz Carpenter. In it, he referred to the fact that he'd talked to Mercury 13 members Jerrie Cobb and Janey Hart, and asked for advice about restrictions for women astronauts and "whether NASA has disqualified anyone because of being a woman." It ended: "I know we both are grateful for the desire to serve on the part of these women, and look forward to the time when they can." When this letter was unearthed almost forty years later, it revealed Johnson's true feelings. Instead of his signature, there was a handwritten, "Let's stop this now!" and then the instruction: "File."

"When she said 2018 I was shocked," said Wally in a taxi to St. Pancras station for our train to Cologne. "I thought it was going to be this year."

She was understandably dejected. If you were thirty, forty, even fifty- or sixty-something, the delays were a setback, but no more than that. Wally was close to eighty. She had a more pressing deadline. Although her mother had lived into her nineties, there was no guarantee for anyone in life, and Wally, despite her physical and mental fitness, had less time left than most. After all the years of hype, suborbital space tourism is now a genuine possibility, but if the delays go on for another five or ten years, Wally might not live to see it happen. I felt both sympathy and empathy for her situation. She could be exasperating company at times, but I liked Wally. The longer we spent together, the more I understood her lust for life and impatience to get into space. In her position, I'd be equally driven and no doubt as difficult, demanding answers and continually putting on the pressure to ensure that the momentum of her race to space continued.

These warm, fuzzy feelings hardened slightly when she continued her usual part-monologue, part-commentary, part-interrogation on the Eurostar—especially when we changed trains in Belgium and had to find a restroom.

"I thought we were going straight to Cologne."

"I did say we were changing at Brussels."

"Well . . . we're here now. I can't believe you had to pay sixty cents for the john."

On the next part of the journey to Cologne, I ordered wine from the drink cart. Wally chatted and mostly I just listened. I wondered sometimes if she needed an answer, because as soon as I responded there was always another question.

After a while, the constant verbosity subsided into background noise and, to maintain my sanity, I started the stopwatch on my iPhone whenever she stopped talking. The longest period of silence recorded throughout the five-hour journey was two minutes and fifteen seconds. The drink cart trundled along the aisle.

"Wow," noticed Wally. "You sure like your wine."

That night I switched from wine to beer in Gaffel am Dom, a brewery and pub in the shadow of the cathedral and across the street from our hotel, which itself was next to the train station. Wally, who had visited Cologne in the 1960s, was thrilled by the pub's hubbub, the decor, the colored glass on the ceiling, and how the waiters carried miniature glasses of beer on handheld drink carousels.

"I've never been in a place like this before."

"Not in a bier keller?"

"No. Never. I don't drink."

And I realized that, despite her extensive travels, she was also—in many ways—an innocent abroad.

The next morning we popped inside the station so that I could record Wally walking out into the square, describing the cathedral in front of us. After our first radio program together, I realized that this was one of her broadcasting strengths. She might not be able to read a script with ease, but her commentary was natural and spontaneous. "This is incredible. We're at the Cologne train station and we're gonna walk outside and then right to my left is the cathedral, which is fantastic. I saw that, oh, forty years ago, and it's so outstandingly beautiful. All the spires reaching to the sky," she enthused, "is absolutely fantastic. And we're here to interview the European Space Agency folks. I just love it here in this town square."

Perfect. Once inside a taxi headed toward the nearby European Space Agency (ESA) Astronaut Training Center, Wally got out her research notes and interview questions for the day. "What's the name of the astronaut we're meeting again?"

"Samantha Cristoforetti."

"Samantha Cristoforesti."

"Foretti."

"Foresstiti . . ." There was a considerable pause. "Do I have to say her whole name?"

"Yes . . . Nice try."

Wally grinned. I admired the way she took each interview seriously, rehearsing and practicing over and over, working on her delivery or pronunciations. As with everything in life, she wanted—and was determined—to do her best. I'd begun making interview notes myself once we were inside the taxi, but had gotten sidetracked into writing down her questions to me instead.

My parents had unwittingly ignited a future journalism career by buying me a notebook. They ordered me to "write everything down" to reduce trips to the lost and found. Despite having a good memory for faces and numbers, I was incredibly forgetful. So forgetful it cost me a position of responsibility. Age eleven and newly enrolled at a local grammar school, I was shortlisted to become class captain. One of the other six girls was elected, but decades later an old school friend, now a breast cancer surgeon, confided that I had won the vote. The teacher had questioned the decision. "Don't you think she's a bit too absentminded?" The hands came down one by one.

"Are you concentrating?"

Wally had noticed I was no longer listening to her. "I want to ask you about the truck. Oh look, a Shell gas station. I wonder how much their gas is."

As I paid the taxi driver, I glanced up and noticed Wally was beside a car in the middle of the road. For a brief moment, I thought she'd jaywalked in front of it. But there had been no squealing of breaks and, as I got closer, I recognized the driver chatting with Wally through the car window. It was the European Space Agency astronaut, Samantha Cristoforetti.

Cristoforetti had been an Italian air force captain and a fighter pilot, part of the 101st Squadron, 32nd Bomber Wing, in Italy. The only woman selected for ESA's class of 2009, she trained alongside fellow astronauts from a range of European countries: Alexander Gerst (Germany), Andreas Mogensen (Denmark), Tim Peake (UK), Thomas Pesquet (France), and Luca Parmitano (Italy). Like most astronauts, she was a dauntingly impressive superhuman. Cristoforetti has a degree in aeronautical sciences and a master's in mechanical engineering (with a thesis on solid rock propellants), speaks at least five languages, is a qualified scuba diver, and—like Wally—is a pilot. But it's not just space tourists who are on a waiting list. Astronauts too must patiently await their turn for the ultimate adventure. Cristoforetti had to keep her skills current for five years until her first mission into space in November 2014. When she returned to Earth in June 2015, after a stay on the International Space Station as a flight engineer, she set a record for the single-longest time by a woman in space—a few hours short of 200 days.

For the sci-fi fans among us, Cristoforetti reached legendary status before her mission even ended. While living on board the Space Station, she was photographed giving the familiar V-shaped Vulcan salute shortly after the death of Leonard "Mr. Spock" Nimoy and was also pictured wearing a *Star Trek Voyager* uniform in a tweet saying "There's coffee in that nebula." This was a reference to both a quote from the USS Voyager's captain, Kathryn Janeway (the first female captain in the Star Trek series universe), and the Space Station's newly delivered espresso machine after years of instant coffee. If that wasn't enough, she wore a towel around her shoulders in a tribute to Douglas Adams, writer of *The Hitchhiker's Guide to the Galaxy*, on May 25, known to fans as Towel Day.

I had a good professional relationship with Cristoforetti. Within six months of arriving back on Earth, she had agreed to present her first ever BBC radio program via our production company. Called *A Home in Space*, it was about living and working on the Space Station. She had also presented *Songs from Space* for us, which we produced for Project Everyone. This venture by Richard Curtis, the film director and one of the cofounders of Comic Relief and Red Nose Day, was to publicize the United Nations' Global Goals for sustainability. We used a combination of astronaut recollections and space-related music to get the message across since Cristoforetti, like many astronauts before her, had experienced a heightened awareness of the fragility of our planet and its thin blue protective atmosphere when viewing it from orbit. Between the music there were interviews with astronauts supporting sustainability goals such as gender equality, climate action, and clean energy. The astronauts included Canadian Chris Hadfield, NASA's Cady Coleman—a chemistry graduate from MIT and veteran of three missions who took three flutes and a pennywhistle into space (two instruments were from the Irish group The Chieftains)—plus Wally's favorite astronaut, Eileen Collins.

Cristoforetti was our first ESA interview for *The First Woman on the Moon* and, due to her record-breaking feats in space, had been featured in *Women with the Right Stuff* too, although I had done the interview rather than Wally. Cristoforetti autographed a photo for Wally, however, which I'd posted to the States. This was their first face-to-face meeting, and Wally had been looking forward to today. So, it appeared, had Cristoforetti. She had not only recognized Wally driving past her on the road, but greeted her like an old friend.

As Cristoforetti parked her car, we walked past the bronze bust of Yuri Gagarin into the ESA Astronaut Training Center (EAC). This is where European astronauts like Cristoforetti completed their eighteen-month basic training. Inside a giant hangar-sized hall were full-scale mock-ups of the European-built components of the International Space Station, such as the Columbus science laboratory containing models of its experiment racks, and also the Automated Transfer Vehicle (ATV). Europe's Ariane 5 rocket launched a fleet of five twenty-ton double-decker sized ATVs into orbit between 2008 and 2015 to ferry cargo to and from the International Space Station.

"We train on the ground in mock-ups," said Cristoforetti. "We also train in other mock-ups in Houston and Russia. When you get up there to the space station, it's almost like you've been there already."

There were also medical facilities along one of the walls, since astronauts had to both be monitored physically and also learn how to treat each other in an emergency. Wally enjoyed seeing the nearby fitness center and the Neutral Buoyancy Facility. This was a giant swimming pool containing a full-size mock-up section of the Space Station for Extra Vehicular Activity (EVA), for spacewalk training. When underwater in a full astronaut suit, the right combination of weights and flotation devices can give the body neutral buoyancy. You neither sink nor swim. It may not be exactly the same as a spacewalk, but it was the nearest an astronaut could get on Earth to practicing moving around in microgravity while moving large objects for prolonged periods of time. Naturally, although it wasn't on her question list, Wally wanted to know how Cristoforetti's experience in space compared. "Did it feel any different to just walking on air?"

"It does because you're not really walking, you're floating," she said. "You're weightless and you can inhabit the space in three dimensions. You're not just walking on the floor. On Earth we live in two dimensions, unless of course you fly, like you and I do. But there you don't need to jump in an airplane—you can float with your body and fly and have dinner on the ceiling. It's very special."

"What did you fly in the Italian airforce?"

"I flew a light ground attack fighter called an AM-X."

"Wow. You're so lucky. You're wonderful. You're very smart."

"You're wonderful, Wally."

It was a heartwarming start, even if I was sitting silently between them with a recorder, wearing headphones. Cristoforetti was well aware of the Mercury 13's history and the barriers that Wally and the other female aviators had broken. She had been back from space for two years and was now working on an initiative called Spaceship EAC. "The idea is we are very well set up for training astronauts for the space station, but what's coming after that is hopefully going back to the Moon. So we're working on being ready for that. It's going to be an international endeavor but we want to create a niche of expertise, and that involves working with young people, students, encouraging innovative technologies."

The European Space Agency's director general, Jan Woerner, was a prominent advocate of a "Moon village"—a base on the Moon for a community from Earth. ESA was also building a lunar dome in Cologne. The inside of the dome would replicate being on the lunar surface to test rovers and help train astronauts. It would be the Moon version of the Mars Yard, but on an even larger scale. And with people as well as rovers.

Cristoforetti saw the Moon as a "proving ground" for journeys further afield, and also admitted she would jump at the chance to be the first woman on the Moon. "If I had to choose between going back to the Space Station and going to the Moon, I would definitely pick the Moon. You want to go where you haven't been yet."

"Well, I think you'll make it," Wally declared.

I felt a sympathetic pang at the realization that here was Cristoforetti, a woman with all the right experience and credentials in place to have a realistic chance of going to the Moon, alongside a woman who might have become the first woman to walk on the Moon if history had panned out a little differently. The accumulation of fifty years of women's rights had made all the difference.

Cristoforetti expected the training for the Moon would be similar to what astronauts currently undergo. Operations would be a similar challenge. "You're still interacting with complex machines and interacting with a crew," she said. "When I went to the ISS it was a very well-oiled machine. There was nothing new to invent. Now we're looking at Moon missions. I think astronauts are going to have a bigger responsibility and will need to be flexible and interactive and give feedback to do things better."

"Are the kids going to have been smarter than anticipated now?"

"There are a lot of smart kids around, so I'm not worried about that. It's just a matter of getting them ready."

"Good, because I don't see that in America."

Wally was doing well and, as prompted on her crib sheet, asked about China. Cristoforetti was already adding Chinese to her impressive list of languages. ESA and China had shown an interest in working together, and shared plans for putting astronauts and a base on the Moon. By the spring of 2016, the China National Space Administration had launched three successful lunar missions—Chang'e 1, Chang'e 2, and Chang'e 3—

all robotic. Chang'es 1 and 2 were lunar orbiters. Chang'e 3 had included a lunar lander and a rover, called Yutu, which rolled onto the surface on December 14, 2013. The chances were high that, in this renewed race back to the Moon, China could put the first woman on the lunar surface.

English and Russian were the two main languages currently used on the Space Station, but with the rise of China and India's ambitious space programs, there will certainly be other languages heard on the Moon or in space in the future. When the interview was over, Wally discovered that Cristoforetti had first visited Russia for her master's thesis in 2001, a year after her own weeklong trip paid for by a TV channel. "I took all the tests with the cosmonauts," she said. "They told me I did just as well or better than the guys."

This sounded suspiciously like the Lovelace clinic story and, while I believe Wally was physically capable of anything in her early twenties, I wasn't so sure the same level of fitness applied when she was sixty. Though very little about Wally would surprise me.

Wally continued. "Did you fare better than the guys?"

Cristoforetti laughed modestly. "I don't think they had a ranking. But I performed."

"You made it. You made it."

"According to expectations, I guess."

"Do you know Peggy Whitson? She's a friend of mine so I'm excited for her." Peggy Whitson was an experienced NASA astronaut and its Chief of Astronaut Corps, 2009–12. As we talked, Whitson was circling the Earth at 17,500 miles per hour on the Space Station during her third and final mission. "I watch her on TV," said Wally.

"I know Peggy," said Cristoforetti. "As someone said at JSC [NASA's Johnson Space Center], 'Superman flies in Peggy

Wally and her palomino horse, Victor, in Taos, New Mexico.

Girl Scout in the 1940s.

Age 14 at the all-girls St. Stephens College, Columbia, Missouri (c. 1953).

Preparing to fly a Cessna 195 (c. late 1950s).

Wally with silverware picked up as a member of the winning Flying Aggies student air team at Oklahoma State University (c. 1959).

Twenty-one years old and the first female civilian flight instructor at
Fort Sill Oklahoma, 1960. Wally experienced her first jet flight in this T-33.

The 1951 Rolls-Royce, restored by Wally, that once belonged to the Queen
Mother. Wally is wearing her mother's wedding dress. (c. 1970s).

No Man In Moon

Stephens Graduate Trains To Be Female Astronaut

If a 22-year old Stephens College graduate has her way about things, the man in the moon may be as outdated as hand-cranked cars within a few years.

She is Miss Mary Wallace Funk II, '58 Stephens graduate, civilian flight instructor at Ft. Sill, Okla., and the nation's No. 4 candidate to be the first woman in space.

Miss Funk, in Columbia yesterday to visit Mr. and Mrs. David Easterly and Capt. and Mrs. Philip Semsch, credited her first touch of aviation training to the Stephens flight program.

"BUT I think I have been interested in flying, ever since I tried to fly by jumping off the barn when I was a child in Taos, N. M," she said.

The rigid testing program for future female astronauts began at the Lovelace Clinic in Albuquerque last February where Miss Funk was one of 20 girls undergoing 53 physical examinations in a seven-day period. Five were initially accepted and seven more girls have joined the program to date.

Although the plans for female astronauts have not yet been approved for sponsorship by the National Aeronautical and Space Administration, the tests given at the clinic are as thorough, rough, and exhausting as the tests now being given America's seven astronauts, Miss Funk says.

SUBSEQUENT tests and training schedules for the women have included virtually everything offered the country's space "men" and Miss Funk indicates with a confident smile that the ladies are well on the way to being an authentic part of the Federal program.

The possibility of her whirling in space or being on the moon "by 1964" first dazed Miss Funk's family, though they now encourage and support her in her space-riding ambitions.

As indication of the progress that has been made in the brief history of one American family, Miss Funk points out that her mother's parents are still living and can clearly remember the days when a horse and buggy was considered good, fast transportation.

And they doubtless remember, too, when the man in moon was just an imaginative figure of speech.

Article from a local Missouri newspaper in Wally's scrapbook, dated September 21, 1961.

The *Parade* magazine cover article from April 1961 revealing that more women had passed the same astronaut tests as the Mercury 7 men.

A copy of the telegram received by Wally in September 1961 canceling phase 2 of Lovelace's Woman in Space program astronaut tests just days before they were due to start.

Top: Wally assessing an aviation crash site scene as an NTSB air-safety investigator (c. 1984).

Right: Age 61 in Russia enjoying her first "zero G" experience on a series of parabolic flights (2000).

Class of 2013 NASA astronaut Jessica Meir with Wally in front of a replica of the Orion capsule at the NASA Johnson Space Center, Houston (2016).

Wally with ESA astronaut Samantha Cristoforetti at the European Astronaut Center in Cologne, Germany (2017).

Sue Nelson and Wally at North West Regional airport, Dallas, preparing to fly over Dallas in a Cessna 172 (2016).

Wally at Spaceport America, New Mexico, beside a replica of Virgin Galactic's SpaceShipTwo—her ride into space (September 2017).

Whitson's pajamas.' She's Superwoman."

Whitson was indeed a Superwoman. After her most recent launch, on November 17, 2016, she became the oldest woman in space, at the age of fifty-six. A few months later, she returned, and as of September 2, 2017, her 289 days, five hours, and one minute in space, combined across three missions, meant she would not just break Cristoforetti's record, but would hold the record for the most days in space for any American—male or female. A biochemist who became an astronaut, Whitson had received numerous awards. One of them, in 1995, was the American Astronautical Society William Randolph Lovelace II Award. This particular award, now retired, ran for fifty years— from 1963 to 2013—and recognized outstanding contributions to space science and technology. I scanned the list. Not surprisingly, Whitson was one of the few women on it. Other winners include NASA headquarters' first chief of astronomy in the Office of Space Science, Dr. Nancy Grace Roman, who was recognized twice, first in 1979 and then again in 2011. Due to her role overseeing the planning and development of NASA's programs, she is often referred to as "the mother of Hubble" for her work on the Hubble Space Telescope. The 1976 award recipient was also a familiar name—it was the man who took part in my Mercury 13 radio documentary and called Valentina Tereshkova a basket case: flight director Chris Kraft.

The first award recipient, however, was Dr. Jeanette Ridlon Piccard: a scientist, a consultant to the director of NASA's Manned Spacecraft Center (now Johnson Space Center) 1964–70, the first female priest in the Episcopal Church, and a balloonist. In 1934, Piccard became the first woman to enter the stratosphere.

The flight began from Dearborn, Michigan. She was the hydrogen balloon's pilot, and her husband, the Swiss scientist

Jean Piccard (whose name later inspired Star Trek's Captain Jean-Luc Picard), was navigator. They were joined on board by their pet turtle. The gondola resembled a huge ball or diving bell with a window, and it was surrounded by Geiger counters to measure cosmic rays. They reached 57,579 feet. Perhaps it was the loss of national pride, but when Tereshkova made her record-breaking spaceflight in 1963, some US newspapers alluded to Jeanette Piccard having got into space first. But a quick calculation shows that 57,579 feet is 10.9 miles (17.5 kilometers), which is nowhere near the NASA, USAF, or Karman definitions of space.

When Wally and I were ready to go to our next interview, Cristoforetti thanked Wally for paving the way for women astronauts. I could see from Wally's face that this recognition mattered.

The rest of our interviewees that day were equally charmed. Scientist Aidan Cowley gave us a tour around his labs, where improbably young engineers and scientists experimented with technologies for a future that expanded beyond our planet.

"What do you think of the Astronaut Training Center, Wally?" Cowley said. "It's cool, isn't it?"

"It's better than cool," Wally shouted. "It's fantastic! Do you want to go to the Moon or Mars?"

"I saw a talk by Elon Musk saying Mars is the new America," Cowley replied. "You don't want to be on the first boat. You want to be on the third, fourth, or fifth boat." Wise man.

Cowley's labs are specifically interested in fuel-cell prototypes for energy production and storage, as well as 3D printing for future missions to the Moon. Unlike the Earth, the Moon has a fourteen-day period of daylight followed by fourteen days of lunar night. This makes visiting the Moon for more than two weeks a challenging technical problem to solve. For two weeks at a time, any solar-powered batteries, for instance, would have no sunlight to power them. This was why fuel-cell systems were of interest. They could combine hydrogen and oxygen to produce water, and in doing so produce electricity. At the end of the cycle, water could potentially be split into hydrogen and oxygen again during the day cycle, and then be stored as gas. Hydrogen and oxygen could be isolated from frozen water, for instance, on the Moon. This process could be repeated multiple times to replenish an energy supply, allowing astronauts to survive for long durations.

"It's a brilliant piece of equipment. How many people had to come up with these ideas and make it?"

That question wasn't on the list. My first thought was that it had no relevance. I was wrong. "Fuel cells have a fantastic history with spaceflight, because the original Mercury, Gemini, and Apollo missions, and even the Space Shuttles, were driven by fuel-cell technology," said Cowley. "Unfortunately people have turned away from fuel cells in the last few decades and focused on battery technology, but batteries have significant problems for being on the Moon."

Batteries could be big and heavy. They didn't like extreme temperature variations either. "You've got from 100 degrees Celsius at the equator to -108 degrees on the dark side of the Moon. A fuel-cell system could potentially be a lot more stable and last a lot longer. This is the kind of technology we think would allow humans to be on the Moon."

Shorter stays would not be a problem if the mission was timed for astronauts to land during lunar daylight, as batteries and photovoltaic (solar) panels can provide the energy required for powering any equipment or vehicles. The longest time spent by astronauts on the lunar surface, for instance, was just over three days, between December 11 and December 14, 1972, on the Apollo 17 mission. It was the last time a human being set foot on the Moon, and the first mission to contain a scientist. The Lunar Module Pilot, Harrison "Jack" Schmitt, was a geologist.

Together with Commander Eugene "Gene" Cernan, they drove a lunar rover vehicle in the Taurus-Litrrow valley region of the Moon a total of 19 miles (30.5 kilometers), the longest distance of any rover, and also collected and returned back to Earth the largest amount of lunar material: 243 pounds (110 kilograms). Along with the material from the previous sample-return missions, this lunar material had proved crucial for future plans involving longer-term stays and habitation on the Moon.

Transporting all the parts of a potential lunar base from the Earth to the Moon will be expensive and time-consuming. So a better solution might be to make the materials for shelter there on the Moon, from the available resources. In the same way as someone would build a shelter from palm trees and vegetation if stranded on a desert island, scientists and engineers are figuring out how to build the components of a Moon base out of the materials that are already plentiful there.

Fortunately, as a result of the Apollo missions, we know that the Moon's surface is covered by a fine powdery layer of dust, known as lunar regolith. Once scientists on Earth analyze its composition and grain size, they could then accurately simulate it to an almost perfect match. By using 3D printers and fusing this simulated moondust together, a process known as sintering, scientists at the European Space Agency can literally print lunar bricks. The key then is to get the right size and shape so that they can interlock and produce the most stable and protective habitat for astronauts, since they will need to be shielded from radiation during longer stays.

Cowley brought out a big container of grey lunar regolith for Wally. It reminded me of a huge pile of iron filings. Wally put her hand into it and allowed the grains to slip through her fingers. "It's very fine," she observed. "Like salt."

The fusing, or sintering, can be done using microwave radiation, solar rays, or directed laser light. "Part of our job here at ESA and also DLR," said Cowley, "is to understand what's the best approach to do this, and what kind of parameters do we have to take into account to actually produce a usable material at the end."

DLR referred to the German Aerospace Center, often known as the German Space Agency. One of its buildings was across the road from the Astronaut Training Centre. How odd that two space agencies in Europe differed on the spelling of the same word—the American *center* versus the English *centre*—but agreed on how to make lunar bricks. Scientists from both places were collaborating on the project.

At DLR, Professor Matthias Sperl showed Wally a piece of rock. "This lunar simulant material is mixed out of volcanic ashes to reproduce the physical and chemical properties of lunar dust," said Sperl. "Then we put that material inside a solar oven, and then concentrated solar light basically melts part of the grains and glues them together to make a brick."

The fist-sized piece had taken two hours to make.

"Okaaay," said Wally, underwhelmed. "I was expecting a square brick, but this is a piece."

Sperl opened a glass-cased cupboard and brought out a small black-grey house brick. Its cross-section resembled layers of dark volcanic rock with an almost crumbly but hard texture. "You can see this brick was produced layer by layer, but this [brick] can produce more complex structures on the Moon. It took us about five hours with current technology to produce that," he said. "That may seem awfully slow, but compare that to the funds that would be needed to transfer it to the Moon. Here's a more refined version. It's still a little dusty . . ."

He wiped his hands together, and then held a different brick up so we could see that it wasn't a rectangular block. "It's shaped like a door handle."

The idea was to stack and interlock these door-handle-shaped bricks together. The team was currently experimenting with different shapes and 3D printing them to see if they would produce a stable wall or half-dome shape. Once the most efficient brick design is identified, a robotic mission could take a 3D printer to the Moon and begin building structures before the astronauts even arrive. The structures would also help protect astronauts from radiation. Sperl offered to accompany us to a room where a box-shaped 3D printer was in action.

"That'll be terrific. Let's do it."

The printer whirred back and forth, constructing what would eventually be a simulated moondust brick, a single layer at a time. Wally was an enthusiastic interviewer. She delighted in seeing a 3D printer in action, meeting new people and witnessing the realities of making this future happen. At heart, Wally was an adventurer, but she also had an engineer's brain. She wanted to take things apart, find out how they work, and put them back together again. She started off doing this with balsa wood planes as a child, before moving on to tractors, and the inside of cars, and then real aircraft. Wally often wished out loud that she had the brainpower to understand more of the technicalities of space travel, but Wally underestimated the amount of effort she put in. Often she surprised me with her understanding of the science and engineering involved, particularly if it was engine-related.

After we had returned to the Astronaut Training Centre, Cowley took us to the site of the lunar dome. It was just a huge expanse of cordoned-off grass at this point, but it was going to be transformed into the largest lunar analogue facility in Europe. A lunar analogue was simply a scientist's way of saying that they were building a replica of the Moon inside, about half the size of a football field, for future lunar astronauts to practice on. To do this would require 600 tons of simulated lunar regolith. "Like the dust you saw and touched earlier on," said Cowley. Wally gasped.

"We'll work out what kind of technologies we'll need for surface EVAs, to prepare our astronauts for walking on the Moon, to test astronaut rover interactions, and also we hope to have a small habitat dome attached to it as well where astronauts can spend some time and then transition outside taking samples. There will be a control center too, so it will be mimicking a full mission on the surface of the Moon."

Wally responded: "That is so outstanding." And she was right. Here was a future both new and familiar from the beginnings of spaceflight through to the Moon landings and beyond. Rather like Wally's ambition to get into space after her achievements in the early 1960s, it was as if history had come full circle.

Before a taxi arrived to take us to Cologne station for our train to Paris, I decided to try another impromptu recording outside. Wally's unscripted commentary outside the cathedral first thing in the morning had been great.

"Wally, could you say where we were and why we are here. As if we were going to meet Samantha."

"Sure. Where are we again—the European astronaut center?"

"The Astronaut Training Centre."

"Can I say European Astronaut Training Centre?

"Yes."

"Right now," she began, "we are at the European space training center."

"Astronaut Training Centre."

"Right now we are at the European astronaut training center, and we're going to meet . . ." There was a long pause. ". . . someone who could be the first lady on the Moon."

"Can you not say lady, and say first *woman* on the Moon?"

"I've got to say the whole thing again?"

"Yes . . . but say the first woman on the Moon."

She began again. "Right now we are at the European space training center—"

"Astronaut."

Wally got frustrated. "I need it on paper."

I got out my notebook and she wrote down the exact title of the center. "Right now we are at the European astronaut training center, and we're going to meet . . ." There was another long pause. ". . . someone who could possibly be the first lady on the Moon."

"One more time. Woman not lady."

"Right now we are at the European astronaut training center, which is a fabulous training center from all the things I've seen, and then we're going to meet a young lady . . ." Another pause. ". . . somebody who hopes to be the first woman on the Moon."

"Perfect," I said. At least it would be once it was edited.

5

An American in Paris

When Wally was last in Paris in the mid-1960s, she parked her camper van beneath the Eiffel Tower. "I drove around it first, went up in the elevator—and what a sight that was."

She gazed up around her. "The trees weren't there and I don't remember these buildings. But it's incredible to walk right up to it again and take pictures."

It was a glorious spring day. Not many of the trees around the Eiffel Tower had budded yet, but the sun was out and the sky was almost free of clouds. The color matched her blue cotton shirt. It was the one with an embroidered *Wally* and *Safety Judge* on the right and a "Women Pilots' Wings of Distinction" patch on the left breast pocket. Just around the corner from the Tower, outside the European Space Agency (ESA) headquarters, a line of colorful flags fluttered in the breeze. The flags represented the twenty-two member states that made up this international organization. ESA has facilities all over Europe, including the one that Wally and I had visited in Cologne the day before, but the one in Paris was where all the big decisions were made about policy and which space missions would get funded.

Inside ESA Director General Jan Woerner's office, the planets slowly revolved above his desk in the form of a hanging mobile. It reminded me of the number of European missions that had explored our Solar System, from Venus Express, ExoMars, and the successful ESA-NASA Cassini-Huygens mission to Saturn and its ring system, to Rosetta's extraordinary orbit and landing on a comet. Then there were the ESA missions yet to come, such as BepiColombo to Mercury and JUICE, which will head to Jupiter and its icy moons. None of these involved people. They were all robotic spacecraft—a cheaper and safer way to explore our astronomical neighborhood than crewed missions. Woerner wanted to expand the space agency's vision.

On the table where we were going to sit for our interview was a revolving Moon lamp. This was where Woerner's vision lay, in a "Moon Village." To my surprise, there was also a book on the Mercury 13. Unfortunately, it was *that* book. Wally's face distorted momentarily, as if she'd sniffed something nasty. But what Woerner said next conquered her reservations.

When Woerner arrived at ESA in 2015, he had been chairman of the German Aerospace Center's (DLR) executive board since 2007 and chairman of the ESA Council from 2012 to 2014. Yet, when applying for the DLR position in 2006, he was concerned that his background in civil engineering wasn't spacey enough for them, despite having worked within aerospace. During the interview he therefore felt the need to convince the committee that he was the right person for the job. "I took a risk," Woerner said, "and suggested I could tell them something about space that they didn't know."

That something was the story of the Mercury 13. Since no one on the panel had known about these women and that particular part of space history, it must have been a compelling listen. No wonder he succeeded in becoming DLR chairman and, not surprisingly, he was delighted to meet one of the women he had spoken about. It also explained why my interview request, which had provided Wally's background as well as the aim of

The First Woman on the Moon program to cover current government and commercial returns to the Moon, had been so readily accepted by the ESA director general. "You helped me get that job," he told Wally, "and probably where I am today."

He nodded toward the Mercury 13 book on his desk. "I still use that book in my presentations frequently."

Wally's aversion to some of the book's content caused her to mutter, "Maybe you should try the other one," but fortunately it was lost beneath the banter. Wally never went into detail about why the book irked her so much, other than mentioning that it repeated a few often told but incorrect stories, but I suspected—from my brief glimpse—that it might have been because it contradicted a couple of Wally's statements. I initiated a deflection maneuver, mentioning to Woerner that I'd made a radio documentary on the Mercury 13 in 1997.

"As a child?"

Both Wally and I laughed. The man was on form. Any differences over the book were forgotten. I needed him to sit nearer to me and Wally, otherwise my arm, which held the microphone, wasn't long enough to reach him. "It's not possible," said Woerner jokily, shuffling his chair toward us. "I don't think we can get any closer. Our knees are touching!"

Radio is an intimate business.

Wally prepared to read her introduction. We would also record it outside afterward, in view of the Eiffel Tower, to give me several takes to choose from.

"I'm in Paris at the headquarters of E-S-A, the European Space Agency."

"No," I interrupted. Wally had spelled out each letter individually. "It's *Eesa*."

Mispronouncing the European Space Agency's shortened name was a common mistake. Although I had specifically spelled out Jan Woerner's name phonetically on her script as Yan Verner to ensure the correct pronunciation, I'd forgotten to do the same for ESA. Wally got out her pencil, made some amendments, and started again.

"I'm in Paris at the headquarters of the European Space Agency. The head of ESA, Man Verner . . ."

"Yan Verner," I said.

"Can't I call him Mr. Verner?"

"No," said Woerner. "You can call me Jan."

She took a deep breath and went back to the beginning. "I'm in Paris . . ."

The new start was way too loud in my headphones and the recording display on my equipment peaked into the red. It would be distorted. "Hold on, Wally, I'm going to have to turn the level down."

Woerner was good-natured about the false starts. "For me, it was fine." Sides had been drawn. It was definitely them against me.

"I'm used to talking in an airplane," Wally confided. "That's why my voice is so loud."

"Of course." They giggled together as if in a great conspiracy.

Wally began her link again, but this time she mimicked the much quieter sing-song voice of a small child. "I'm in Paris . . ."

Woerner's laughter nearly burst my eardrum.

Finally, Wally read her introduction and got it spot on. "I'm in Paris at the headquarters of ESA, the European Space Agency, which is within walking distance of the Eiffel Tower. The head of ESA is Jan Woerner who is at the forefront of plans to build an international community on the Moon. He calls it a Moon Village."

Phew. The interview finally got underway, with Woerner explaining how a Moon Village would consist of public and private entities, astronauts and robots, to be an open environment for the world. He wanted an "open concept," and believed that the Moon should become a place where countries around the world could gather, once the International Space Station was finally retired, for science, technology development, and outreach. The Moon would become "the next outpost of humans on Earth."

Woerner agreed that Samantha Cristoforetti would be the perfect person to go to the Moon, and maybe even become the first woman on the Moon. "She's skilled, really smart and I like the fact that she has emotions. She feels we need to take care of the Earth. She is a very strong astronaut."

"I loved her," said Wally.

Woerner also confirmed that all ESA astronauts, not just Cristoforetti, were learning Mandarin "in order to be global players." A more diverse future lay ahead within space, and women, thankfully, were considered an automatic part of it. Wally signed one of the postcards she kept with her for fans. She was in a blue flight suit covered in space patches, standing in front of an American flag. It resembled an astronaut's pose before the Stars and Stripes. It said: "Wally Funk, Mercury 13 Astronaut Candidate" and "Aviation Pioneer." She signed it for Woerner. The head of the European Space Agency was absolutely delighted.

On the way out, while being escorted by a press officer, a woman crossed our path by chance and was introduced to us before we left the building. It was Claudie Haigneré, a medical doctor with a PhD in neuroscience who had developed experiments for the human body in space while working at the French space agency CNES. She was now Woerner's special advisor but was perhaps best known in France as its first female astronaut. On October 21, 2001, she became the first

European woman to visit the International Space Station on the Andromède mission.

Even though I had a specific interest in space and women's history, I had heard little about Haigneré's achievements. In July 1999, for instance, she became the first woman to qualify as a Soyuz Return Commander. This was the Russian spacecraft that could bring up to three astronauts back to Earth from the International Space Station. Since 2011, when the Space Shuttle had been retired, it was their only route home. She later went on to become the Minister of Research and New Technologies in the French government.

It reminded me of the fight women often have with visibility, no matter where they are from or which country is reporting their achievements. Helen Sharman, who became Britain's first astronaut in 1991, is another case in point.

A scientist from Mars—the chocolate company not the planet—Sharman learned Russian and trained for eighteen months before heading to the Russian space station Mir on the Soviet Soyuz TM-12 space capsule. It was the twelfth expedition to Mir, and her eight-day mission was part of Project Juno, a privately funded collaboration between a British company and Russia. While on board, Sharman performed a variety of Soviet-designed experiments on seeds, materials, and superconductors, and how the body adapted to weightlessness. She took up a miniature lemon tree (which stayed alive for three years) and also made radio contact with a UK school as part of her outreach activities.

"Because I was the first British astronaut, the legacy of that means that Britain has been on the map of human spaceflight ever since I flew in 1991," said Sharman, during an interview with me in 2016 at Imperial College, London, where she worked in the chemistry department. "Wherever I go in the world, I represent the United Kingdom. I'll always be that first British astronaut. It's great that I got to go into space, and it sends a very strong signal to girls and women in Britain."

It was not surprising during the 1960s, considering the traditional expectations of women's roles, that reporters often referenced Valentina Tereshkova with a comment on her appearance. But thirty years after Tereshkova, Sharman found that little had changed when it came to press interviews.

"Some of those questions were about the clothes I wore in space. Somebody asked me where I had bought my underwear, or the face cream I used in space," Sharman told me.

"There was one article in a newspaper titled 'Barbarella Come Back' and the whole thing was 'Isn't it terrible that Helen went into space but she didn't even wear any makeup. She wasn't prepared to show herself at her best in front of the cameras.' Come on, guys," Sharman said. "It's like going on a really tough camping trip going to the Mir space station. The International Space Station is a relative luxury. It's sweaty and sticky and," she chuckled, "with 180 grams of luggage, who's going to take a lipstick?"

Unfortunately there was one aspect of her stay in space that Sharman regretted to this day. It related to an item of clothing she was asked to take on board while she was training at the Yuri Gagarin Cosmonaut Training Center in Star City, Kazakhstan.

"Alexey Leonov, the first spacewalker, was my boss in Star City. He's always got a joke up his sleeve somewhere. There was a tradition that, when astronauts arrived at the space station, they share a dinner, and you take up something to dress for dinner. The men often take ties that float nicely in front of them," she said.

Perhaps because Sharman was to become the first woman on board Mir, Leonov—whom she speaks of extremely fondly—

decided to do something special for her. "Alexey had taken it upon himself while we were doing two weeks' quarantine in Kazakhstan to go off to a local dressmaker—totally unknown to me—and he chose some pink material." Sharman laughed at the memory. "It's not really my color."

Leonov then designed what she referred to as "a short blouson frilly combination thing . . . a pink frilly froufrou outfit." Having seen the offending dress, I understood why she found it so difficult to describe. It resembled an awful 1980s marshmallow-style wedding dress with ruches, frills, and a bow at the top of the neckline. Wally would have hated it. Funnily enough, Wally was the only other person I had ever heard use the word "froufrou" in conversation.

"I was given this by Alexey Leonov. My boss," said Sharman. "I couldn't really say, 'Thanks, but I hate it.' The idea was that I'd secretly put it on inside my spacesuit and then, for my first dinner, I would put the dress on and surprise them."

The surprise worked, and Sharman described continuing the tradition of dressing up for dinner with the cosmonauts as "a bit of fun." The downside came later, on her return to Earth. "Sadly, that's one of the images that is perpetuated over and over again. Is that because the world wants to see its women dressed up in pink frills?"

Sharman's moment of invisibility arrived over two decades later, in 2015, when ESA's first British astronaut, Tim Peake, was assigned his flight onboard the International Space Station. Suddenly, Sharman—who had flown the flag for Britain in 1991—read a number of press reports incorrectly stating that Peake would be the first British astronaut. She blamed the media at first, assuming that journalists had not gotten their facts straight, and partly blamed herself for having taken a few years out of the public limelight.

Unfortunately, the mistake had originated from the UK Space Agency. "The UK Space Agency put out press releases when Tim Peake was newly flight assigned that he was going to be the first British astronaut," said Sharman. "I saw it. That was not just shocking to me, but just blatantly wrong. It was the UK Space Agency who actually tried to rewrite history, tried to write me out."

The UK Space Agency made a hasty correction. "The next time I saw a press release it called Tim the 'first official astronaut.'" She found that wording equally problematic. "It was nothing to do with Tim. The UK Space Agency decided my mission wasn't official." Sharman was rightly indignant. "Did I slip someone a fiver so I could do a quick hitchhike into space?"

The UK Space Agency was again mortified by its mistake. "I don't think they were actually trying to demean me, or even my mission. They would have just rather my mission hadn't happened," she said. "I'm a bit of an embarrassment. Not because of being a woman but because it wasn't UK-funded, and they wanted the UK government-funded astronaut to be the first."

It was a historical issue to some extent. The UK Space Agency didn't exist when Sharman became the first British astronaut, in 1991. Between 1985 and 2010, the British National Space Centre (BNSC) coordinated all of Britain's civil space activities. More specifically, BNSC didn't "do" human spaceflight—that was part of their policy—and so naturally it didn't contribute any money toward the International Space Station either. It was only after the formation of the UK Space Agency in 2010 that this policy changed. These changes paved the way for Britain to have its first ESA astronaut.

Sharman didn't think her gender affected that way of thinking, but conceded that it was responsible for the unintentional rewrite. "If it was a man, it wouldn't have been allowed to happen."

She also appreciated that, when it came to a story, the media liked to talk in superlatives. The biggest, the best, the first captured headlines. This was something that Wally had mastered. She knew what journalists liked and, because of the numerous firsts in her career, could provide any number of them. But, quite rightly, Sharman had objected to the demotion of her achievement.

"Tim's the first UK government-funded astronaut. He's the first British ESA astronaut. We were always going to love what he's doing, as he's a great guy, but it was just so wrong to write me out of history. In Britain we are still not used to women doing things before men," she said. "We would like to think we are. Legislation says that women should be paid for doing the same job. Are we paid the same in practice everywhere? Of course not."

Sharman admitted that things were getting better. "Many good organizations are trying to improve things. Many have equal rights and equal opportunities. We've come an awful long way," she said, "but still, when people hear that I've flown to space, now, in 2016, people still ask me who was the first person. You were the first woman; who was the first person? It's often assumed a man must have flown before me. Loads of people out there are getting a very false picture of women's input, and we need to correct that."

The upside of the controversy for Sharman was that she received a lot of public and private support sympathizing with her about the media treatment, praising her dignity and admiring her achievement. It also reminded a new generation of people that Britain's first astronaut was a woman. At the end of 2017, the British government announced that Sharman was made a Companion of the Order of St. Michael and St. George in the New Year's honors list.

Tim Peake was also one of Sharman's supporters and, before his launch, corrected any journalist publicly if they mistakenly called him the first British astronaut. When Peake flew into space in December 2015, he took with him *Road to the Stars* by Yuri Gagarin. The book belonged to Sharman. It was the perfect link between the first and second British astronauts in space. A few months after his launch, I was at a school in North London for Peake's first live televised talk from space. Students and members of the media were on hand to ask questions. One reporter referred to him as Britain's first astronaut. Peake set the man straight.

Sharman's experience with Leonov could be viewed as a joke gone wrong, simply intended to uphold a tradition on board the Russian space station, which had never before hosted women. But the Soviet space agency, to be sure, did not have a good track record when it came to women. Tereshkova, the first woman to have flown in space, in 1963, never flew again, and it took almost twenty years before another woman followed in her footsteps. Or should that be spacesuit.

Svetlana Savitskaya, the second Russian woman to fly into space, on August 19, 1982, was an aeronautical engineer and, like Wally, a pilot, which means, before the first American woman went into space in 1983 not one but two Russian women had gotten there first. If you were being cynical, this was not a coincidence. The Soviet space agency knew that NASA finally had women astronauts and that Sally Ride and others were preparing for missions. After a nineteen-year term of all male cosmonauts, they too had brought women back into the space program. Surprise, surprise, then, that one of theirs, Savitskaya, flew before Ride, and also became the first woman to fly on a space station, the Salyut-7.

Two years later, Savitskaya became the first woman to fly a second space mission and, on July 25, 1984, was the first woman to do a spacewalk when she spent three-and-a-half hours performing a number of electrical welding experiments on the space station's outer hull during her eight-day mission on board Salyut-7.

The *New York Times*'s correspondent in Moscow reported on August 28 for the following day's edition that the Salyut-7 flight engineer, Valentin Lebedev, had welcomed Savitskaya on board with the words: "We've got an apron ready." Lebedev added, "It's as if you've come home. Of course, we have a kitchen for you; that'll be where you work."

The journalist also reported that the government daily newspaper *Izvestia* had listed some unusual attributes in the astronaut's biography. "There are few women like Svetlana," it said. "She is charming and soft, a hospitable hostess, and likes to make patterns and sew her own clothes when she has time to spare."

The similarities between the reports on Tereshkova, Savitskaya, and the Mercury 13's achievements were striking. Yet Wally's experience in 2000, doing a week of cosmonaut training in Moscow, had felt much more modern and unisex. "They had one room, and the guys took off their clothes over here to get checked out and the girls were over here," she said, pointing to either side of an imaginary room. "There was no sex discrimination. Men were getting changed over there and I was getting changed over here. It was no big deal for me. As long as they gave me all the tests they needed."

Wally was unconcerned, especially as the tests were nowhere near as numerous or difficult as those devised by Dr. Lovelace. She got to do a parabolic weightlessness flight, after practicing in a swimming pool beforehand, as well as centrifuge tests. "I excelled in these as, being an acrobatic pilot, I could pull 6Gs."

By 2015, Russia appeared to be making progress on the sexism front, with an eight-day single-sex experiment to simulate a flight to the Moon and back. The mission, called Moon-2015, consisted of six women, all of whom were qualified in medicine, psychology, or biophysics. The experiment consisted of living and performing scientific experiments in a spacecraft mock-up at Moscow's Institute of Biomedical Problems. It was the first study of its kind with women.

One of the science directors, Sergei Ponomarev, told the *Guardian* newspaper: "It will be interesting to see how well they get on with each other, and how well they are able to perform tasks. We believe women might not only be no worse than men at performing certain tasks in space, but actually better."

Unfortunately, during a press conference before the study took place, the Institute's director, Igor Ushakov, gave the women some advice: "I'd like to wish you a lack of conflicts, even though they say that in one kitchen, two housewives find it hard to live together."

Reporters also asked the women how they would cope without makeup. Some things never changed. Anna Kussmaul, one of the participants, responded to a question about their hair with wonderful sarcasm. "I don't know how we'll survive without shampoo," she said, "because even in this situation, we really want to stay looking pretty."

The four women who spent thirty days together in a laboratory a year later, as part of NASA's Human Exploration Research Analog (HERA) IX program simulating a mission to a near-Earth asteroid, fared better. But the public undermining of women's abilities persists to this day.

It must have been even worse for the Mercury 13. Pilot Jerrie Cobb, the first woman to pass the tests, gave several press interviews at the time of the hearings. One TV journalist asked her: "Why does a pretty girl like you want to become an astronaut?"

Did Wally ever feel bitter that the Mercury 13 women weren't taken seriously?

"Bitter? No. Not at all. I'm not that kind of a person. I'm not negative. I'm always positive. Why would I feel bitter? I've had nothing but great things happen."

She was definitely positive. Glasses were always half full. Certain facts were rounded up, not down. Her response to the program's cancellation was to "throw it a fish." She often used this expression. It was from the Taos Indians, she said, and meant "to not look back."

Sitting in the sunshine on a park bench, with the Eiffel Tower in front of her, Wally recalled staying in a campsite four or five miles south of Paris fifty years ago, making friends, and going to museums and the Louvre. In a way, Wally's travels to Europe and beyond during her mid-twenties had been a positive form of escape from America when all avenues to becoming an astronaut had been officially closed after the 1963 hearings.

Wally had bought a VW camper van in 1965 and arranged for it to be delivered in Brussels. "Mother sewed a thousand-dollar bill in my underwear," she said. "Father gave me cashier's checks."

She arrived with her friend, Ann Cooper, armed with an outgoing nature and a *Fodor's* travel book. "I'll show you the map of my travels. I have three different ones: Europe, Middle East, and Africa. Where I stopped every night, I put the date. It's a great conversation piece. I have all my passports," she said excitedly, "and when they ran out they would just attach another page and it would get stamped. I have great passports. They'll have to go to a museum one day."

Wally wrote to her parents regularly as she traveled from country to country—fifty-nine in total, she said—for over two years between 1965 and 1967. During this time, she was either alone, with her friend, or with a small poodle called Toot. Some of the people she stayed with were artists with connections to the artistic community in Taos, New Mexico. Others were associated with the military. She stayed at the homes of her parents' contacts, at campsites, or slept in the van on the road. Despite the thousand-dollar bill safety net and cashier checks, she was on a budget. If the showers were too expensive at campsites on the coast, Wally said she would "go into the ocean to get a bath." It was a liberating experience. "My parents didn't give it a thought. Here I am, twenty-something years old, and I'm overseas by myself. It was great. I could do anything."

The *Taos News*, her parents' local newspaper in New Mexico, printed a piece on her travels on December 15, 1966. Headlined "Mary Wallace Funk Sends Letter as Christmas Greetings to Taos," it referred to a letter Wally had mailed from Cape Town, South Africa.

While in Morocco she visited bazaars in Marrakesh, and spent three months on the coast in Agadir. She saw Roman ruins in Italy, traveled through Angola, and rode an ostrich in South Africa. She was staying for a few months in Cape Town, where she had a job teaching flying.

The camper van was sold when she couldn't get it out of Kenya, and another one acquired. Wally collected a new and now iconic Volkswagen Mini Mansion II camper van at the factory in Hanover, Germany. "Then I toured some more, took it on a ship, and sailed to New York."

Again, the *Taos News* published her plans, this time on October 12, 1967, from a letter written on board the Kovacic, a Yugoslavian freighter in Genoa, Italy, waiting to return home. By then Wally, Cooper, and Toot had driven up through the east coast of Africa through Europe and were threatened with jail at the Tanzanian border. While in Uganda, they "did have an unfortunate situation in Kampala of having our front and side windows smashed completely out while we were in the camper. Fortunately we could get away, as our lives were in danger."

Since Wally had always said there had never been any trouble on her travels, this came as a surprise later when I read it. But it was clear that it had been what most people would consider the trip of a lifetime. "Two-and-a-half years of travel have slipped by too fast, but I feel we have collected a wealth of knowledge and gone through all types of experiences," Wally wrote. "I feel the best gain from your dollar is to travel and see the struggle of the world, and also to witness the well-meant but often misplaced American aid."

She finished her travelogue with a patriotic flourish. "The American who never ventures abroad fails to experience the grat-ification of being an American. In all of our travels, the grandest sight to behold is the glory of the flying American flag!"

As she reminisced about her travels from half a century ago, Wally's attention was constantly distracted upward to the sky and any air traffic. There were planes, too, on the back of her shirt and the belt she wore, which was tipped with leather but primarily made of canvas. Multicolored aircraft circled her waist. This was her obsession. Her life. She pointed out the con-trails of different aircraft. "Military traffic leaves more contrails than airlines. It's the different way the air goes over the wings, the heat and the cooling process which mixes with the atmos-phere, and that's what leaves the white line. That must have been a heavy jet." I wasn't sure of the science but, not in the mood for a dispute after such a good morning, I took her word for it.

Wally was qualified to fly all manner of aircraft, from sea-planes to gliders. The most important rating was the Airline Transport Pilot license, or ATP, which she earned in 1970, and was often referred to by others as the crown jewel for a pilot. "That is the highest rating anyone can get, because you can be hired by an airline," said Wally. "You know me, I want the highest, biggest, best."

Wally had continued flying during her travels, viewing many of those fifty-nine countries from the air as well as the ground. "When I came back, I started instructing right away at Hawthorn airport in California and did that for a couple of years. Then I wrote a letter to the boss of the Federal Aviation Administration, John Glenn."

"The astronaut?"

"No," she laughed. "Different one. I wrote and said I wanted to go to Alaska and be a bush pilot, and would he give me a commendation letter. He said, 'Wally, you be in my office on Monday for a meeting.'"

That Monday deadline felt awfully familiar. She'd often used the Monday line for Dr. Lovelace too, even though the timings were longer. Call it poetic licence.

"For some reason I knew I had to be dressed up in hose, heels, the whole bunch. He interviewed me for two or three hours and at the end he said, 'I want to put you up with the FAA in Washington to be our first girl FAA safety inspector.' I said, 'Holy cow, really? I don't know that much about a lot of things.' He said, 'We will teach you, we will send you to schools.'"

Wally completed her General Aviation Operations Indoctrination Course for FAA inspectors in Oklahoma City in 1971, the first woman to qualify. The *Los Angeles Times*, on November 28, 1971, wrote a short piece on her achievement entitled "Wally Funk: Success is the Name of Her Game."

That qualification allowed her to "investigate accidents, test applicants for pilot licenses and apply aviation law to whatever circumstances may arise." The article also noted that, while teaching five aeronautical science classes at Redondo Union High School in California the year before, she was the first teacher in twenty-three years to reach a "69 percent success in having students pass the FAA private pilot and basic ground school written examinations."

She also became the first woman in the FAA's System Airworthiness Analysis Program two years later. "It was great fun. It was kind of a desk job, when needed, I would go to different schools and give written tests for private pilots, or give check rides to see if they would get their private licence. Then I would be checking schools and aircraft. Whenever I would have my paperwork ready I handed it to the secretary, Helen. She would type it up and Glenn always liked it."

While an FAA inspector, she had also worked on a couple of accidents with the National Transportation and Safety Board (NTSB), but as an observer. In 1974 the NTSB asked her to become a full-time investigator. Wally was genuinely surprised. "I didn't believe it," she said, and told them she wasn't qualified enough. "But the guy said: 'You will go to every aircraft manufacturing school, every engine school, or any other school we want you to go to. When you have an accident out in California, Arizona, Nevada, or Hawaii and you have to take that wreckage and put it in a place and inspect it, as well as the inspection you've done on ground or on site, you will have help and you will have a place to do this work in.'"

She accepted and completed her training. Her first assignment was the Whittier midair collision in January 1975. A Cessna 150 and a small DeHavilland commuter aircraft had crashed into each other above Whittier, California. Fourteen people died. She was quoted as saying: "I found the tragedy hanging with me. Since then I've learned that an investigator can't let emotion get in the way—not if the job is to be done right." The January 15 article about the crash in the *Los Angeles Times* referred to Wally as "NTSB's only woman crash investigator."

A later article, on July 21, 1975, in the same newspaper but about a different crash, described Wally, then age thirty-six, as the NTSB's "newest and only woman investigator." According to the current US Department of Transportation website, however, Wally was "one of the first" inspectors.

"I was the first woman," said Wally. Either way, she broke more boundaries and delighted in her new role. "It was great. I loved being an investigator."

When asked about her job for the newspaper in the July edition, barely six months after she had started her new role, she admitted that it was a "tough, hard job at times," but also rewarding. "You pursue an end result that hopefully will prevent another crash and save other lives." The article showed a black-and-white photograph of Wally with shoulder-length hair and a center part, doing her job framed by plane debris, and described as an "air crash detective."

She wore what looked like a cross between workman's overalls and a flight suit. "That was our uniform," Wally said. "I wore a regular uniform with my name on one side and NTSB on the back. It was either blue or grey, I think. It was a bit like a flight suit."

Forty years later, perched on a bench in the Parisian sunshine, Wally outlined the main reasons for air crashes. The biggest causes, she said, were usually pilot error, weather, gas—"Many people that crashed did not have enough fuel"—or an engine malfunction. Wally then outlined the procedure for me after a plane had crashed.

"Okay, we're sitting here. Let's say we have an accident in front of us. Let's say the guy wasn't paying attention and the aircraft stalled. He doesn't know how to get out of a spin and crashes. When an airplane comes down, if it hits the ground back and forth several times, part of the aircraft comes apart and gets buried. So knowing that, I have to dig around looking around for parts. If it crashes straight and level it's no big deal. If it comes straight down, then holy cow, that's a mess."

Based in the Los Angeles office as a five-member team, everyone carried electronic beepers for crash alerts and was on rotation—twenty-four-hour on-call duty. Through covering four states, Wally would travel to an accident site by all forms of transport. Sometimes she flew her own plane there, or traveled in the jump seat of another. If they were closer, she drove. On one occasion, when there was an accident in the San Fernando Valley close to the NTSB Los Angeles office, Wally drove her Rolls-Royce—the one that had once belonged to the Queen Mother—to the crash scene. "They all loved it," she said, but Glenn told her: "I think you need to take the government car next time."

Once the police had left the accident, Wally would then take command of the site. "The first thing I do is take pictures all around—photographs were very, very important—and then I start with the engine. I don't really start pulling things apart yet. I want to investigate all the way around the aircraft, the wings, the elevator, the rudder."

It certainly sounded like being a detective. "Exactly like a detective. Then it was up to me to let people know what I needed. If it was out in the boonies, out in the middle of nowhere, I needed to have a truck come and take the wreckage to a hangar or a garage. When an aircraft crashes at a forty-five degree angle . . ." She hesitated, as if to reformulate her words, and then continued. "Well, if four people are onboard, they're all going to die and the front two people are going to be all smashed up. The coroner wouldn't always get there for a while, and sometimes

they would leave stuff and I would have to get it out myself."
I realized that by "stuff" and "it" she meant body parts. "I've
pulled bodies out when coroners didn't do a good job."

The aircraft's manufacturer would usually send a representa-
tive to the site as well. "If it was a Cessna, then the Cessna man
would come and we would work together and I would learn from
all this. Every month I had an accident to go to. The way our
office worked was you were on call every other weekend. If I was
number two on a Friday, by Saturday night I was number one."

Her job also involved interviewing and investigating what
went on away from the crash site in order to get a fuller picture
of events. "You have the tower, ATC, the air traffic control, the
radar people, the weather people, and you need to check what
they know of that aircraft's number. So I had to get all of that
data that goes with my report."

These reports were meticulously detailed. "A report could be
anything from three to four inches thick."

What was it like, yet again, working as a woman in a man's
world? "You have to remember they're working with a girl. They
don't think I know what I'm doing," she said. "But I got the
confidence of all those people in those states within three years
because I made a name for myself as a good investigator. And
the men never spoke bad language to me either. I said, if you're
going to speak that way, I'm going to excuse myself."

To begin with, as a field investigator on smaller crashes
involving light aircraft, she was on her own. "I didn't get a team
from NTSB in Washington, DC, until later in my career. They
even had people that would travel to help an investigator in
the field out. The only people on the site would be firemen and
police officers and people who would help move the aircraft.
When I come upon an accident and there's been a fire, the fire
department is in charge. I am not in charge until the fire depart-

ment says the accident is mine. Then I start in and by that time phone calls are coming in."

Despite the nature of investigating what was usually a fatal accident with lives lost, Wally enjoyed her work. "It was great. Never a dull moment," she stated. "I enjoyed my job. Many of the guys I was working with at NTSB were retired military and they just wanted to get it over with."

She also had an advantage when it came to dealing with civilian air crashes. "I had a one-upmanship over these guys civilian-wise because I flew general aviation aircraft. I did very few jets because jets weren't in vogue. People didn't have that kind of money back then. I was very lucky, honey. The men didn't know if I knew my beans. But within two or three years I was on top of the heap and my boss, John Glenn, said, 'Wally you're doing a great job.'"

Wally would go on to investigate hundreds of accidents covering the three mainland states and Hawaii. Most of them took about a week. Some planes crashed into trees, buildings, mountains, or even a volcano.

Her childhood outdoors helped her to detach herself from the reality of these crashes. "I dealt with dead animals and buried them," she said, "so for me to pick up a body or part of a body was like picking up a frog."

Wally's attitude, thoroughness, knowledge of different aircraft, and attention to detail aided her work. But there was the emotional aspect to deal with, too. "I had all the people who talked to me who had lost their loved ones."

Relatives of those killed were not allowed onto or near the scene of the accident. "I met them later but not on the site. They were still so much in shock."

I asked her how she dealt with it. During difficult situations Wally said she would "talk to them just as natural as you and I are talking. I certainly didn't show them pictures. I'd just gently say it was weather and they got into cloud . . . or they probably didn't pay attention to instruments and the aircraft wasn't capable of continuing flying . . . something like that."

Wally needed to draw on all her reserves of strength and professional detachment a few years later with a crash that made headline news on September 25, 1978. "That was the longest and hardest investigation I've ever had to do."

Flight PSA 182 was a popular morning commuter flight for Pacific Southwest Airlines from Sacramento via Los Angeles to San Diego. At 9:01 AM, the Boeing 727 was descending toward Lindbergh Field airport in downtown San Diego preparing to land. Airborne at the same time, a flight instructor was helping his student with instrument training in a private Cessna 172. This was a small popular plane, the same type Wally had taken me flying in the year before in Dallas.

As the passenger jet approached the runway just a few miles away at 2,600 feet, the PSA 182 collided with the Cessna. The light aircraft exploded immediately. The larger aircraft was fatally damaged. A county photographer attending a news conference caught the PSA flight with his camera. Fire and smoke poured from the right wing as it plunged at an angle toward the middle of a residential area. Witnesses watched horrified as bodies plummeted to the ground. According to the flight recorder onboard the jet, the time between the midair collision and hitting the ground was just thirteen seconds. This was the first crash in Pacific Southwest Airline's twenty-nine-year existence. But it was the worst recorded aircraft disaster in California and US aviation history.

The wreckage destroyed twenty-two homes, and 144 people died, including all 135 on the passenger flight, the two on board the Cessna, and five adults and two children on the ground.

Wally, the lead NTSB investigator on duty that day, arrived on the site two hours after the crash.

Even decades later, basking in the Paris sunshine, it remained at the forefront of Wally's memory. "It was horrendous. The PSA overtook a Cessna 172 coming from its right. The people in 172 never knew because the PSA was descending. The PSA took about twenty blocks of homes out when it was skimming along and crashing. Where the 172 crashed was about four or five blocks away."

Wally compiled photographic evidence of the wreckage to help piece together what had happened, and also recorded witness statements. She collected what remained of the Cessna 172 plane into a hangar to document all of its parts. She then started documenting the much larger passenger jet plane remains on site. "It was scattered for miles, and we finally had to have help getting it out of the area and into a hangar. It took me weeks out there getting all the airplane pieces in different hangars and seeing what happened."

The investigation even involved measuring the angles of treetops, since the jet had sliced some of the trees on its fatal decline.

It was a test of Wally's fearsome will not to let emotion get in the way of doing her job. She wanted to help others by performing the investigation to the best of her ability. Body parts were everywhere: on streets, in people's backyards, in trees. A flight attendant's body had fallen through a car windshield, flying glass injuring a woman and baby inside. The authorities placed pieces of human flesh and bone in plastic bags that were taken to St. Augustine High School gym, which was being used as a temporary morgue.

The investigation involved more than collecting physical pieces of wreckage. It was a puzzle to be solved from all aspects of the accident. "I listened to the ATC—air traffic control, ground control, radar control."

In the flight recorder transcriptions released to the press, four voices were heard in the cockpit: all male. The last words to be heard from the cockpit were "Mom, I love you."

Wally insisted that at least one stewardess was also in the cockpit. "I flew PSA from time to time. They always had a party in the cockpit. I knew this because I always rode in the cockpit so we always had a good time. So they were having too much of a good time. I heard the woman laughing."

It was difficult to square this contradictory information or corroborate her claims. The presence of anyone else in the cockpit was never reported in the press. The transcripts did not feature any female voice. Wally was adamant that she was telling the truth. "I don't know what's out there, but you could hear four or five boys and the girls laughing. I know it was in there."

She wasn't happy with her portrayal in a Canadian TV series that documents air crashes, which reenacted the aftermath and showed lessons learned. "The film people came to me and I told them everything just like I'm telling you. I listened to all the ATC stuff, and when this movie came out they had a stupid girl instead of a good-looking girl in uniform like I was. And she talked stupid," said Wally unhappily. "I was in charge. When the fire department left, I was in charge. She was not in charge. They said that there were only four people in the cockpit. They listened to the ATC and nobody answered. The PSA came down a little too quick. They did not tell the truth to the public how that accident really happened."

When I watched the relevant episode of *Air Crash Investigation* on YouTube, also known as *Mayday* or *Air Accident* in other countries, I scrutinized the reenactment. The woman who took photographs and represented Wally as an NTSB inspector asked "Any survivors yet?" and was not in a uniform. She wore a pale peach trouser suit and her long dark brown hair was tied back in a ponytail. She resembled a fashion photographer more than an air crash investigator. No wonder Wally was critical. Later, when an older, male NTSB investigator arrived, presumably from Washington, he was shown taking control. Wally's TV reenactment role was depicted as minimal from then on, although her youthful stand-in was at least present around the discussion table.

The crew in the cockpit were shown joking and laughing before landing. "Even though they were fun and laid back, they were highly professional," a contributor said. "'Catch our Smile' was their motto. It was an experience. It was fun."

There's no doubt that this was a complicated and controversial case. The location of San Diego's Lindbergh airport, in close proximity to housing, had long caused objections from concerned residents. In February 1980, as reported in the February 27 *Los Angeles Times*, PSA captain Robert Chapman had just resigned, age forty, over safety issues. He cited "dangerously high" levels of fatigue due to short turnarounds on flights. He blamed tiredness for the air crash, and put the blame for the accident on the PSA 182 cockpit crew. The organization, which lost thirty-seven crew members and employees in the crash, dismissed Chapman as a "disgruntled former employee." There had certainly been issues with communication between air traffic control and the PSA 182. There had also been reports of a third plane in the vicinity of the crash, but this theory was dismissed due to lack of evidence.

The official NTSB report concluded that the probable cause of the accident was the failure of the PSA flight crew to follow proper air traffic control procedures, alongside a number of other contributing factors. Later I examined the transcriptions again. There were only four voices listed from inside the cockpit, but, I realized from the time codes, these were only partial transcripts from the minute just before the crash, ending with the crash itself. Wally must have been mistaken about the presence of a stewardess in the cockpit, as the official report did not include this either.

Wally worked at the NTSB for just over ten years, until her retirement in 1985. During that time she continued flying both privately and as an instructor. "Teaching people was really my thing. Even at NTSB, I was still teaching flying on the side after work. I never really told them I was doing that. But after 450 accidents, picking up bodies and doing investigations, I wanted to make great pilots out of my students," she said. "I thought, all these people are dying and what are you doing? You're investigating, but you're not helping people get better—and I've never had a student have an accident."

Wally was never short of students, but admitted to finding it difficult to find work as a pilot during the 1980s because she was a "girl." I'd tried and failed to get her to say woman. "I had one airline tell me I'd done excellently on all the tests, but they said, 'We can't hire you.' I asked why. They said, 'We don't have a girls' bathroom.'"

Years later she read that one of the first female airline pilots had prepared for that interview question. Her solution, which the pilot brought to the interview, was a piece of paper with "girls" written on one side and "boys" on the other "to put on the john." The ingenious woman got the job.

I followed the trail of another plane overhead. "Flying was your first love, wasn't it?"

"There's no other discussion," she said. "That's all I've ever done."

Her favorite plane was either a Cessna 182 or a Stearman—a biplane—which she owned in her early twenties. "When I had the Stearman I was teaching acrobatics," she said, before admitting that she could also put a 182 through a loop even though it wasn't rated for acrobatics. "I could not do it in a 150 or 172 because they don't have the horsepower. My preference is to fly high-wing aircraft."

What about flying highlights? "I loved racing," she said. "I can't even tell you how many races I've raced. The Powder Puff Derby, the Palms to Pines Air Race, then another down into Mexico. There was one called the Poker Run where you had to land at five different airports and pick a card up at each one and see what hand you had when you got to the terminus."

It was a whole new world. One where a pilot could play a game of cards across hundreds of miles.

The ludicrously named Powder Puff Derby, a favorite race of Wally's, was officially known as the All Women's Transcontinental Air Race (AWTAR), but its nickname, courtesy of humorist Will Rogers, had stuck. "It was coast to coast, so you have to refuel every three-and-a-half hours," Wally explained. "Then you take back off again, and in the evening they flagged your time. Everything was precisely timed on the clock. Say you go from A to B to get gas—that time goes against your handicap. I probably gassed up four or five times in an air race that took two to three days. You have to look at your charts carefully and know your copilot."

The Palms to Pines Air Race was also women-only. This was a race from Santa Monica, California, where you found palm trees, to Independence, Oregon, where there were pine trees. A particularly good year for Wally was 1975. She came second in the Palms to Pines and beat seventy-nine other competitors to win the Pacific Air Race from San Diego to Santa Rosa.

How did you beat someone if they were flying the same plane as you? "Different airplanes had a handicap because the engines were different. You might have a Stetson that had 100 horsepower or a Cessna 182 that had 200 horsepower. You had a chart, so I would find a plane that had a good handicap and fly them over a low course, say 1,000 feet, and see what their speeds would be. Then I'd take them up to 5,000 feet, because sometimes on a race you'd go over hills and mountains. I would spend months sometimes picking the right plane. I wanted perfection."

Even if women were racing against each other in the same plane, it was up to the expertise of the pilot to choose the right altitude and course to get the best performance from the engine. "You paid a month ahead for your hotel room, meals, everything. It was very expensive, the rental of the aircraft, the gas, and getting the mechanic for an annual inspection before you took an airplane up. So there's a $2,000 bill right there. *Ms.* magazine sponsored me several times. I had the name painted on the side of the airplane. They loved it, as they would write the race up."

Was there any prize money? Wally snorted. "I only got trophies."

And the prestige, I suggested. "Oh my word, yes! I would give anything to take you on a race," she said. "You would holler and scream all the way."

I assumed Wally meant in excitement. When asked what gave her the most excitement, she responded quickly. "Parachute jumping was fantastic. The other time was being in a glider at Stillwater, Oklahoma, when I went up to 14,000 feet."

Back on the ground, a guy wouldn't believe she'd gone that high. She told him to look at the instrument on board that would give her altitude. "He did and said, 'Oh yes.' So I said, 'Hi'"—her tone suggested a firm farewell rather than a greeting—"and walked away."

Proving someone wrong had played a consistent part in Wally's life. As had the support of her parents, especially her mother, Virginia Shy Funk. Wally referenced her often and, when she first gained her private pilot's license at Stephens College, her mother was one of the first people she took flying. "I was thrilled she was going with me and she was thrilled to go up. A dream had come true for her."

Her mother died at age ninety-five in January 1998. "We had a wonderful relationship," said Wally. "I found out about four or five years into my career, when I took her to a race, that she had flown in 1919 in a Stearman-like aircraft in Olney, Illinois. A guy had landed his plane outside the school house and she wanted to fly. He said, 'You have to have a dollar a minute,' so Mother ran back to her friends, got ten dollars, and went back to the pilot. He took her up and she did turns and loops and rolls. So she had her first experience flying as a youngster."

The effect it had on Wally's mother was instant. "When she went running home to her father, she said, 'I wanna fly.' Grandfather was a business entrepreneur and he owned a bank. He said, 'No daughter of mine is going to fly,' and that really put the crush on her. So when I came along—and it was the spirit of that Taos Mountain—they were so happy that I had that instinct. My parents were overjoyed about it, as I was living her dream."

It felt as if we could have sat on that bench, in the warm sunshine with the Eiffel Tower alongside us, talking and staring at planes all afternoon. But we had a train to catch from the Gare du Nord. Wally took one last look at the sky.

On the Eurostar from Paris to London, Wally chatted about everyone we had met over the last few days. "We did so much. I learned so much. I'm worried I won't remember it all."

Her return trip to Texas was the following day, so I made a mental note to print off the itinerary for her, with photographs and names and a summary of our discussions before she left. As usual, Wally had a busy schedule ahead. Month after month, there were trips planned across the United States. There were talks on aviation or space to give, and ceremonies to attend. In just a few weeks, in May, half a century after taking her astronaut tests, the name Wally Funk was going to be inscribed on the National Air and Space Museum's Wall of Honor in Washington, DC, in recognition of her "contribution to our aviation and space exploration heritage."

Wally mentioned she had a short trip planned in September to New Mexico. The trip, she explained, was one of several events that Virgin Galactic arranged for their Future Astronaut customers. Its aim was to visit Spaceport America.

This was going to be the space equivalent of an airport. It had only been completed five years ago, and was part of the nascent future of commercial space travel. The spaceport would eventually house a number of privately owned spaceplanes from a number of different organizations that would take small satellites and paying passengers into space.

It was also where Wally's journey into space would begin. And it sounded incredible.

"I can take someone with me," said Wally. "Why don't you come along?"

6

Spaceport America

September 2017. The car was parked in front of my hotel in Albuquerque and, if I was being kind, it had seen better days. If I wasn't being kind, the small red Honda looked ready for the scrapheap. The only positive was that Wally would not be at the wheel. The vehicle, as I understood from our conversations before I left the UK, belonged to the couple who had collected her from the airport that morning. They would then drive us to a friend of Wally's on the other side of town.

When Wally got into the driver's seat, I couldn't disguise my panic.

"Aren't your friends driving? Isn't this their car?"

"No," said Wally cheerfully. "It's mine. They keep it at their place for whenever I'm in New Mexico."

My voice went up an octave. "I thought they were taking us."

"It's okay," she added soothingly. "I'll be driving."

The male friend must have recognized the fear on my face because, while lifting my luggage into the trunk, he whispered "Good luck," and left, grinning.

The passenger seat was extraordinarily low, and any spring in it had long sprung. The last time I'd sat this close to the road's surface was in an MGB GT. It was a British two-door sports car, 1969 vintage, with chrome bumpers, a wood-paneled dashboard, and an "overdrive" switch that only converted into fifth gear on a downward slope, in a prevailing wind, at a very specific speed. Sadly, the car, the one I'd owned when I first met my husband, was exchanged for a people-carrier after the birth of our son because there was no space for a child seat. No one waved, I discovered, when you hit the road in a Renault Scenic.

A further pang of nostalgia for the MG arrived when I saw the Honda's rotary handles. The air conditioning wasn't working, Wally informed me, and the temperature was already in the 80s, so I wound down the window. After the car coughed and spluttered a few times, I recalled that the MG also had a habit of not starting. It also had a habit of breaking down. In the middle of London. During rush hour. At major intersections. After several grinds of the ignition key, the Honda's engine finally turned over. Then the beeping began.

"That shouldn't happen!" shouted Wally.

I was trapped in a scene from *Groundhog Day*. "It's because you haven't got your seat belt on."

"No. It shouldn't happen because I got him to rewire it so that it didn't beep with me not wearing the seat belt."

After a quick call and a heated discussion over what wire to pull, the beeping stopped. The car journey across town could begin and, whether I liked it or not, Wally was driving. Despite this terrifying development, I was genuinely happy to see Wally again, and not just because it meant our road trip to Spaceport America would soon be underway. Simply put, I had missed her. By now we spoke reasonably regularly over the phone and e-mailed often, but nothing could beat the full face-to-face, larger-than-life experience. Somewhere along the last six months, this voluble, stubborn, generous, occasionally difficult and eminently likeable woman had become a friend.

The invitation to visit Spaceport America as Wally's "plus one" had been a fantastic surprise. Unfortunately that invitation turned out to be a surprise for Virgin Galactic, too. They had informed me, with some confusion, that Wally had already designated her plus one to someone else. Perhaps because it was Wally, Virgin Galactic made an exception. A pretty generous exception as it turned out. Wally could have two plus ones. I could go to the ball after all.

The deal was that Wally, plus one, and plus two made their own way to the Spaceport in southern New Mexico. There would be some treats, but guests paid for their own accommodation and meals. The trip included a pickup from El Paso, if arriving at the nearest airport, an outreach event or hike, and a guided visit to the Spaceport for an update on how Richard Branson's SpaceShipTwo was progressing. All Wally wanted was a date: When would she be going into space?

Before our shared journey into Wally's future, I wanted to make a short trip into her past. The Lovelace Foundation for Medical Evaluation and Research, where Wally and the rest of the Mercury 13 had taken their astronaut tests, no longer existed, but the site where it used to be was close by. Often referred to as the Lovelace Clinic, this was the civilian facility where human spaceflight in America began. William Randolph Lovelace II oversaw the original Mercury 7 astronaut physical selection process there and, through his enlightened attitude for the time, almost gave thirteen women the opportunity to follow in their footsteps.

Lovelace saw a Russian become the first woman in space in 1963, but sadly, despite his best efforts, would never see an American woman do the same. In 1965, a year after he had been made NASA's director of Space Medicine, Lovelace died near Aspen, Colorado, in a private plane crash, along with his wife and the pilot. Other members of his family continued the business, however, and from the freeway, I glimpsed the Lovelace name on a number of medical and health-related buildings. The New Mexico native had left a legacy in more ways than one.

The short drive to the former site of the clinic felt much longer. On several occasions, Wally was either driving in the middle of the road or across more than one lane. The vehicle behind us hit his horn aggressively after we swerved into a central lane. When Wally turned off the main road into a side street, I felt marginally safer.

"I think it's near here."

In a huge parking lot, Wally circled several medical buildings until we reached a dead end. She was flummoxed. "Well, I cannot believe this has happened."

"Do you think this is where it used to be?"

"No, they tore the whole thing down." Wally sounded impatient. "I have to ask."

She waved down a passerby. "Hi. Is this the old Lovelace Clinic?"

"No," he replied, "that was over there. If you go to that old parking lot, that was it. That big thirty-story building."

Wally was dismayed. "I never thought it would take me this long to find it. I'm going in there to check. I think I saw a door back there..."

A warning sound erupted from the car. A different one from the seat belt alarm. And it worried me. "What's that beeping?"

But she had gone. The driver's car door was open and we had stopped in the middle of the parking lot. Luckily it wasn't busy.

Wally returned to the driver's seat within minutes, having learned that only the front portion of this huge modern complex was part of the old building. "Well," she said triumphantly. "I was right. It was right here, but it's changed. You got your camera with you?"

The beeps had stopped while she was on her mission, but they restarted again. Wally had jumped out of the car, and was marching into the distance, shouting at me to come this way or that. She barked instructions on what angle to position my camera and warned me not to get the Pepsi sign in any photo. The beeping continued.

"Wally, you've left the car running."

She ignored me. "I recognize this part here. We'll drive around the front. This part will be more accurate."

How did she remember the building from 1961? "It was two or three stories. Stairs at the front. Nice entrance on the roadside. Now, there used to be a motel across the street. I don't remember the name of it. That was all open space . . ."

After we'd driven across the busy main road for the front view, Wally finally noticed the noise. "What's that beeping?"

"I think it's because your seat belt isn't on."

"It hasn't beeped before. And I told you. He fixed it."

"My seat belt is on."

We took a few more photos. It was impossible to get Wally contemplative because in each shot she beamed, mouth wide, immaculate teeth on show, with her arms outstretched and upward. "You're doing that pose again."

"Yeah. I did that for somebody outside church the other day and the guy said, 'That was the greatest pose anybody's ever given me.'"

Back in the car, the beeping continued like a metronome. Wally was dismissive. "It should go off in a minute."

It didn't.

Thankfully the journey to the plus one's home only lasted around ten minutes. I clutched my seat again as several vehicles were forced into evasive maneuvers. We entered a distinctive neighborhood. Each house was architecturally different, mostly single-story, with curved arches or walls and a small garden leading down to the pavement. However, they all had walls of the same smooth salmon-pink or terracotta-red facade. "These are made of adobe brick," said Wally. "Just like my adobe house in Taos." I found Taos difficult to pronounce. "Rhymes with house, louse, and mouse."

In the front garden of one of these beautiful adobe houses, an unfamiliar bird with a spiky hairdo and a distinctive long tail ran in front of several clusters of prickly pear cactus plants. Without thinking, I yelled, "What is that?"

Wally slammed on the brakes and leaned across me to look out the window. Within a few seconds she started to laugh. "What—you've never seen a roadrunner before?"

"You mean *meep meep* roadrunner—like in the cartoon?"

"Yeah!"

"No, I haven't. A roadrunner! I love it."

As I chuckled at this ludicrous-looking bird wandering among the cacti, Wally laughed at my response to the roadrunner.

It must have been an odd sight, as two women guffawed sitting in a car by the curbside. Her simple pleasure at my simple pleasure only enhanced our mutual enjoyment. This was where our personalities overlapped. Both of us were quick to see the funny side of most things, and to enthuse about anything that tickled our fancy, whether it was a cockpit, a space capsule, or, as on this occasion, a roadrunner.

Wally had met her plus one at a Women in Aviation conference the year before. Loretta Hall was giving a talk on the Mercury 13 when she discovered that one of the Mercury 13 was in the audience. They'd kept in touch ever since. Loretta introduced herself to me via e-mail and, since both of us were on a budget, we opted to share a room where Virgin Galactic's

Future Astronauts were staying: the Hotel Encanto in Las Cruces. It was a risk considering we'd never met each other before but, via e-mail at least, Loretta seemed friendly, and we had several things in common. We both shared a keen interest in space and, like me, she viewed a glass of wine as an essential form of relaxation. She had also offered to provide transportation during the three-day trip, and rooms at her home for Wally and me before and after the trip, to save us money. This was a welcome relief for the bank balance. Three months earlier, in June, I had taken an unexpected trip to New York. The *Women with the Right Stuff* documentary on women in space that I'd made with Wally the year before—which had almost prompted a nervous breakdown—had won a New York Festival's International Programs Radio Award. At the awards dinner, I collected a surprisingly heavy but magnificent art-deco-style piece of hardware, and paid tribute to Wally and "all women who aimed high" in a short acceptance speech.

Loretta greeted us in the driveway of one of the adobe homes. For some reason, I'd assumed she'd be in her thirties or forties, but Loretta was seventy-one years old; Wally, a slightly more mature seventy-eight. I was about to undertake a road trip across New Mexico with not one but two septuagenarians. It would be an elderly version of *Thelma and Louise*. Plus one.

Trim, with short grey hair, Loretta's gentle and intelligent manner made me warm to her immediately. She had met her husband, Jerry, as an engineering student and became a high school math teacher. In 1985, after being a full-time mother for a number of years, she began writing on architecture, engineering, and construction. Since her retirement, Loretta had discovered a love of space history, particularly in the state she lived in. Her most recent publication was *Out of This World: New Mexico's Contributions to Space Travel*. She had also written a book for children about the Spaceport, illustrated by her daughter. In short, I couldn't have asked for a better guide throughout New Mexico.

She produced a road map and spread it out on the kitchen island. Wally nodded with approval at the chia-flax-quinoa granola bars nearby and the packets of instant Quaker oatmeal. She opened the fridge and examined the bottles and cartons. One of them contained pomegranate and blueberry juice. Not cranberry, but Wally was happy. Loretta pointed out the bottle of sauvignon blanc to me on one of the shelves. "That's for later," she said.

Loretta talked us through a suggested route for the following day. The aim was to break up the three-hour-or-so-long journey to our hotel in Las Cruces with a side trip to the Very Large Array (VLA) radio telescope. The VLA is not one telescope, but an array of twenty-seven antennae (plus one spare) spread across twenty-two miles (thirty-six kilometers) in the plains of San Agustin. Each dish is eighty-two feet (twenty-five meters) in diameter, but they work together as if they were one much larger telescope. Combining their data gives the equivalent resolution of one giant antenna twenty-two miles (thirty-six kilometers) across and the sensitivity of a dish 422 feet (130 meters) wide.

The telescopes study the universe using radio waves which—like microwaves, infrared, and visible light—are a type of electromagnetic radiation. Radio waves are the basis for radio communication on Earth, but we can also detect radio waves from space. If an astronomical object has a changing magnetic field—like a star (sun), planet, cloud of gas, or a spinning neutron star known as a pulsar—then it will emit radio waves that can be detected across the universe.

Most radio telescopes, like the VLA, are situated in dry desert locations to avoid humidity, because water molecules in the air distort the radio waves passing through them, which causes problems for radio astronomy. But there was another reason why this facility was a particular draw for women who worked in the fields of astrophysics and astronomy, as well as science fiction fans like myself: the movie *Contact*. In it, actress Jodie Foster plays Dr. Ellie Arroway, a character indirectly inspired by a real-life astronomer, Dr. Jill Tarter, from the Search for Extraterrestrial Intelligence (SETI) Institute. There the similarities end, as the film covered humankind's first encounter with intelligent life from another solar system through the detection of a radio signal.

What made the film memorable for me was the fictional female astronomer's intensity, intelligence, and determination. To my surprise, Wally hadn't seen it. "I've heard of Jodie Foster."

I scurried into my bedroom and got onto my laptop. It turned out that 2017 was *Contact*'s twentieth anniversary. Perfect. Within half an hour, I'd secured an interview with VLA astronomer Dr. Rick Perley for the monthly Space Boffins podcast I'd been coproducing and presenting since 2011 with my husband and fellow space and science journalist, Richard Hollingham. Perley was based in Socorro. I was assured it was close to the VLA, and was where the main work got done as, unlike in the film *Contact*, no astronomers were based by the telescopes anymore, sitting beneath them in a straw hat gazing meaningfully toward the sky like Jodie Foster's character.

The next day, Wally herded us impatiently into Loretta's car. Our first pit stop was the National Radio Astronomy Observatory in Socorro to meet Dr. Perley. According to Loretta, it was about an hour's drive away. Not long after the journey was underway, the commentary and questions began. This time Loretta, as driver, was in the firing line. Wally's attention jumped from building to building, subject to subject.

"What do you think these apartments run to . . . ? Do libraries, museums, whatever, would they buy paintings? Do you have an air circulator at all? Okay, we've gotta keep our eyes out for shoe stores." One of her shoes always had to be built up with a higher heel, and it required a minor repair.

"We've left a little early," remarked Loretta carefully. "They might not be open yet."

"I gotta get some copper wiring, maybe, to wrap around my wrist. What's the name of the hotel in downtown Santa Fe? The one that was the old hospital . . . Do you have an emery board in your purse? I have a nail that's snagging . . . What are these mountain ranges?"

Loretta was much more patient than me. But that doesn't take much. She handed Wally a map.

Wally examined it. "This map says 1912."

"We got it when we moved to Albuquerque," Loretta deadpanned. I liked this woman.

Wally made several phone calls, leaving loud messages for several friends, explaining who she was with and where we were going, and then resumed her questions.

"Can you still go to Carlsbad caves? Do either of you recall a Beverley Bass? I taught her kids to fly. She helped people out in Gander after 9/11. I was in the air on 9/11 and control tower said, 'Get down now.' Her story was made into a play." Later, thanks to Google, I discovered that Beverley Bass, now retired, was American Airlines' first female captain. She had been in the air on duty during the terrorist attacks on September 11, 2001. Bass had been flying long haul from Paris to Dallas when, along with many other airplanes, she was told to divert to Gander,

Newfoundland, on Canada's east coast. Her exploits, along with those of other pilots, were made into a Broadway play, *Come from Away*.

It was a sharp reminder that Wally may appear like a hard-of-hearing, eccentric elderly woman at times, whose stories sometimes seemed so far-fetched as to include poetic licence, but more often than not they contained a surprising truth. It was just that her life had been so extraordinary, and so beyond what most people experienced, that sometimes it presented itself like fiction. Or the ramblings of a madwoman.

But then I've often wondered how I would appear to people if, sitting under a plaid blanket at age ninety, in a nursing home, I told anyone who would listen: "I used to be on the television ... I went in a Moon buggy with an astronaut..." or "I've floated in the air ..." Most people would assume I, too, had lost the plot. Instead, that grumpy old woman who kept demanding white wine instead of tea was a former BBC TV reporter who had ridden on a replica lunar rover with Apollo 17's Gene Cernan, and who had, in her fifties, achieved a lifetime goal of floating like an astronaut by experiencing weightlessness on a European Space Agency Zero G plane.

Heaven knows how Wally appeared to those who didn't know her background or history. I asked her if she had ever worked for an airline. "One and a half months, honey. For Sierra Pacific in Arizona. It didn't make it."

I did a fact-check on Sierra Pacific Airlines. It had been set up in the early 1970s in Tucson, Arizona, and was apparently still in business. You win some, you lose some.

"When you park, can you park the nose away from the sun? That's what mother always said. Park north away from sun into the shade."

We were at the Science Operations Center at the National Radio Astronomy Observatory in Socorro, and Wally was issuing parking instructions. As Loretta reversed into a space, there was a familiar refrain, but this time the query came from Wally. "What's that beeping?"

"It's the car," Loretta replied. "It lets you know if you're near something."

Both women sat silently in the room as I interviewed Dr. Perley. He had also been the scientist for the upgrade project, transforming the VLA into the Karl G. Jansky VLA. Naturally, my first question was: Who was Karl G. Jansky? The answer was the American engineer whose discovery of radio waves coming from a source outside the Earth led to the development of radio astronomy. The distance between the dishes, we also learned, could be altered since they were mounted on rail tracks that could put the VLA into several different-shaped configurations. We'd see what configuration it was in on our approach.

The remaining hour's drive was not easy for Loretta.

"How many feet away do you have to be before something sets it off? Is Karl Janksy still alive? What are those mountains?"

The speed limit signs changed relentlessly too—thirty miles per hour, fifty miles per hour, forty miles per hour, thirty miles per hour—and my stomach protested with the brakes each time a new one approached. When we heard sirens, Loretta knew immediately why and pulled over. "I was speeding."

The police car waited behind us. In Britain, traffic cops don't carry guns and I'd seen too many American films where trigger-happy police officers shot people as they reached for a driver's licence from a glove compartment.

"Why isn't he getting out?" I was getting nervous.

"He has to do vehicle registration checks."

While the officer was still in the car, Loretta retrieved a driver's licence from her handbag. *One less shooting possibility.* Finally a cop approached, peered at its three occupants, and addressed Loretta through her open window.

"Did you know you were doing forty-eight miles per hour in a thirty-mile-per-hour zone?"

She did. Seventy-one year old Loretta received her first-ever speeding ticket and an $80 fine. The officer left with a parting platitude none of us appreciated: "I hope your day gets better."

But we knew it would. Even from a distance, the Karl J. Gansky Very Large Array was stunning. The twenty-eight white telescope dishes were spread out for miles in a Y formation. On the approach, we could see the rail track stretching into the plains or toward the San Mateo Mountains. There was even a railway caboose at the visitor center. As we walked toward the closest telescope, there was a straining, grinding, metallic groan. The 230-ton telescope was slowly shifting into a new position.

"Well, well," said a fellow visitor. "I've been here on and off for over ten years and I've never seen one of them move."

It was a magnificent sight. And the movement caused an eerie sound. Behind the groans, the metal almost produced a slow melody. It reminded me of *Close Encounters of the Third Kind.* Perhaps E.T. was trying to make contact after all.

Among the stills and posters that publicized the movie *Contact,* two were instantly recognizable to its fans. Apart from Jodie Foster in a straw hat, the other was of her holding a pair of headphones up to her ears. The backdrop for both was one of the huge white telescopic dishes, just like the one that was in front of me. Since I didn't have a hat but carried headphones for my audio equipment, I copied that particular pose and later, when I posted it online, discovered many other women who loved science and astronomy had done exactly the same thing. There was a lot of love for *Contact*.

"Do either one of you know the bunch of wiring that's inside the VLA?"

The response to Wally's question, in unison, was: "No."

Back in the car, heading south, Wally got excited. "The Spaceport's on the map!"

"That makes it real," Loretta replied.

Wally also located El Paso, from where most of the other Future Astronauts were being collected to be transported to their accommodations. I assumed many of these ticket holders would be on domestic rather than international flights.

"How big is El Paso airport?"

Wally considered my question. "Well," she said. "If you overshot the runway, you'd end up in Mexico."

Spaceport America, according to its website, is the world's "first purpose-built commercial spaceport." Although it is often mentioned in the same breath as Richard Branson, the state of New Mexico owns the spaceport, which is on 18,000 acres of land and has 6,000 square miles of restricted air space.

Virgin Galactic is a permanent tenant, along with SpaceX, UP Aerospace, EXOS Aerospace, and EnergeticX Pipeline2Space. I looked the last one up. EnergeticX Pipeline2Space "enables projectiles to deliver payloads to space." The company was started by young engineers and plans to put small "cubesats"— miniature versions of satellites often not much bigger than a shoe box—into a pointed bullet-shaped container, inside pipes 1,000 feet underground, and use a jet engine to fire them upward into suborbital space. A pipeline to space indeed. It did exactly what it said on the tin. Or pipe.

The trip hosted by Virgin Galactic for ticket holders and plus ones was not only for their clients to see the Spaceport and be updated on any progress, but also presumably to maintain a level of interest. Some of their ticket holders, like Wally for instance, had been on the waiting list for seven years. "There's gonna be a lot of people within my time frame," Wally said, "who will be getting pretty anxious."

Located several hundred miles south of Albuquerque, there's just one main road to follow, Interstate 25. I tuned in and out as Wally told an anecdote about skiing while playing the bass drum. I heard the name Branson, but she was referring to Branson, Missouri, a city she visited annually after her church had taken parishioners there on a bus tour. "Branson in November has all the Christmas shows. Anybody who's anybody goes there to perform. They have three shows a day. I love it."

She stayed in the same room in the same hotel. "Number 135, first floor on the left. And I go ziplining. Been there each year for the last six years. I get ten runs."

That would be a sight to see. Wally on a zipline. I imagined the photographs at the end showed her smiling, arms wide open. But then a road sign made me read it out loud in disbelief. "Elephant butt?"

Wally roared. "It's pronounced *bute* not *butt*."

I took a photo of the "Elephante Butte" sign nevertheless. But that was just the start of it. The Spaceport's closest town is called Truth or Consequences. Despite knowing that Britain contained towns or villages named Scratchy Bottom, Bell End and Brown Willy, somehow Truth or Consequences—"T or C" for short—seemed even more ridiculous. Better still was the name's origin. The town was originally Hot Springs, until

1950, when it changed its name simply so that a radio program, called *Truth or Consequences*, would broadcast from there for the show's tenth anniversary. Not that any of this mattered, because we were not staying in T or C but about forty miles further south, in Las Cruces. Apparently its hotels were more appropriate for Virgin Galactic's Future Astronauts.

Technically, Wally became a non-Virgin Galactic branded and lowercase "future astronaut" in 1960, when she first read *Life* magazine's article about Jerrie Cobb and the opportunity for female pilots to become astronauts. She became a branded Future Astronaut in July 2010, when she bought her $200,000 ticket. It was another leap of faith for Wally, reflecting a belief that, in the future, space travel would be accessible to all and not just the men. All women needed was the price of a ticket.

Her flight into space will begin on board Virgin Galactic's SpaceShipTwo. Some ticket holders, including Wally, had already examined the spaceplane close up and personal at a hangar in California's Mojave Desert. A month earlier, while on a family holiday in America to see a total eclipse, I'd even seen the Mojave facility myself. Not the spaceplane, just the outside of the hangar, as—despite trying—I wasn't allowed inside. Too much engineering work was going on, apparently. Instead, I drove around the area, loitered outside, and took a few photographs of my son doing a handstand in front of the Mojave Air and Spaceport building. We couldn't get in that either, as it was locked. Then we noticed the warnings. They said "Don't even think about it," and surrounded the Virgin Galactic and nearby XCOR Aerospace hangars.

XCOR made the Lynx spaceplane that, in 2013, offered future commercial astronaut seats as prizes in a worldwide competition by the men's grooming product Axe. Naturally I entered—partly to raise the profile of women, as its sexist ad campaign raised a lot of feminist hackles, and partly to get into space. The first stage involved securing online votes. After reaching the shortlist of 250 out of 87,000 applicants from the UK and Ireland—much better odds than those of becoming a European Space Agency astronaut, according to Tim Peake—I then endured public humiliation in the form of an inflatable British Army assault course at a London shopping center. I was one of the oldest women competing, and ended up with one of the slowest and most undignified times. Not exactly Project Mercury standards, but it was worth a try. Unfortunately for the winners, not to mention the scientists and engineers who worked on the spaceplane, XCOR laid off its entire staff in June 2017 "due to adverse financial conditions."

Fortunately there was a spacecraft on display, just not the one we'd expected. In Legacy Park, a small grassy area in front of the Mojave Spaceport, stood an unusual traffic cone–shaped vehicle. It was a Roton rocket ATV (atmospheric test vehicle). Entrepreneur, engineer, and former NASA consultant Gary Hudson set up the Rotary Rocket Company in 1996, in Mojave, to produce this commercial spaceflight vehicle. The Roton rocket would be a piloted vertical take-off and landing vehicle. Post-orbit, it would use a motor mounted on its nose with three rotary blades—rather like a helicopter—to land upright back on Earth. Hudson's idea, which was considered fanciful by many, was going to sell launch slots for satellites wanting to get into Low Earth Orbit.

Hudson was decades ahead of his time. Unfortunately, the company closed its doors in 2000, when the finances ran out, and the Roton rocket never went into space. Four of the company's staff, however, went on to found XCOR.

However, according to reports, XCOR's doors were not yet closed. At the time of the lay-off, industry analyst Bill Ostrove told *Forbes* magazine that the slow growth of demand for space tourism was partly to blame, and also that "their primary competitor, Virgin Galactic, pivoted to focus on launching satellites rather than human tourists into space."

This referred to Virgin Orbit, which was set up in March 2017. Two years earlier, Virgin Galactic announced that it would launch small satellites into space from a rocket called LauncherOne, which would be launched from beneath a Boeing 747 Branson had nicknamed "Cosmic Girl." Virgin Orbit was a spin-off of the LauncherOne program, and would run in parallel to Virgin Galactic.

This was a good tactical decision, but what happened to XCOR was a reminder of how good ideas can falter. Even with the right technology, backing, and almost twenty years of expertise, the company still couldn't make it work commercially. No wonder Wally was anxious.

The Spanish colonial-style Hotel Encanto de las Cruces welcomed the three of us with refreshing drinks and the tinkling of fountains. Up in our room, Loretta and I giggled at the pairs of white toweling slippers on the carpet in between our beds. There were also two matching bathrobes and two totally unexpected goodie baskets containing fruit, snacks, soft drinks, and—best of all—a silver Virgin Galactic spaceplane-branded water bottle. Being easily pleased by space swag is the secret to a happy life.

Wally's room was in an adjacent corridor. She came to visit when Loretta and I were both post-shower, wearing the fluffy robes and matching towel turbans on our wet hair.

"Look at you two," she exclaimed, and then, with a touch of sadness, added: "I'm all on my own."

Our decision to share a room would have been, I realized, Wally's preferred choice. Wally was totally independent, but she loved company. I made a mental note to pop in and see her whenever I could.

Freshened up an hour later, we headed to an area by the outdoor pool to meet our Virgin Galactic hosts and some of the other Future Astronauts for welcome drinks. Wally had met Richard Branson and his mother on a prior trip and, while his presence was never guaranteed, we knew in advance that he would not be attending this one. A few days earlier, Hurricane Irma had wrecked his home on Necker Island, alongside thousands of others, on its path through the Caribbean.

A small bar was set up near a low table and chairs, as waiters hovered nearby with canapés. Wally, as usual, chose a non-alcoholic drink. Loretta and I dived into the margaritas. As this was a private trip, I'm not releasing the identities of other Future Astronauts, but the first person I spotted caused some personal excitement. For a brief moment, I thought one of the ticket holders was Stan Lee. This was the man who, along with artist Jack Kirby, created Spider-Man, Ant Man, Black Widow, the Hulk, Black Panther, Iron Man, the X-Men, and the Fantastic Four. As a child, I had pretended to be Invisible Sue from the Fantastic Four in the school playground. Apart from the remarkable physical resemblance to Lee, the elderly man seated on the chair in front of me sported the Marvel comic icon's familiar tinted glasses. Most surprising of all was that he looked much older than Wally.

My mistaken assumption had been that Wally was the oldest Future Astronaut on the waiting list. But "R"—who incidentally was not Stan Lee—appeared to be in his nineties. I discovered later that R was in fact a youthful eighty-nine. His elegant and glamorous plus one was in her nineties. Initially I was surprised to see so many other older ticket holders but, after talking to one

Swiss father and son, learned that it was the thirtysomething son who had bought the golden ticket.

The Virgin Galactic personnel included a Dutchman, Martijn, and two British women, Tiff and Clare, who I recognized from the London HQ. Everyone present gave a brief introduction. This included a Japanese guy who had hedged his bets by buying tickets into space from several companies. His female plus one was involved in a space venture in Japan that took people's ashes into space. The Virgin Galactic reps sat up and took notice. Another ticket holder, a friendly retired American man in about his early sixties, had once sold Virgin Galactic tickets to others. He was with his male partner, a bearded blond. We were also joined by a former NASA employee. She was a woman of an uncertain age, feisty, wearing a designer shirt. She reminded me of Mercury 13 member Jerri Truhill with her deep voice, constantly wisecracking. Afterward, at a communal table in the hotel's restaurant, one of the ticket holders lowered himself into the seat next to me. "I'm not sure I've got the energy to sit next to Wally," he joked under his breath. "She's a pistol, a fireball, a force of nature."

It was true. Her energy levels were off the scale—not just for a seventy-eight-year-old, but for a thirty-eight-year-old.

After our starters there was a late arrival: a young British woman, "B," who had gotten her master's at seventeen and made her money in property development abroad. She was successful, vivacious, and extremely likeable, and wore an eye-catching black-and-white scarf covered in astronauts. It was like nothing I'd ever seen—and I knew my space merchandise. Both Wally and I coveted it, so I asked the woman if she didn't mind telling me where it was from.

"Chanel," she replied, and all my hopes of owning a similar scarf disappeared. B's young daughter had also saved up and bought her a matching Chanel space pin, which was a reminder that wealthy people inhabit a different world. The scarf designer was Karl Lagerfield, whom she knew and frequented for his clothes. The space theme was going to be big, apparently. That night I did an internet search and noted that Lagerfeld's space collection had hit the catwalk six months earlier in March, and that space will indeed be this season's look. I checked the cost of the scarf. It was over $800. Thankfully, I own a few NASA T-shirts so, despite being unable to afford the scarf, I will still be *en vogue*.

The next morning, Wally admired my shift dress. "You dress like me. Simple. My mother was all about town, elegantly dressed, immaculate, and on committees. I was the complete opposite. She wanted me to come out in New York. Well . . . I wasn't having any of that."

I'd never seen Wally in a dress. She wore her usual uniform of cargo pants and a crisp, freshly pressed shirt. This time the shirt was blue denim, and "WALLY" was monogrammed in red capitals on the right breast pocket, just above the words "safety judge." On her left pocket was embroidered "SpaceShipTwo" and "Virgin Galactic."

People divided into groups for either a hike to Dipping Springs or a local outreach event. Naturally, Wally chose the latter. It was a trip to the Las Cruces Challenger Center. Challenger Centers were set up after the January 28, 1986, Space Shuttle accident. It should have been a routine tenth launch for the Challenger shuttle. This was the shuttle that had taken Sally Ride, America's first female astronaut, into space three years earlier. But seventy-three seconds after liftoff, a booster engine failed. To everyone's disbelief, the shuttle exploded in a huge ball of white smoke and produced two further plumes that splintered off in opposite directions. The NASA launch commentator understated the issue when he said it was "obviously a major malfunction."

All seven crew members on board perished. Their collective deaths were witnessed by the astronauts' friends and family on the ground at Cape Canaveral and by millions of others, including school children, live on CNN. It was a shocking moment in US space history. The dead included Judy Resnik, a seasoned astronaut and America's second woman in space, plus a woman who would have become the first teacher in space, Sharon "Christa" McAuliffe.

Much of the pre-publicity in the media had focused on McAuliffe, the school teacher from New Hampshire who had been selected from a pool of 10,000 applicants to be the first US civilian in space. She had planned to give school lessons while in orbit and, partly as a result of the educational aims of this mission, in the aftermath of the fatal accident, the crew's families helped create the Challenger Center for Space Science Education a few months later. The first Challenger Learning Center opened in Texas in 1988, and now there are over forty across three continents. I reported for the BBC on the first Challenger Learning Center to be opened outside America in October 1999. It was in Leicester, in the UK. As a result of making that television report, I was familiar with the format: students undertook a variety of mission scenarios in a realistic setting of control rooms, off-world bases, or space station laboratories, completing tasks that promoted science and engineering. Wally had no idea what was coming, but when she saw the room full of school kids and our mission leader dressed in a blue astronaut flight suit, she was hooked—especially since our three-hour mission was to go to the Moon.

For the first half of the session, while Wally was in mission control, I was in a space lab paired with a ten-year-old girl performing science experiments to test water system samples for contamination. Every so often, an emergency interrupted the routine and we responded accordingly. It was great fun.

"I could see you!" Wally said excitedly, when we switched and I entered mission control. There, I spied on Wally through the monitors as she enjoyed the social side of simulated space travel and chatted with everyone, no doubt asking plenty of questions.

Later, over lunch, we discussed our mission with those who had been on the hike; they hadn't realized that the outreach trip would be so good. It inspired one of the Future Astronauts to help fund and set up a Center in his hometown.

After lunch, four white Land Rovers—one of Virgin Galactic's sponsors—waited to drive us to the Spaceport. Wally immediately got on her phone to leave a message for a friend. "It's 3:40 PM New Mexico time and I'm on the way to the Richard Branson Spaceport..."

Technically it was the state of New Mexico's Spaceport, of course. We were waived through a border stop and turned off at a sign for Uphorn. The smooth road soon deteriorated into a dirt track, and the four identical cars, one after the other, kicked up clouds of dust. It resembled a scene from a thriller where a covert mission was about to happen. The whole road will eventually be smoothed over, but in the meantime, during twenty-four miles of bumps and sand, with a landscape of desert scrub and mountains in the distance, Wally kept up a stream of questions to John, the driver: "What do these lines do on the rear window? How do I see a film back here? How do we open this cold box?"

Like many of her questions, most of them were asked without pausing to see if she could answer them herself and, before John had finished explaining, she had started the next question. Finally, we could see the Spaceport in the distance. But only just.

It blended in with the landscape, low and brown. It was an unusual shape, too, and reminded me of a pair of old-fashioned sunglasses, or a butterfly with two wings and two large, circular eyes.

"I've heard butterfly before," said John. "I've also heard female lady parts and a ladybug." He laughed. "It's whatever you want it to be."

I took a long, hard look at the Spaceport. Despite owning lady parts myself, I couldn't see the resemblance.

The location of the first private Spaceport in the world is in the Jornada del Muerto Desert, near the White Sands Missile Range. This is advantageous for future spaceflights, as there will be no commercial planes overhead due to the Range's restricted airspace. Even though the Spaceport is currently empty, there was a security gate, and we handed over passports or driving licences. For some reason, this made Wally unhappy and, uncharacteristically, she snapped at the guard. "Don't damage my licence."

It was held together by tape and already falling apart. I'm not sure she noticed that he looked more than a little upset. Closer to the building, before reaching a giant, brick-red sculpture in the shape of a half-crescent moon, we stopped to take photographs.

A few of us walked the remaining few hundred yards to the entrance, alongside road signs saying Asteroid Beltway and Half Moon Street. From the ground, the Spaceport wasn't particularly impressive. It was plain, brown, and understated, with curved walls leading toward a locked door between the two butterfly wings or bug eyes. Our Virgin Galactic guide provided a few facts and figures—it was on 18,000 acres of land and the runway was 12,000 feet long. That converted to over two miles, or 3.6 kilometers. Wally was astonished. "I can take off and land six times!"

She had already flown over the Spaceport, and had landed and taken off again from the runway twice before it had officially opened in 2012, but couldn't recall when.

When the doors opened, it was a theatrical moment, but there was nothing to see. An empty, rippling, curved corridor tempted us forward. It didn't take long before the walls changed into windows. There on our right, looking down below, was SpaceShipTwo. It was a thrilling sight. The entrance at ground level was an illusion. Our corridor was actually a bridged walkway several stories above the hangar.

The spaceplane was the only vehicle in the hangar, and smaller than I expected. It was white with a black underbelly, and resembled a private jet. There were four rows of three round porthole-style windows along the fuselage for the passengers and five windows for the cockpit. Pin-up art of a female astronaut, similar in style to that seen on conventional Virgin aircraft, decorated the curved nose beneath the cockpit. She appeared to be doing a Fosbury Flop over an invisible high jump. There were no wings in the middle section of the plane. Instead, at the back were large, upturned tail fins resembling those from a 1960s Cadillac. Cameras flashed, but it was the light at the end of the corridor that drew me. It was an unbelievable sight. We were now at the front of the hangar behind an enormous three-story window overlooking the runway, with distant mountains as a backdrop. Stunning doesn't begin to describe it. We had effectively entered Spaceport America through the equivalent of an unmarked back door. The spaceplane was cool, but this view of blue sky, sandy scrub, and distant mountains was a showstopper. The Foster and Partners–designed building was also an amazing location on Earth to begin a journey into space. It was otherworldly.

There was an overwhelming amount of natural light and, since the building was in a desert, there were eleven boreholes for water—of which four were active. As the guide Martijn provided some facts and figures, his voice echoed around the building, making it difficult to hear. Wally struggled while I gazed out the enormous windows. The Land Rovers were now parked on the runway apron.

We got inside the cars again and were driven along the vast empty expanse of the Spaceport's runway. It was over two miles long and forty-two inches (107 centimeters) thick, including a fourteen-inch (35.5 centimeter) layer of concrete. I stuck my head out of the roof window and the skin on my face rippled backward with the buffeting wind. I had simulated my own launch into space. Wally was busy examining the windsock.

"See the wind going into the windsock? That's coming from the west. So if we were taking off north we'd have a left crosswind. If we were taking off south we'd have a right crosswind. Always wing into the wind."

When the four vehicles reached the end of the runway, they lined themselves up and started revving their engines. Side by side, it felt like we were either going to be part of a race or a car commercial. Wally was told to put on her seat belt. It was going to be a race.

The acceleration took us all by surprise. After the initial shock, Wally, Loretta, and I whooped with delight as the car reached 130 miles per hour. It was the fastest any of us had ever been in a car. We had not won the race, but it was another first for three young-at-heart women with a combined age of over 200 years.

Back at the Spaceport building, a lift took us to an area on the third floor that will become the Future Astronauts Lounge, which will also be open to friends and family. The huge, cavernous space, with a massive curved section consisting of multiple vertical windows extending from the floors below, overlooked the runway. We were witnessing the baby steps of commercial space tourism, and I was full of admiration for those who had bought tickets as they, along with the entrepreneurs, scientists, and engineers, were an integral part of this future. Without these ticket holders and the promise of their business, none of this would be happening.

I asked if the SpaceShipTwo we had seen from the overhead bridge was flight-ready and, to my surprise, discovered it was not the real thing. It was a full-scale model from the UK's 2012 Farnborough Airshow. Most of the ticket holders had seen the real thing in Mojave, but it still felt like a bit of a cheat. Martijn informed everyone that a replica of the front part of the spaceship would eventually be displayed in the lounge so that people could sit inside and get an idea of what the real spaceship was like. Wally grumbled below her breath. "They said that last time."

The briefing also outlined the procedure for Future Astronauts and their flight profile, which involved the White Knight mothership circling and climbing slowly to around 50,000 feet, with SpaceShipTwo carried beneath it. "Once there, the pilot will give the signal to release. It's quite a dramatic separation of the two." SpaceShipTwo would then go from zero miles per hour to the speed of sound in around fifteen seconds.

At the height of their journey, Wally and her fellow passengers would be able to see the curvature of the Earth, the blackness of space, and "the whiteness of the stars," which everyone can see already at night—though it seemed churlish to point this out. The time from takeoff to landing would be between 90 and 105 minutes. The guide gave more information. The astronauts would fly "eighty miles high" and then, for several minutes in space, their dreams would come true. Then it would be time for reentry, "belly down, feathers up."

Clare also gave an idea of timelines, though she was naturally reluctant to give definite dates. "We should be in space by the beginning of next year [2018] if all goes well, and after that we will prove repeatability with flights around the middle of next year. Then there will be another three months of test flights."

Wally's face was utterly crestfallen. Reassurances that "things are going extremely well at the moment in Mojave" and that they were "hitting our interval timelines and milestones" made no difference. After we broke for cocktails, I overheard Wally give the guide a hard time. The schedule was too far ahead. Why weren't they getting things done faster?

As the sun set over the mountains, we toasted the Future Astronauts with champagne on the balcony, but Wally was clearly unimpressed. It wasn't that she was ungrateful. It was because she had done this visit before and, in her eyes, there had not been enough progress. Understandably, time, for a seventy-eight-year-old, was not in unlimited supply.

"I heard that same thing five years ago from Branson," she grumbled. "And now Branson's not going to go up until the end of next year. It's just bullshit."

Wally often used the British word "bloody," but this was the first time I'd heard her swear properly. Yet it was clear that there had been progress. A link from Mojave to the Spaceport had been installed, and there was now a Spaceport Operations Center, which was the small curved-roofed building erected nearby, next to the fire station, which, hopefully, would never need to be used.

After reporting on space missions for decades, one thing I had learned was that any launch date attached to a space mission nearly always slipped. In the space industry, whether it was the scientific instruments, a satellite for the payload, or the launcher itself, delays were an accepted part of the process. You had to be prepared to play the long game. And be patient.

I discussed some of these issues with her and, begrudgingly, Wally admitted that there had been progress. "Yes, the windows weren't here, the lights were not here, they were just building the fire station, and all the trucks were out." She still looked miserable.

I took one of the Virgin Galactic reps aside. "Isn't there any chance Wally can fly earlier? She's so much older than everyone else. This has been her dream for over fifty years."

There was nothing they could do. "Technically, we can't. There are people ahead of her on the list." Clare was genuinely apologetic. "We love Wally and if we could, we would."

Downstairs, on the hangar floor, a table had been set for dinner behind the tail fins of SpaceShipTwo (the model). It had seventeen windows: five for the two pilots and twelve circular portholes above and to the side of the six passengers. It looked like a cozy fit. "I'm going to be sitting on the right-hand side, right behind the first officer," Wally said. If she was lucky, she would be sitting behind a woman, too, since former NASA test pilot Kelly Latimer was one of Virgin Galactic's pilots.

Up close, I examined the spaceplane's pneumatic painted astrobabe more closely. Floating down from the woman's arched back was a long blonde ponytail. The female astronaut wore a fishbowl helmet and a tight-fitting black-and-white retro spacesuit, Barbarella-style, sporting elbow-length gloves and a basque. I wondered what Helen Sharman would make of it. More disturbing was finding out that the design was based on a woman Wally had met at the Spaceport dedication in 2010: Branson's mother, Eve.

Wally was featured in many of the press photographs taken on the runway at the dedication, alongside Branson, New Mexico Governor Bill Richardson, and Apollo 11 astronaut Buzz Aldrin. "We had all of about ten minutes to talk," she said. "They were all very nice and very polite. We were talking business, when we were going to go. Branson has always said it was going to be next year . . ."

Did her trip into space always feel constantly out of reach?

"It's getting closer, but I didn't want to wait another year. I want to go up in an even-number year like 2018."

"Are you superstitious?"

"No, I like even numbers. I'm not seeing as much happening here as I anticipated when we drove here. For me, they're not doing it quickly enough. I want to see it happen fast. Everyone says there's wiring and all kinds of technical stuff, but I know better, being kind of a mechanic. They can do it faster if they want to."

My reassurances about safety considerations were dismissed. "No. I don't think that's anything to do with safety. I've been to Mojave. They're not working quickly enough because they've got other things going on and they're building two more."

Virgin Galactic was indeed building two more, at the Mojave facility in California, to make up a fleet of spaceplanes. This made economic and business sense, since over 650 people had bought tickets and, once the spaceplane had proved itself safe with passengers, and space tourism flights were underway, the company reckoned that demand for the flights would only increase.

After dinner, which included a space-style dessert in a glass bowl resembling an astronaut's helmet on a bed of dry ice, we all went outside the Spaceport and admired its curved lines against the night sky. Its lights promised a bold future in commercial spaceflight among the darkness.

It had been an amazing trip but, the next morning, while waiting for Loretta to bring her car around to the hotel entrance,

Wally was in a rare reflective mood.

"I've not got many years left," she said.

It was the first time I'd heard her acknowledge any possible limitations of her ambition as a result of her age. It almost made me cry. After that unusual and unexpected moment of vulnerability, I wanted more than anything to see her get into space.

7

Storage Space

Not far from Spaceport America and Roswell, the birthplace of the world's extraterrestrial conspiracy theory, I saw my first UFO. At least, that's what the craft resembled. As might be expected, the Unidentified Flying Object was housed in a military base: the White Sands Missile Range in New Mexico. It is the United States' largest military installation, covering over 3,000 square miles within the Tularosa Basin and extending into five counties. Apart from playing a key role in developing the country's missile and atomic weapons capabilities, it was also where a number of German scientists, including Werner Von Braun, a former member of the Nazi party and SS officer, had been spirited away from Germany as part of Project Paperclip and helped form America's space program.

After passports and driving licences were handed in to security for a background check, our instructions were to stay within the Range Museum area and only take photographs with the San Andres Mountains in the background, not toward the Range Museum itself. Despite it being a glorious day, Wally, Loretta, and I were the only visitors: three women in the ultimate man's world, in a spectacular—if ominous—playground of war.

The missile park contained all manner of military projectiles, displayed at various jaunty angles. These missiles had all been tested at White Sands, from a couple of Pershings and a Patriot, to a yellow-and-black Vergeltungswaffe 2 (more commonly known as a V-2 rocket) to a Redstone. But some of these agents of war had produced a different outcome: one that resulted in robotic probes exploring the Solar System, enabling people to live and work off-world on the International Space Station. They were also partly responsible for today's emerging business of commercial spaceflight—a business that had allowed Wally Funk to purchase a trip above the Earth into space.

The Redstone was originally designed by Von Braun as a surface-to-surface ballistic missile. It was later used as the first stage of the Jupiter C rocket, to put America's first satellite, Explorer 1, into orbit, on January 31, 1958, over three months after the Soviet Union had beat them to it with Sputnik 1. Redstone boosters then went on to blast a member of the Mercury 7, Alan Shepard, as the first American in space in 1961. It was the same year that Yuri Gagarin made space history as the first man to orbit the Earth, and also the same year that Wally passed her tests and became a member of the all-female Mercury 13—the women who had wanted to join the men among the stars.

The flying-saucer-shaped UFO appeared totally out of place among the missiles. If you discounted the extraterrestrial possibilities, the craft also resembled a large, squat, open, metallic parasol with four short legs. It was, in fact, a Balloon Launched Test Decelerator Vehicle, one of four that NASA used at the White Sands base in 1972 to test the Viking Mars Lander Decelerator. A helium balloon lifted the craft to the required height over the town of Roswell, over 150 miles east of the missile range, and released the Test Decelerator Vehicle. This unusually shaped craft then flew to White Sands using its four rockets at just over the speed of sound, while spinning for stability. This fact had not passed me by.

On July 8, 1947, several eyewitnesses reported the crash of a UFO at Roswell. The Roswell Army Air Field (RAAF) attended the scene and quickly secured the site. The story later made headlines across the United States, but the front page of the *Roswell Daily Record* stated: "RAAF Captures Flying Saucer on Ranch in Roswell Region."

The US government dismissed these reports as relating to an experimental weather balloon. But witnesses persisted. It also happened at a period of time when there had been several UFO sightings across the United States, so interest was high. There were tales of bodies by the wreckage in Roswell, including one that may have even been alive. These hairless child-sized bodies could only have been extraterrestrial, people claimed, since they resembled small, inhuman, grey creatures with large almond-shaped heads and enormous eyes, but without any ears or a nose. There were even rumours that an alien autopsy had taken place and had been filmed.

It was now seventy years after that incident, but that image has persisted to this day. The "grey" has now become the go-to alien in modern science fiction, from the movies *Close Encounters of the Third Kind* and *Paul* to the television series *Stargate*. Roswell was now the UFO capital of the world. Nevertheless, in 1972 the military released a never-before-seen, spinning, flying-saucer-shaped craft from Roswell to travel at great speed in the skies toward a US military base. And some Brits thought Americans didn't do irony.

Von Braun wasn't the only connection to space at the military base. Robert Goddard—the American engineer and father of modern rocketry—and Dr. Clyde Tombaugh—the astronomer who discovered Pluto in 1930—also worked there. Tombaugh was employed there for nine years, starting in 1946, and improved an experimental missile-tracking telescope that supported the White Sands rocket-testing program. Some of the sounds of the Range's later missiles being test fired—including a Lance and a Nike Tomahawk—even made it into *Star Wars*. Ben Burtt, from Lucasfilm, visited White Sands several times in 1978 for the studio's sound library before the release of *Star Wars: The Empire Strikes Back*. He had already won an Academy Award for the first *Star Wars* film, and presented the museum with a Darth Vader helmet that had been used during filming in appreciation of their help.

White Sands had an incredible museum. It was full of unexpected space snippets alongside some impressive missile hardware. The Space Shuttle Columbia had even landed on the White Sands runway in 1982. Yet Wally was uncharacteristically listless and quiet. She wanted to sit in the shade for a while, but I suspected her lethargy resulted from more than just the heat. Perhaps, I wondered, it was lingering disappointment after yesterday's visit to Spaceport America and the realization that her trip into space was not as close as she'd expected. Wally wandered off without a glance at the vast array of missiles by her side. Later, after exploring the site for half an hour or so, I located Loretta in one of the museum buildings, but not Wally. By now I was used to Wally's meanderings. At some point, she would always run off full speed in an unexpected direction.

When we all finally reconvened in one of the areas that detailed the history of the Range, Wally mentioned she'd been out for a walk. I reminded her that we were on a military base and restricted to the museum—exploring elsewhere might get her arrested. The expression on her face said it all. I decided not to inquire further. That sort of information was on a need-to-know basis.

Wally requested Loretta's car keys to retrieve something from her car, and my internal alarm bells were triggered. Once

Wally was out of earshot, I warned Loretta that Wally would probably drive her car.

"She can't." Loretta was confused.

"I know. But she will. That's what she does. She did it to me in Texas last year and in Florida a few months ago. Whatever Wally said she was getting, it's an excuse. I'll put money on it. Trust me, your car won't be where you left it."

From Loretta's face it was clear I sounded ridiculous, paranoid, possibly both. Like a conspiracy theorist, for instance, who believed that a simple Balloon Launched Test Decelerator Vehicle was a UFO. There would be numerous reasons, I persisted, but Loretta mustn't believe any of them. I began to feel embarrassed. *Maybe I'm being unfair?* Then, upon leaving the building, we discovered that Loretta's car was no longer in the parking lot, a good few minutes' walk away, but right in front of us in a disabled spot. Wally leaned against the vehicle, casually scrutinizing the map. Loretta was visibly shocked.

"Wally," I said indignantly. "You're not insured."

She mumbled something about what a wonderful museum it was and how she'd wanted some shade. "I was doing you a favor," she added sheepishly.

Our next pit stop before returning to Albuquerque was the New Mexico Museum of Space History: a bright, modern building resembling the bottom stage of a rocket. Its windows reflected the cloud-free blue skies and the Sacramento Mountains overlooking the town of Alamogordo. Outside the entrance was a welcome surprise: a full-scale replica of the Mercury capsule Wally would have flown in if history had been kinder to her. Better still, unlike the real Mercury capsule that Wally and I had seen at the Kennedy Space Center in Florida earlier in the year, she could sit inside this one. Wally went up the few steps, climbed into it, and, despite its being designed for only one person, beckoned me to join her on board. I wedged my bottom into the seat beside her as she examined the controls.

"Okay," she explained, "first you have up here roll, yaw, and pitch—that's what you do with your stick—there should be a stick here. Then you have your temperature, your clock, control fuel, descent . . . how fast you're coming down. Your air speed indicator. Gosh, it starts at 40 miles per hour and goes up to . . . I can't read it . . ."

"100."

"Okay. Over here we have cabin pressure, then humidity percent, oxygen, emergency switch, DC volts, ammeter, and the auto bus and the AC volt switch . . ." She reveled in the technicalities and joked at the control lettering's condition, no doubt worn from hundreds of eager fingers pretending to fly a Mercury space capsule. "Some of the switches I can't read. I'm sure this would be the trim."

"So you could have flown this?"

"Yes! I'm so surprised. These instruments are the same instruments I have in a Cessna 172. Now over here they're a tad bit different. I don't know jet tower and capsule . . ."

"So just a few buttons you don't know?"

"Yes, on the left-hand side. Oh!" She raised her voice in delight. "This is so INCREDIBLE!" She spotted some more dials. "Time to go . . . retrograde . . . time elapsed . . . This tells you exactly what you need to do. Oh man, this is exciting." Her raucous cackle filled the capsule.

"This would have been a piece of cake for you."

"Yeah. Now I've got to figure out how to get out of here. Push my butt up, honey." Wally took one last look. "Oh man. TO SIT IN IT! I've watched it so many times."

Inside the museum, Wally found the Space Shuttle simulator unexpectedly difficult. "Discovery Houston, you're a little high," a voice warned. "You need to get down as soon as possible."

Wally asked, "Where's the gear?" Before I could answer that I had no idea, a loud crashing sound emanated from the machine. "Uh oh," Wally said.

Despite crashing the shuttle, Wally recovered and examined the mission patches among an array of cloth circles in a glass case. Every NASA space mission, and many others around the world, issues an embroidered patch that represents it in some form of artwork. It could be a Space Shuttle leaving the Earth in a stylized arc or, as with the Apollo 11 patch, an eagle landing on the Moon. The surnames of astronauts from that mission are sewn around the edges. Wally was searching for Eileen Collins's name. When she couldn't find it, she informed a member of the museum staff and told them to update their collection.

She then scrutinized the framed photographs on the walls of the museum's Hall of Fame. The few women on display included Valentina Tereshkova, the first woman in space; Anousheh Ansari, the first female private space explorer; Eileen Collins, the first woman to command the Space Shuttle; and Susan Helms, who became the first woman from the US military to fly into space, in 1993. Helms still held the record, from March 11, 2001, on her fifth mission, for the longest spacewalk. Together with her NASA colleague Jim Voss, they did an EVA (extra vehicular activity) for 8 hours, 56 minutes.

NASA's Peggy Whitson was not yet on the wall, but I assumed she'd be a shoe-in, since a few months earlier she had completed her eighth spacewalk, a record for female astronauts. Surprisingly, there was no recognition for any of the women from the Mercury 13. Not even Wally, a New Mexico native. But there was a tribute to Edward Dittmer, who trained Enos and Ham, the first chimpanzees in space. Ham became the world's first astrochimp on January 31, 1961, performing a sixteen-minute suborbital spaceflight in a Mercury capsule, just days before Wally reported to the Lovelace Clinic in Albuquerque to take her astronaut tests. This time it was my turn to be annoyed. I was indignant on Wally's behalf. An astrochimp trainer had been elected into that Hall of Fame before Wally and the other pioneering women from the Mercury 13. Not even the first Mercury 13 member, Jerrie Cobb.

Wally took it in stride—she was rather taken with Ham's doll-like flight suit on display in a glass case and, back outside, Ham's grave. Ham was short for "Holloman Aero Med," because he was trained at the nearby Holloman Airforce Base Aeromedical Center. A dedication plaque at the gravesite records Ham's birthplace as Cameroon in 1955, and his death at North Carolina Zoological Park in 1983.

The area outside the museum was designated the John T. Stapp Air and Space Park, named after Colonel Stapp, a US Air Force medical researcher and thrill seeker who put his body through some extraordinary extremes in the name of science. The section of blue sled track on display was from a "daisy track" decelerator that was used to subject a human or animal to G-force testing. A pneumatic piston device—the Daisy BB airgun used one to fire pellets, which is how the track got its name—shot the subject with an explosive force along the track at up to 150 miles per hour, until they were stopped equally abruptly. The device tested aircraft and spacecraft seats, including the Apollo command module, but was best known for its contribution to seat belt safety. Stapp often used himself as a human guinea pig before he expected others to do the tests, and once reached a mind-blowing and dangerously high 35G.

It reminded Wally of the Martin-Baker ejection-seat trial she had undergone after the phase two tests had been canceled and she decided, under her own steam, to travel around the US to complete the same small number of additional tests as Jerrie Cobb and the Mercury 7 men.

Martin-Baker was a British aviation firm that had devised a way to save pilots' lives by detonating explosives beneath a chair to eject the pilot out of the aircraft and out of harm's way. A parachute then brought the pilot safely back to Earth. The test was the vertical equivalent of a human cannonball or, indeed, the daisy sled. The pilot strapped himself into a seat knowing that there were explosives underneath him meant to accelerate the chair upward along a supporting tower of guide rails. He pressed his feet and head against the rests, held his elbows inward, and then pulled the charge. Boom! As gravity pulled downward, the spine was at risk of being compressed. The ejection seat was designed to balance out these forces so that the pilot could evacuate a plane in an emergency without damaging his back. Otherwise it could result in ruptured discs, fractured vertebrae, or, in the worst cases, a severed spine.

It sounded terrifying. Or, as Wally put it: "That's just when they put you in a seat, shoot you up a pole, and you come on down real hard."

She recalled that she had various wires stuck all around her body. "They wanted to see what your body will do in that kind of motion, going up hard and fast and coming down hard and fast, and it was kind of a shaky landing. I had a tremendous headache."

She also neglected to tell them that she'd severely injured her back in a skiing accident the year before, resulting in the use of a back brace. Otherwise, of course, they might have said no.

On the final stage of our drive back toward Albuquerque, a giant nut advertised PistachioLand near a horse hotel. New Mexico was a fascinating state. I was starting to relax, but Wally continued to worry about her position on the spaceflight list.

She'd obviously spoken to a few Future Astronauts about it, as she knew several of their positions—thankfully behind Wally—and that one of them was placed sixty-seventh, much higher than her. "But he is one of the founding investors," she said generously, "so they get priority."

Loretta's car made a warning sound. This alarm was not related to seat belts. It went off if her tires hit the white lines at the side of the road. "I stay away from the white lines all the time," said Wally, and my eyebrows couldn't have arched any higher. She went back on her bright pink phone. Its screen wallpaper showed her swimming with a dolphin. Both of them were smiling.

The call had obviously gone to voice mail as she muttered, "I never get through," before leaving a message. "Hi, Eileen. It's Wally . . . I've just been to the New Mexico Museum of Space History and I saw your face everywhere and the patches you gave me. I just wanted to say I'm so proud of you. I wish you would call, and I'm so thankful I know you. Give Wally a call."

The call, it was clear, was to Eileen Collins, first female commander of the Space Shuttle. Wally asked for everyone's phone number. After initially being taken aback, people usually gave it to her. She dialed another number. "Hi honey. I think it's 4 AM in South Korea. Richard Branson kept us so busy it was incredible. Up until midnight. I need to tell you all about it. I expected you to call me before you left but you didn't . . ."

She telephoned another friend to check some dates. It was confirmed that Wally had flown over and landed on the Space-port runway in 2009, did two touch-and-go landings, and circled around it. Then she examined Loretta's camera. "When we get home, I'd like to see what kind of a battery charger you have for your camera. I've just had an idea. Do you have a CVS or a Walgreens where I can get my pictures done?"

The following day, back at Loretta's house, we watched several short films from the space museum archives. The museum had kindly allowed Loretta to view them for research. One of the films showed Colonel John Stapp himself on a full-length daisy track. The forces he'd experienced left the whites of his eyes blood red within bruised eye sockets. Colonel Joe Kittinger Jr had commented: "He was brave and had no fear . . . tenacious and never gave up . . . He never made general because he wasn't a politician. He rubbed a lot of people up the wrong way and ignored his superiors . . ."

I couldn't help thinking that some of Stapp's characteristics applied to Wally. She was from that era of brave, fearless pioneers. She reminded me of the role Chuck Yeager played in Tom Wolfe's *The Right Stuff*. The man who broke the sound barrier was a test pilot and a candidate with the right skill, bravery, and flying experience to become a Mercury 7 astronaut, but, because he didn't have a college degree, wasn't eligible for the tests. Technically, neither were John Glenn and Scott Carpenter, yet they made it. Perhaps it was also because Yeager didn't consider sitting in a capsule to be flying. It was obviously a question he had often been asked because, on October 12, 2017, Yeager tweeted: "Q: Why didn't NASA ever select you to become an astronaut? A: They knew I didn't want to wipe the monkey crap off the seat before I sat down."

Wally may not have had the engineering or math degree required by NASA when she applied through the proper channels to become an astronaut, but there was no doubt that she too had "the right stuff." In her own way, and without the swearing, she also had a touch of Yeager's feisty attitude.

Loretta was also full of surprises. Two years earlier she had volunteered to be part of a National Aerospace Training and Research Center (NASTAR) space experiment in Pennsylvania.

The Center, an air and space education and training facility, was the first to be approved by the Federal Aviation Administration to meet training requirements for commercial human spaceflight. The training involved testing the effects of G forces on the human body using a centrifuge—exactly the same test that Wally underwent in the early 1960s.

It was an experience all three of us had in common. In 2013, I had taken several rides in the UK's only human centrifuge. Based in Farnborough and formerly part of a government military facility, the centrifuge was now operated by the defence and space company QinetiQ.

The centrifuge itself opened in 1955. It was built to simulate the G forces experienced by pilots and—at the time—possible future astronauts. It was located in a circular room, and consisted of a low horizontal arm, pivoted in the center where a medical officer sat. There was a windowed gondola at the end of the arm. It resembled a small cable car for a single seated passenger. The glass-fronted control room was gloriously retro. It contained the same grey panels, black rotary dials, and circular glass instrument display as when it opened in the mid-1950s.

The instructor strapped me in and ordered me to relax, but I wasn't nervous. If anything, I was overexcited. If it felt unpleasant, he told me to tense my body. I would undergo three spins inside the gondola, starting at 2.6G, the sort of gravity you might feel at Jupiter. Each lasted fifteen seconds. On the first one, my ears popped. When the centrifuge stopped, my stomach lurched as if on a rollercoaster and my ears popped again. At 3G, it was more of a rush and made me feel slightly light-headed. The instructor told me to try and touch my nose. My arm felt a resistance, as if swimming through a strong tide, as I placed a finger on my nose. When we finally reached 3.4G, my body experienced a force almost three-and-a-half times its weight.

The pressure was uncomfortable, nowhere near as pleasant, but still thrilling.

At this point I was unable, when instructed by the control room operator, to raise my hands from my lap, let alone touch my nose. I felt the skin on my face being stretched and forced toward the back of my head. The instructor's disembodied voice from the control room echoed in the gondola. "We know what you'll look like when you're fifteen years older now."

Going up to 3.4G was more than the G forces experienced by a Space Shuttle crew on either launch or landing. It gave me a newfound respect for what astronauts experienced. Crop sprayers or acrobatic pilots, like Wally, could easily pull 5, 6, or 7G. Fighter pilots, the instructor told me, experienced up to 9G, but they would wear a protective G suit. I was dressed in the clothes I'd arrived in.

Thankfully, I hadn't boasted about reaching 3.4G to Loretta. She was sixty-nine when she participated in the NASTAR experiment. "I did 6Gs in the centrifuge," she said matter-of-factly, "as well as the flight plans for the Virgin Galactic spaceplane. It wasn't as bad as I thought."

Loretta had not only withstood far more G forces than were experienced by astronauts during a launch to the Space Station, she had also sampled exactly the same reduced forces of 3G that Wally and all Future Astronauts would encounter on their Virgin Galactic spaceflight. I was in the presence of not one, but two extraordinary women.

During her course Loretta had learned the "hook." This was the anti-G straining maneuver that was taught to fighter jet pilots to help prevent loss of consciousness.

"Six extra deep breaths, another . . ." Wally gave a demonstration. "Hold it for five seconds and let it out. It's when you experience G forces head-to-toe direction and the blood drains out of your head. You go . . ." Wally took a sharp breath, ". . . to force the blood back into your head."

Loretta showed us a DVD of her spins in the centrifuge and explained that she was part of a medical study experiment, which included using meditation and relaxation to counter any feelings of anxiety. Many of the study's findings were interesting. People with heart problems or diabetes, for instance, could cope with the G forces on a commercial spaceflight. This boded well for the future of space tourism. Although anyone who has bought a ticket into space from a commercial company would need to undergo a medical beforehand, it meant that the experience of space would not be restricted to those with superhuman fitness and health, like today's astronauts. Once more commercial spaceflight businesses are up and running, it is expected that the ticket price will come down too, since this is probably the most prohibitive aspect of the venture for many people.

When the films ended, Wally jumped up. "My back is hurting. I have to go for a drive. I need some exercise."

Loretta looked exhausted. I certainly was, so I suggested a walk around the neighborhood instead. Of course, Wally had a reason why we couldn't do it my way. "I haven't got the right shoes. I need some air, honey. A change of scenery."

"How can you exercise when you're in a car?"

Wally changed tack. "I need an ice cream. I want something sweet."

Stalemate. Never short of friends, Wally had nevertheless lived alone most of her life. Perhaps that explained why she seemed unused to compromising. If she wanted to do something, that's all there was to it. Someone had to back down.

"Okay, Wally. Where are we going?"

"Anywhere."

"How long for?"

"Only thirty minutes."

The drive would be to Albuquerque's historic old town. I lowered myself into the passenger seat of Wally's battered red Honda. Because I'm from the UK, it took a minute or two before I realized that we shouldn't be on the left-hand side of the road in the United States. This memory was prompted by the sight of a car headed straight toward us. Fortunately this was the only vehicle we encountered on the quiet streets that surrounded the adobe residences, but on the main road Wally gradually straddled two lanes, and the tension in my back got a whole lot worse.

From the overpass, two tall buildings stood out: the Lovelace Heart Clinic and Medical Center. Another reminder of Wally's incredible history. Recently, I'd noticed that whenever she retold the story about receiving the call for the astronaut tests, she would always say, "Dr. Lovelace said, 'Be here on Monday.'" I recalled an oral history transcript from an interview she had given to NASA. I'd printed it out a few months ago, and I was sure the time line was longer than a few days. Wally backed down slightly. "It could have been a week . . ."

The old town was founded in 1706. In a leafy part of the city dominated by an adobe Catholic Church, Wally insisted on driving around the area several times until we could park closer to the ice cream parlor. So much for the exercise. Luckily, someone finally vacated a spot right outside the shop, but by then Wally had had a change of heart.

"I don't want an ice cream. It's too sweet."

"We've come here, so let's go in."

There was no doubt the flavors were tempting. She opted for a single scoop and grumbled at the size of the portion. "That's going to be too much."

Wally ate every last drop of it. "That was delicious. Thank you."

In the jeweler's next door, the intricate Native American turquoise and silver earrings, necklaces, bracelets, and belt buckles were an unexpected reminder of her childhood. "I sold all of mother's pieces," she said regretfully, and for the first time I noticed that she was wearing a delicate gold chain holding a solid gold letter W around her neck. It must normally have been hidden behind one of her scarves or high-buttoned shirts. "My mother gave it to me when I went to Stephens. She told me never to take it off, and I never have."

I examined the other gold chain around her neck. This one held a sizeable diamond. "That diamond belonged to my Nana. I had my mother's diamond made into a ring. It's the chunky one."

One of her rings was a memento of an air race, one long forgotten, with an offset diamond surrounded by leaves made from multi-colored gold. "It was one of the states where they mined three different types of gold," she said.

That other gold ring with the pilot's wings held the central diamond that once belonged to her mother. Wally looked rueful.

"You must miss your mother."

"I dream a lot, so I'm in constant . . ." She trailed off again for a few seconds and then quickly recovered and stated firmly: "I speak to my mother."

I was glad we'd taken this drive. Although Wally's hyperactivity could be draining at times, she was also energizing, kind, generous of spirit, and totally lovable. She was 99 percent strength, 1 percent vulnerability, so sometimes it was a tough call between a shake or a hug. Back in 1997, I hadn't been entirely sure whether I liked Wally or not. The relentlessly cheerful and confident loudness of her presence, perhaps unintentionally, acted as a barrier. Independence combined with an apparent lack of vulnerability can be off-putting. Or so I've been told. But she was also open and honest, and there was a sweetness there, too, that made Wally Funk something special. She was unique. No one has ever lived a life quite like hers. She has lived a thousand lives already. Sometimes it felt as if there was almost too much life. The expression *carpe diem* didn't even begin to cover it.

I returned to Loretta's home feeling refreshed. Her husband Jerry was on the sofa. Fox News blared from the television.

"I don't want to be any trouble," said Wally, "but do you have Headline News?"

On our final full day in New Mexico, Wally's red Honda died and refused to restart. It was abandoned in a parking lot, to be dealt with by her friends later. Definitely a lucky break. She had some storage space in a locker facility on the other side of Albuquerque, not far from where she once had an apartment close to the airport. Wally unlocked the climate-controlled room, and together we delved into the mementos from her extraordinary past.

The room contained over half a century of memories in cardboard, plastic, and wooden boxes. There were a couple of chairs, a filing cabinet, and, across the back wall, stacks of framed prints and paintings, a pair of skis, and a narrow, long, red sign with bronze lettering.

"Oh wow." Wally scrambled over the trunk. "I'd forgot about that. It's Funk's 5 and 10!"

As she struggled to lift the heavy wooden sign, refusing all offers of help, I examined the back of her black polo shirt. It had been a gift from Virgin Galactic, and was decorated with a vertical line of white silhouettes showing the evolution of an Icarus-style winged human figure, through early types of aircraft advancing to a jet, a spacecraft, and then, naturally at the top of the pile, the distinctive outline of SpaceShipTwo. Wally heaved the sign into the corridor and rotated it horizontally on the floor, right way up.

The sign—almost as long as she was tall—used to hang outside her father's store in Taos, New Mexico. At either end of "Funk's 5 and 10" were the words "Curios" and "Jewelery" at a forty-five-degree angle. It was under this sign that Wally shined shoes, sold rabbits, or carved bows and arrows so that she could begin saving money for the future. The saving habit had never left her.

We went through each box methodically. One was filled with aviation awards and trophies and a "Most Elegant in Show" award for her 1951 Rolls-Royce; another housed skiing boots, overalls, and multiple pairs of thermal underwear and thick socks. She picked up some Indian pot shards. "This must have meant something to me at some time."

There were *Life* magazines, photograph albums, and scrapbooks. She found three sheepskins bought in New Zealand, a model of a Stearman biplane, homemade candlesticks, and a brass Moroccan water carrier from her travels through Africa. There were giant wall stickers that said "A woman's place is in the cockpit" and "The Powder Puff Derby." A metallic rattling revealed a collection of personalized vehicle license plates from different states, with different variations on her Mary Wallace Funk initials. They included a yellow "WF" and "MWFII" for New Mexico and some blue Californian plates with "F II," "I MWF," and "MWFII."

She pulled out a huge, long board. It had maps of the United States, Europe, and Africa, and was edged by hand-painted emblems of the flags and names of the countries she had visited between 1965 and 1967, before her return to the US. It was the same board I'd seen in the December 10, 1967, edition of Santa Fe's *New Mexican* newspaper. There was the emblem for South Africa. During the drive back to Albuquerque, Wally had regaled us with stories of being in Kruger National Park with the poodle, Toot. In one of them, she had left her van to photograph elephants on foot.

"You're lucky the dog wasn't eaten by a lion," I said.

"Little Toot? No. Never had to chastise her because she was so easygoing. Maybe she got that from me or my mother, I don't know."

For once, I held my tongue and instead asked how she got the dog through customs. "When we got to England, I knew I couldn't bring the poodle with me so I put her in my purse, went to the bathroom for a long while, and got through."

The racks of artwork contained prints, a tiled scene of adobe houses, and a huge black-and-white photograph of a parachutist about to land on the ground. It was Wally on her first parachute jump. One framed photo showed seventy-eight graduates from Oklahoma State University's sorority Alpha Chi Omega, 1959. Each woman wore an identical black off-the-shoulder dress.

Numerous certificates revealed Wally's competitive life of ambition and achievement. She was sixteen years old in 1955, when she received her National Rifle Association (NRA) junior diploma qualification as a "Distinguished Rifleman" for "demonstrating unusual skill while firing in the prone, sitting, kneeling, and standing positions." An image of Wally as Doris Day's Calamity Jane resurfaced in my mind. There was even a photograph of her dressed as a cowgirl by her palomino horse, Victor, as "The Taos Kid." When she was older, she even rode in a rodeo.

"I wanted to be a cowboy. A cowgirl. My mother got chaps for me, boots, my gun, a belt. When I started shooting, I did cowgirl action shooting in Taos every Wednesday or Thursday night with my heavy red bag, with all my ammunition in it," she said. "I carried my gun and walked to the armory down about half a mile, and I shot for two or three years."

The NRA diploma required pinpoint accuracy. "When I was fourteen, I shot perfect bullseyes. Five bullseyes in each target. A ten point. You had to do it when you were prone, which meant when you were lying down; sitting, kneeling, and off-hand—that's standing. So in those four positions, I made ten targets in each position in a perfect bullseye."

The NRA club she belonged to forwarded the results to Washington. President Eisenhower sent her a letter of congratulations. "That was a big part of my life. I did everything active and did it well. That's what led me to be a shooter on targets in California. I've shot in competitions in Australia and New Zealand, too. I took my gun," she said. "I would ride on a horse with a pistol and shoot balloons containing a powder."

Naturally, Wally had kept a record of gaining her commercial pilot's licence, age twenty, in 1959. This was the qualification that opened up the start of her long professional career as a pilot within aviation. Even today, Wally flies weekly. She unearthed the application form. There was not much that Wally threw away, but this meant I knew that, in April 1959, she stood at 5 feet 8 ¼ inches, weighed 136 pounds, and had brown hair above those bright blue eyes.

The Department of Transportation Federal Aviation Administration certificates included an eighty-hour flight standards inspector workshop in Los Angeles from October 1971; a seventy-two-hour course for a 22,100 Air Taxi Operation Certification and Inspection Indoctrination in 1973; and a flight instructor's revalidation course in 1977, sponsored by the Los Angeles chapter of the Ninety-Nines—the organization for women pilots set up by Amelia Earhart and other female aviators in 1929.

Wally believed that Earhart had not died at sea, but had been spying on the Japanese in 1937 when she had run out of fuel, had to land on a beach, and was captured. A Japanese prince, who she had taught to fly, released her. She had apparently returned to the States in secret and lived the rest of her life in Florida under the name Irene Bolam, and died in the 1980s. The whole story sounded crazy, but it had been a popular theory since 1965. One thing I had learned since knowing Wally was never to throw any of her outlandish claims out the window. It turned out that she had simply lived an outlandish life. Who knew whether this claim was also true?

There was a Supervision and Group Performance certificate from the Office of Personnel Management in 1979, and later certificates from the National Transportation Safety Board showing that Wally had completed her Aircraft Accident/Incident Report course at Washington, DC, in 1982, and a helicopter orientation course in 1983. Then there was one for Technical Writing from the United States of America Office of Personnel Management, and a South Bay Adult School certificate for an Orientation Computer Programming course in California, both from 1984.

All these certificates and trophies were a record of a life that had been spent continually learning and striving for a combination of adventure and self-improvement. In a framed color photograph of an NTSB Basic Aircraft Accident Investigation Course from 1975, Wally was the only woman among seventeen men. It was the longest I'd ever seen her hair. It just about rested on her shoulders.

The photographs from Wally's younger years—either framed, in albums, or accompanying newspaper articles—were revelatory. I had only ever known her in the later part of life, from her fifties onward, when she had white hair. There was a relaxed, carefree nature to these photos. This last year or so, I had often witnessed Wally anxious because she wanted so badly to be able to take her spaceflight.

Would I have been as doggedly persistent as Wally if I were her age and had a ticket into space? Would I have sent regular e-mails and made telephone calls to Virgin Galactic to check on their progress? So many that they would instantly know my voice and I would know all their names? Would I have appeared as single-minded and even possibly difficult in the process of checking up on my dream? Yes, yes, yes, and absolutely, yes. We were more alike than I'd realized.

The newspaper cuttings revealed a woman who had persisted with her dream right from the start. I found a clipping from the *Taos News*, dated June 1, 1961. I recognized the photograph. It was taken at the Fort Sill military base, and showed Wally in a flight suit holding her helmet in front of a US Airforce T-33 jet. Its headline was "Mary Wallace Funk Passes Space Tests." It began: "The first woman in space may be a Taos girl who already has put wings on her future."

Wally had been making headlines for most of her life. The year 1961, however, was a crucial one for both Wally and human-kind's endeavors to explore what lay beyond the Earth's atmos-phere. For it was the year Yuri Gagarin became the first person in space. It was also an important year for me, as I was born thou-sands of miles away from Wally in the UK a few days after that wonderfully evocative photograph was published. Since it was a forceps delivery, I was literally dragged kicking and screaming into the space age.

These clippings, however, also gave an insight into the social life of her parents. Her mother was often on committees, volunteering, speaking about bonsai in one instance, and—a particular favorite of mine—at a garden party where she displayed "a daffodil with a twenty-four-inch stem which had been picked from the Taos plaza." These activities were religiously recorded by the *Taos News*. "She was the matriarch of Taos," said Wally. "Dressed beautifully. Always entertaining."

One article from Wally's collection, brown with age and labeled "1958" in one of her scrapbooks, said: "The Lozier Funk home was the setting for an open house the evening of Dec. 26th when Mr. and Mrs. Funk . . . charmingly welcomed 125 guests. Dancing was enjoyed during the evening." It gave me an idea of how large their family home must have been.

"There were all kinds of parties," Wally recalled, sorting through another box. "Here's my nana and grandaddy. Nana was always beautifully poised. That was in 1955. See?"

A group of well-dressed men and well-coiffed women posed for the camera. "My parents had a lot of parties." Her father even kept up the sartorial standards when relaxing. "When he went fishing, Father dressed as he was for the store. Vest and bow tie."

Wally came upon a letter from her mother, sent in March 1973, and read it aloud. The handwriting was difficult to decipher in several places. From the way it began, Wally must have included a newspaper cutting of her exploits in a prior correspondence.

"Dear Wally," her mother wrote. "Your marvelous letter and that great write-up was something every parent prays for, but few are so blessed . . . How few young people have enjoyed so much praise . . . you are the true blue, family-loving American, unselfish, willing to learn and not afraid to grow with self-criticism where needed . . . with unending pride in our daughter . . ."

The letter diverted into their social life, meeting friends and going to lunch and an antique show. It ended: "Call us collect Wednesday. Love, Mother."

Wally chuckled. "I always called collect as I didn't have the money."

She picked up an old black-and-white photograph of a young girl in a white dress, black stockings, and laced-up boots with white ribbons in her hair. She was standing on the steps of a house in front of a porch, with a rocking chair on the veranda. Wally turned over the photograph and discovered it was her mother, Virginia Shy, age seven, taken in Olney, Illinois, in 1907.

The *Oklahoma City Times*, from May 19, 1960, revealed Wally with short hair, smiling beside two men and in front of several trophies. They were all pilots from Oklahoma State University's (OSU) Flying Aggie club. Wally "moved Aggie girls ahead by winning the top co-ed pilot award at the recent meet in Columbus, Ohio."

By the end of the year, the *Daily Oklahoman* was reporting that Wally was "the only girl ever enrolled in OSU's flight instructor training program." In another scrapbook press cutting from 1960, four cowboys surrounded Wally, who was riding something that was, at first glance, a bucking bronco. Her back was arched and one of her arms was held aloft holding a cowboy hat. The "bronco" turned out to be a saddle on a fifty-five-gallon gasoline drum pulled by ropes and operated by the four men.

Another newspaper article reported that Wally was about to compete in the National Intercollegiate Flying Association Air Meet at the University of Illinois. "Attending the meet will be Mary Wallace's mother, Mrs. Lozier Funk, who has been in Mattoon, Ill., with her parents, Mr. and Mrs. W. C. Shy, the last few weeks, and who will attend the National Garden Club Convention at St. Louis, next week."

Wally didn't just take her mother to races. She once took her to an air-crash investigation. "She helped me dig and look for a compass."

To my delight, there was an original copy of the April 1961 edition of *Parade* magazine. This was the Sunday newspaper magazine, distributed across the United States, that featured Mercury 13 members Jan and Marion Dietrich on the cover in matching orange flight suits as the "first astronaut twins." All the successful women who had passed the astronaut tests had been warned by Lovelace, several times, to keep it a secret. Their phase-two tests were still ahead.

Somehow, that advice seemed to have eluded the Dietrichs and Jackie Cochran, who wrote the article. After that, all the women—including Wally—felt free to speak to the press and tell their stories. "Because the twins spilled the beans to *Parade* magazine," reasoned Wally. "Although Lovelace was very upset, and so were we."

The *Parade* article showed a white-haired Jackie Cochran, who had partially funded the tests, observing Jan Dietrich on a treadmill, breathing into a mask for a lung-function test. It was an interesting read considering Cochran's later role in the committee hearings—a role that helped prevent the women from going into space. She opened the article with: "Women will fly into space just as certainly as men will—only not so soon."

Cochran's words appeared to be partly waving the flag for women and yet also partly holding them back. She predicted that a woman would go into space by December 17, 1963—a peculiarly specific date, because it was the one hundredth anniversary of the Wright brothers' first flight. She then gave a more realistic time frame of within six or seven years. As it turned out, her first prediction was correct, as a woman did fly into space in 1963. She just wasn't American.

Cochran also wrote: "Women can be just as good 'astronauts' as men." But in the next paragraph she argued, "Economically, this country can't afford right now to have women pilots flying as a part of the Armed Service. It's considered too expensive when there is no emergency or shortage of this kind of talent. It costs the government several hundred thousand dollars to qualify a jet pilot. Such a government-trained pilot cannot be a sporadic flyer; he must fly regularly. And with women, marriage and children are likely to interrupt their flying careers."

Wally had underlined "Mary Funk" in the article, as well as highlighting two sections: the paragraph that said that the women who passed "may later receive specialized training to participate in space flight as astronauts or as engineers or skilled technicians" and the description of the program as being the "first 'launching pad' for women in space."

Four-and-a-half months after that *Parade* article was published, the program was canceled.

Cochran, the first woman to break the sound barrier, had been a divisive person for the Mercury 13. She had been born poor in Florida, but was now—primarily through marriage—an extremely wealthy woman living in California. Through her financial backing, she gave these women the opportunity to achieve their dreams of becoming astronauts, yet simultaneously contributed to putting them on hold through her testimony in Congress. Jerri Truhill had been outspokenly negative about Cochran when we'd met in 1997. What was Wally's view of Cochran?

"She was always nice to me because I came from Taos," said Wally. Cochran liked the town and often visited. "We talked about the people we knew there and the artists. She was always okay with me and the fact that I was doing so well and how physically fit I was. You know what, you take women that are married with two or three kids, they couldn't do what I did. I don't think the twins were married."

After the *Parade* magazine revelations, Dr. W. Randolph Lovelace himself was quoted in a May 28, 1961, edition of the *Daily Oklahoman*. The article announced: "Oklahoma's second lady astronaut has completed the medical and physical competence tests of possible future space flights, one of the nation's top medicine experts disclosed here Saturday."

The first Oklahoman was Jerrie Cobb. As Wally was an OSU graduate and working in Oklahoma, she was the second. Cobb had just been announced as a NASA consultant by the space agency's head, James Webb. Interestingly, the writer noted that "Dr. Lovelace, expressing a view contrary to that expressed privately by some scientists here, said women will make space flights eventually."

"Sometime in the future," said Lovelace, "we don't know when, women will go into space—just as they have gone into everything else." He had also heard rumors that the Russians were possibly preparing to send women on space flights.

A month later, in the June 27, 1961, issue of the *Daily Oklahoman*, it was announced that Wally Funk "Dreams of Becoming First Woman in Space." It noted her flying achievements and included the fact that, the year before, the Ninety-Nines had named Wally "the top woman aviator in the nation."

The article also quoted her OSU Flying Aggies coach and flight instructor, Tiner Lapsley. Wally was the only female member of the club, and had also stayed with Lapsley and his wife. The piece provided a professional and personal insight into what this energetic, determined seventy-eight-year-old was like as a twenty-one-year-old.

"She always wanted to compete with the boys," Lapsley said. "She was an extremely active girl. There's not a lazy bone in that girl's body . . . She tried to help the mechanics, mowed the grass around the airport, and gassed up the airplanes—most boys don't like to do it because it's too hard."

In other words, over fifty years later, Wally hadn't changed. The article noted that Wally "dressed like a boy, always wearing blue jeans, baggy flight shirts, and hair cut short." While growing up, Wally "played tackle football with the best of them."

There was a reference to her job at the time as a flight instructor at Fort Sill. "Never in Fort Sill's history had a woman been contracted by the government to instruct both male and female pilots."

Officials had told Lapsley that Wally was "the best flight instructor they have."

The final sentence said: "In addition to a thorough medical check-up, special tests are given dealing with resistance to stress of various kinds, such as the tilt-table test, bicycle test, Master 2-Step tests, and the cold pressure tests of which Miss Funk made an almost above average mark on all tests given her."

At the time of that article, only five women had passed the astronaut tests. Wally believed her dream of getting into space was close to being fulfilled. She was cycling sixteen miles each day to get to and from the army base, in order to keep up her fitness. But she knew even then that it would take something extra to realize this dream. "It will take faith in mankind and God to get me up," she said.

A few months later, on September 21, a follow-up article related: "No Man in Moon. Stephens Graduate Trains to Be Female Astronaut." It was already out of date. Nine days earlier Wally had received the telegram canceling the program.

When we left the storage room, I glanced at my watch.

"Good grief. We've been in there for four hours."

Wally said goodbye to the sullen receptionist she'd tried, and failed, to engage in conversation when we'd arrived. "Thanks a lot, honey. We've been in there for six hours!"

Those "extra" two hours sure went fast.

🚀

That night, after fond farewells with Loretta, Wally and I shared a hotel room near the airport. I had a 4:30 AM start for a return flight to London. Wally's flight to Dallas was also the next morning, but at a more reasonable time. The television was on, and every few minutes Wally flicked the remote back and forth between several channels. "I often watch several movies at once," she said. "I don't watch romantic movies though. Too much kissing."

I was in bed, in pajamas, zoned out on my laptop, and prepared for an early night. Since Wally usually watched television at a high volume until about 11 PM, the deal was that when I was ready to sleep, she would watch the television in reception before her own bedtime. I heard her unpacking toiletries in the bathroom. She was talking again, but the combination of the air conditioning and the television turned her words into a blur.

"I can't hear you," I shouted.

Wally's raised voice echoed from the bathroom tiles. "I said, have you checked the times of the airport bus in the morning? You don't wanna miss it."

I glanced upward from my laptop to answer, and was confronted by a vision of Wally on the toilet. The bathroom door was wide open and there was a mirror on the wardrobe opposite the bathroom entrance. Eyes averted, we continued the conversation. She had a shower. The bathroom door remained open, as did the shower curtain, and I marveled at her total lack of modesty. Wally was a complete contradiction sometimes. Always conservatively dressed, occasionally demure, and prudish if the conversation veered off into anything remotely sexual, Wally was also completely comfortable in her own skin.

For a brief moment, I watched her bathe and admired her naked body. At seventy-eight, Wally's constant activity had kept her in shape both physically and mentally. Underneath the baggy cargo pants and shirt, she had the physique and skin of a much younger woman.

The night before, I had encountered another unexpected view of Wally as a younger woman. It resulted from checking the NASA oral history transcript to ascertain the correct timing between Lovelace's selection call for the tests and her arriving at his clinic. It was, as I'd thought, not days but four weeks. Not an important disparity, as the aging process often blurred timings, and, over the years, Wally had always been totally transparent with the media. It was just that, like most of us, later stories differed from their earlier versions by small details after being retold hundreds of times.

Then, as is often the case with the internet, I got diverted. It turned out that, in 2001, the Australian band Spiderbait had specifically called their fifth album *The Flight of Wally Funk*. Inspired by the female aviator, it included the tracks "Inner Ear Infection," "Most Boys Suck," "A.D.D.," and "Arse Huggin' Pants." After listening to a couple of the tracks on YouTube— disappointing, but then I'm not a big rock fan—up came the NASA oral history interview among Spiderbait's list of songs. The interview had been filmed. It was dated July 18, 1999, at the NASA Johnson Space Center, two years after Wally and I had first met. I pressed play and watched for just under an hour, fascinated by a younger version of Wally. At that stage in her life, I realized, she was only a few years older than me.

Astonishingly, despite the time since it had been filmed, she didn't look that different. She wore a crisp blue shirt with "Wally" monogrammed on the right and an airplane referencing an air show event on the left. Around her neck I recognized the delicate gold "W" chain from her mother. When she gesticulated and her hands came into the shot, I noticed the same two heavy gold rings, one with the diamond from her mother, on her fingers. Even at sixty, Wally's hair was as toothpaste-white as her smile. The white hair, as today, reflected her luminous skin. She was truly beautiful.

More interestingly, her distinctive high-decibel voice was softer, more gentle, and, apart from the usual familiar burst of laughter, much quieter. She remained warm and vivacious, but it was as if Wally's volume had been turned down low. Her overly loud, conversational level today resembled mine if I forgot to take off headphones while editing and answered someone's question. It made me realize how much age-related hearing loss had affected her tone and presentation over the years.

I recognized some of the same stories she'd been retelling since the 1960s—the Superman cape she wore when jumping off the barn at four years old, the Merry Widow girdle refashioned into a G suit for the centrifuge at 5G—but the tales had more nuance and, because they were told in a more normal conversational tone, came across as less eccentric. Since her memories were closer to the event itself, more details were intact, too. But what came through most clearly of all was that this was a warm, smart, considered, determined, and accomplished woman, a tremendous pilot and a feminist role model. She was full of encouragement for her sex, and advocated for "girls" to study math, science, and engineering and to achieve their dreams if they wanted to go into space. "A dog did it, a monkey did it, a man did it, a woman can do it."

Watching Wally dry herself brusquely in our motel, I averted my gaze and contemplated how lucky I was to know her, as well as the complex reality of the woman that is Wally Funk. She combined an inability to concentrate in some areas with a complete focus on others: primarily aviation and her goal of becoming an astronaut. This focus had led her to both break barriers as well as open doors for other women within aviation and the space industry, not to mention being an inspiration for others.

She has spent almost sixty years determined to complete her goal of getting into space. Those sixty years have not been easy for women. Achieving mass representation within many industries has been a slow process, and remains ongoing. Scientist and British astronaut Helen Sharman was almost written out of history when the first British male astronaut flew into space with the European Space Agency, but the first South Korean and the first Iranian in space had both been women, as a part of the Russian space program. In 2012, almost fifty years after Valentina Tereshkova made her historic flight, China sent Liu Yang, its first woman, into space.

Women, like men, have given their lives to further our desire to explore beyond Earth. Apart from astronauts Judy Resnik and Christa McAuliffe, who died in the Challenger shuttle accident, Laurel Clark and the first Indian-born woman in space, Dr. Kalpana Chawla, were the two women in a crew of seven who died on board Space Shuttle Columbia when it disintegrated while making a landing approach on February 1, 2003.

Although around 550 people had become astronauts at this point, only around one in ten were female. And, despite the trailblazing heroics of Valentina Tereshkova, fifty of the fifty-nine women who have flown in space were from the United States. The fact that there had been so few female cosmonauts testifies to the continued issue of sexism in Russia. Only four since 1963.

It took until 2013 before the issue was even addressed in public. Scientist and former cosmonaut Yelena Dobrokvashina said that Russian women rarely went into space because Russian men feared that their heroism would be diminished if shared with members of the opposite sex. A year later, in September 2014, Yelena Serova prepared to become the first Russian woman on the International Space Station, and had to fend off questions during a press conference about leaving her daughter and taking care of her hair. She turned the tables and gestured toward her male cosmonaut colleagues. "Aren't you interested in the hairstyles of my colleagues?"

NASA astronaut Karen Nyberg got so tired of being asked how she washed her hair on the ISS that she eventually took control and made a much viewed video showing how it was done. But there has been progress. In September 2014, India successfully placed its Mars Orbiter Spacecraft into orbit around the red planet. A photograph of the control room made even more impact around the world. It showed a group of space engineers celebrating the mission's success. Most of these engineers were women dressed in colorful saris. For many, that image was a visual redefining of the once traditional all-male preserve of mission control rooms. At several space agencies now, there are women flight directors, engineers, robotics experts, scientists, and doctors.

But while only around sixty women have gone into space at this point, the pool of countries that they are from is even smaller—just ten: the UK, France, Italy, Canada, the USA, China, Japan, India, Russia, and South Korea. Once commercial spaceflights are up and running, the number of women who will have gone into space will increase dramatically, and their nationalities will diversify. It may be a business for the space tourism entrepreneurs, but for women it is also a highly visible opportunity to claim their rightful place alongside men in space. Yet again, Wally will be breaking boundaries.

There are few who deserve a spaceflight more than Wally, except maybe Jerrie Cobb who, by being the first woman aviator to pass the astronaut tests in 1959, made the Mercury 13 and Wally's space ambitions possible in the first place. But at eighty-six, Cobb's opportunity has likely passed. Meanwhile, Wally has been saving and preparing to become an astronaut by studying space travel and taking every opportunity available through the media, from a zero-G flight or a week's training alongside cosmonauts, to get a little closer to realizing her dream.

What if ill health prevents her from going up? It was a question I'd hesitated to ask. I hadn't wanted, like her, to even consider the possibility. "I wanna go, I wanna go," she said. "I'm in great health, and I take vitamins and I keep going 100 miles per hour every day. One woman said the other day, 'You walk too fast.' No. I'm gonna go. There's no doubt about it. I'm in perfect health. The only tablets I take are vitamins."

Wally does her exercises each morning, and moves at a pace that often causes me to canter to keep up. But even the longevity of her legendary fitness sometimes gives Wally cause for concern. "I put a ladder against the fence at the back of my yard and climbed over it the other day to clean it up," she said. "But something happened that I hadn't felt in the last year. It was hard for me to swing my leg over my fence. I had to get a guy to help me hold my butt up."

Not bad for a seventy-eight-year-old. "I will fly until I'm ninety-one," she said laughing. "After that I probably won't pass the physical. I just wish I was flying ten hours a week. I'm only getting two hours every other week at the moment. I go up to 5,000 feet, doing stalls, and I take one guy in his Cessna 182 and we can do a loop."

There is no doubt that Wally is ready to become an astronaut. It's why she keeps so fit. It is also fortunate for her that commercial space flights are now being offered, because the career path for would-be astronauts has become far more competitive and demanding over the decades. Today's near-superhuman requirements would probably squeeze out talented pilots like Wally—even those, again like her, who had reached an Olympic standard of athleticism.

Nowadays astronauts have multiple degrees, master's degrees or PhDs—usually in physics, medicine, aerospace, or engineering—and the ability to speak several languages. By today's standards, it is highly likely that not even all the Mercury 7 men would meet the criteria to fly into space. Although, by yesterday's standards, those harsh physical tests might have poleaxed a few modern astronauts' careers too.

But back in the 1960s, talented pilots in peak physical and mental health made great astronaut candidates, able to handle the conditions and requirements they met with at the time. Wally Funk, and the rest of the Mercury 13 female pilots, had the right stuff. Wally was—and is—exceptional. This remarkable woman was denied her destiny as one of the first women in space. But what a life she has had while fighting to right a wrong. Wally has shown a generation of women that we could—and can—do space travel and, whether behind the scenes or in the pilot's seat of a spaceplane, that the history of space consists of a number of immensely brave women who were ready to strap themselves on top of a rocket to explore the unknown. Women have always aimed high and, eventually, women reach those heights—even if it must have sometimes felt as if the world wanted to punish them for their ambition.

Wally is now approaching eighty. This is a race against time. Time that history owes her. Wally's whole life has been heading toward those final moments when she will launch from Spaceport America in New Mexico and enjoy those precious few minutes in space. Minutes that will feel like a lifetime. Minutes that will achieve the lifetime ambition of one truly extraordinary woman.

We rarely discussed her age, but it was often there, unspoken in the background. She told me over dinner once, out of the blue, that she had booked her spot at the Portal of the Folded Wings Shrine to Aviation at Valhalla Memorial Park Cemetery in North Hollywood, California. That was my chance. Is there anything in her life she would have done differently? "Absolutely not," she said firmly. "I've loved everything I've done, sweetheart. I wish I was born twenty years later so I could have been in the military and gone into space. That's what I wish. Now I can't do anything but support space or lecture in schools about STEM. But honey, I wouldn't change my life for one minute."

When I left the motel room in darkness the following morning, Wally was asleep. Seeing this woman, who is normally in constant motion, calm and lying still was a strange sight. It felt as if she was suspended, like Schrödinger's cat, in a quantum state where anything was possible. A state where dreams of space travel could come true.

Sources and Further Reading

There are several books published about the Mercury 13. I started two of them, as they were extremely useful for cross-referencing and checking dates, but then became worried that their tales about Wally would influence my own experience of her, and so deliberately put them on hold until after the writing for this book was finished. Those books are: *The Mercury 13: The True Story of Thirteen Women and the Dream of Space Flight*, by Martha Ackmann (Random House, 2003) and *Right Stuff, Wrong Sex: America's First Women in Space Program* by Margaret A. Weitekamp (Johns Hopkins, 2004). There is also *Promised the Moon: The Untold Story of the First Women in the Space Race* by Stephanie Nolen (Basic Books, 2004), and *Almost Astronauts: 13 Women Who Dared to Dream* by Tanya Lee Stone (Candlewick, 2009).

Obviously, I'm not going to reveal which one Wally was unhappy about. But it's fair to say that her reasons were personal and, for what it's worth, from what I have read of that particular book so far, it's excellent. Although Tom Wolfe's book *The Right Stuff* (Jonathan Cape, 1980) was about the Mercury men rather than the women, it is a fantastic read about the space race that took place from the 1950s onward. The tests that the men endured were exactly the same as the ones the Mercury 13 women took, under the same medical supervision of Dr. Lovelace. So there is a connection. Just think of the women when you read it. The film version, made in 1983, is definitely worth watching, too. Somehow seeing the indignity of those tests being reenacted, makes it all the more real and jaw-clenching.

Any quotes I have used from newspapers or magazines have been referenced with dates and titles along the way. Any space facts and figures have been checked using NASA or ESA, or both.

There's a good summary of the Woman in Space program written by a relative of Dr. Don Kilgore (who worked at the Lovelace Clinic). It's called *A Forgotten Moment in Physiology: The Lovelace Woman in Space Program (1960–62)* by Kathy L. Ryan, Jack A. Loeppky, and Donald E. Kilgore Jr. (Adv Physiol Educ 33: 157–164, June, 2009). If you have a specific interest in New Mexico's space history, you can hunt out Loretta Hall's *Out of This World: New Mexico's Contributions to Space Travel* (Rio Grande Books, 2011). If you want to inspire younger women (and men) by what women have done in the past, then I'd recommend *A Galaxy of Her Own: Amazing Stories of Women in Space* by Libby Jackson (Century, 2017).

Hidden Figures: The American Dream and the Untold Story of the Black Women Mathematicians Who Helped Win the Space Race by Margot Lee Shetterly (William Collins, 2013) does not cover female astronauts or aviators, but it is an excellent book and a great example of women who made a difference and persisted in what was then the male-dominated environment of space travel.

I have lived with stories of the Mercury 13 for over twenty years now. The result in print form is part travelogue, part biography, and part history of women in space. The main source for this book is my travels with Wally Funk, of course, which resulted in multiple interviews and recordings between 1997 and 2017. Along the way, I double-checked dates and facts, helped by a number of original documents that Wally has stored either in Dallas or Albuquerque. During this period of time I also interviewed Mercury 13 members Jerri Truhill, Sarah Ratley, and Irene Leverton, legendary NASA flight director Chris Kraft, and Dr. Don Kilgore from the Lovelace Clinic. Most of the quotations from astronauts and scientists are also taken from firsthand interviews. Having original source material on audio was a huge help. Watching Wally's 1999 oral history interview with NASA on YouTube is a fascinating step back in time, even if it's not the full Wally experience, volume-wise, as she talks a lot louder now.

The 1997 radio program I made for the BBC about the Mercury 13, *Women with the Right Stuff*, is still available to listen to online via the BBC website. Sadly, two of the women I interviewed for it, Jerri Truhill and Irene Leverton, are no longer with us, so it's a poignant listen, but also, hopefully, remains an inspiring one.

Acknowledgments

First and foremost, I'd like to thank Wally Funk for her time, energy, enthusiasm, friendship, good humor, and ever-present laughter. She is the aviation equivalent of the Unsinkable Molly Brown and an inspiration to women everywhere, young and old.

The BBC has played an enormous role in my life. I've worked for the organization as a staff member twice, resigned twice, and continue to work for them as an independent producer and broadcaster in between resignations. In one of those periods, when I was freelance in 1997, they commissioned my idea for a radio documentary on the Mercury 13 via the independent company Partners in Sound. That set off twenty years of intermittent relationships with several of the women, including Wally, and it also cemented my interest in making programs that cover women's history or have a feminist angle.

Two other, more recent documentaries I made for the BBC effectively resulted in the book, since it was traveling with Wally that gave me the idea of doing something different from a straightforward biography, which was nowhere near as appealing to write. But if it hadn't been for Steve Titherington suggesting Wally as my presenter, this book would not have come into being.

Thank you to Virgin Galactic's Clare Pelly and Gemma Vigor for answering my questions and facilitating my trip to Spaceport America. There's nothing I'd like more than to see SpaceShipTwo succeed and for Wally to be seated where she wants, behind the pilot, and finally go into space. Thanks also to Jeremy Close and Abbie Hutty at Airbus, Defence and Space for delighting Wally (and me) by hosting a visit to their Mars Yard at short notice; Elena Filippazzo, Samantha Cristoforetti, and Jan Woerner at the European Space Agency; and NASA for inspiring me to aim high when I wrote to them, at age thirteen, wanting to be an astronaut; Nicholas Booth deserves a big shout-out for his early and consistent encouragement of this book idea; thanks to Loretta Hall for opening her home to a stranger and allowing me to depart as a friend; and my gratitude goes to Peter Tallack at the Science Factory and my editor at the Westbourne Press, Lynn Gaspard, for believing both in the book and in the appeal of the magnificently named Wally Funk.

Apart from Wally, I'd also like to identify four women whose lives have always been a personal inspiration: Barbara Young, Nicola Kerr, Melanie James, and Penny Hollingham. In a world where women sometimes have to fight for equal opportunities or simply to be heard and acknowledged, their advice, strength, and voices have always rung clear.

Finally, for the two men in my life: my husband Richard Hollingham and our son Matthew. Richard, as a science journalist, gave invaluable advice and editing suggestions on early drafts. Matthew couldn't have been kinder or more understanding. Thank you both for the constant support and for living with my obsessions.